150+ Inspirational Low-Carb, High-Fat Recipes to Maximize Your Health

the EVERYDAY KETOGENIC KITCHEN

Carolyn Ketchum

VICTORY BELT PUBLISHING INC.

Las Vegas

Farmers' market photos taken by Rebekah Hubbard

Author photo taken by House of Bonas

Front and back cover photos by Hayley Mason and Bill Staley

Interior design by Yordan Terziev and Boryana Yordanova

Printed in Canada

TC 0518

TABLE OF CONTENTS

This book is dedicated to my dad, John R. Currie.

Any man can be a father; that's simply biology. But not every man can be a Dad.

Thank you for always being a Dad.

FOREWORD

When Carolyn Ketchum asked me to write the foreword for her book, I was excited to do so. It wasn't just because I have followed her excellent website for many years, and it wasn't just because we share the same publisher. It meant that she was writing a book, and I was going be among the first to see it.

Carolyn and I both became interested in a low-carb, high-fat ketogenic diet through our experience with diabetes—her experiencing gestational diabetes while carrying her third child, and myself through my work over the last quarter century to wipe out type 2 diabetes (a form of accelerated aging!), starting with the first centers for metabolic medicine. We both have dedicated ourselves to the goal of promoting a low-carb, high-fat diet to mitigate many of the health problems our society is facing today.

In addition to our shared history, what made me want to provide the foreword for this book is the fact that Carolyn's approach to a high-fat ketogenic diet is so complementary to my own. I endeavor to discover the truest and best science behind health and nutrition, but without delicious ways to implement that science, compliance can be difficult. This is where Carolyn shines. She is well known for her low-carb baking skills, making incredibly tasty treats that many of us thought were out of reach on a healthy diet. The only willpower necessary for *The Everyday Ketogenic Kitchen* is to refrain from trying the next great recipe immediately.

The recipes in this book are truly a treat, whether you strictly adhere to a high-fat keto lifestyle or you are just looking for new ideas for making healthy and satisfying meals. Carolyn covers all the bases, from sauces, snacks, and main courses featuring a variety of proteins to what she has become very well known for, everyone's favorite: sweets and desserts. I wholeheartedly recommend *The Everyday Ketogenic Kitchen*. Carolyn is an excellent representative for the low-carb community, and I can say with confidence that you'll enjoy her recipes as much as I have, and be healthier for it.

Ron Rosedale, MD

PREFACE

A few years ago, my father asked me how I would feel if I didn't have diabetes anymore, or if my diagnosis had all been a big mistake and I never really had diabetes in the first place. Wouldn't I feel like I'd missed out on all the carbs I had denied myself over the years? My response surprised even me. I just laughed and said, "Dad, you don't get it. I love this way of life. I love what I do and what I eat. I wouldn't change it for the world."

How often do you hear someone say that they are happy to have been diagnosed with diabetes? It's certainly not a common sentiment. This insidious disease affects almost 30 million people in the United States alone. It can cause neuropathy, blindness, kidney disease, heart attack, and stroke. Diabetes is responsible for an estimated 1.5 million deaths worldwide each year. So why on earth would anyone be happy about it? I am happy about it because it led me to a lifestyle that I truly enjoy—one that I intend to pursue for the rest of my life. And I wouldn't have come to this lifestyle without a serious intervention, such as a diagnosis of diabetes.

But make no mistake, I was anything but happy about it in the beginning. I would even go so far as to say that I went through a distinct grieving period—shock, denial, anger, the whole shebang. Acceptance would come in time, and happiness would come quite a bit after that. But it would come.

I was first diagnosed with gestational diabetes during my third pregnancy. Because I had a slender build with an active, healthy lifestyle and no significant risk factors, the diagnosis came as quite a shock. My doctors reassured me that it would resolve itself instantly upon the birth of my daughter. And so it did. Or rather, it seemed to for the first few months. At the advice of my endocrinologist, I continued to test my blood sugar every so often, and I began to see a disturbing upward trend. Both my fasting and postprandial (after-eating) numbers were on the rise. I was eating what was considered to be a healthy "standard American diet" filled with vegetables, fruits, and whole grains. I'd lost all my baby weight and had committed to regular exercise, becoming a dedicated runner at the ripe old age of thirty-seven. So why was my blood sugar continuing to creep upward?

I know now that my story is not all that uncommon. Type 2 diabetes is on the rise, even among slender, seemingly healthy people. Our modern diet is heavily carb-centric and has become steadily more so over the past sixty years, thanks to the low-fat dogma inherent in most nutritional advice. It makes you wonder if all those grains and sugars that replace the fats in our diet have severely taxed the collective pancreas of the Western world.

However, before I truly understood any of this, my glucometer was telling me that something wasn't right despite my best efforts, and I was simply heartsick about it. I couldn't imagine what I was doing wrong or why this was happening to me. Because I am an information junkie, I took to the Internet in hopes of finding ways to manage my blood sugar without resorting to insulin or other medications. And the obvious answer was staring me in the face: a low-carbohydrate diet.

I didn't want to believe it at first, and I confess, I cried. I actually sat on my kitchen floor and cried, thinking that this was the end of my enjoyment of food and, by extension, life. Food had always been a pillar of my life. Not just eating it, which of course brings great pleasure, but also creating it—cooking and baking, measuring and mixing, seasoning and tasting to bring out just the right flavors. Since I was a teenager, I've spent much of my free time putzing around in the kitchen. When a new issue of *Bon Appétit, Gourmet,* or *Cooks Illustrated* would arrive in the mail, I would read it cover to cover. I would spend hours creating elaborate menus for our annual holiday party. It might sound trite to use the phrase "the joy of cooking," and chances are it's trademarked anyway, but for me, cooking was never just a means to an end. The whole process brought me joy. Some people cook to have something to eat. Others, like me, cook to have something to cook.

However, with a diagnosis of type 2 diabetes, all that joy would be denied to me, wouldn't it? Like so many of the uninitiated, I thought low-carb, ketogenic diets consisted mainly of eggs, meat, and cheese. I like these foods, but I certainly wouldn't want to subsist on them alone. What about bread? What about muffins? What about dessert??? How could I possibly enjoy life without cooking and eating those things? It turns out I couldn't. More to the point, I didn't have to. There was a whole undiscovered world out there devoted to alternative cooking and baking. People were using new ingredients in different ways, and I could hardly wait to get in on the action.

I had started my blog, *All Day I Dream About Food,* in March 2010, a few months before I realized I was truly a diabetic. It wasn't something I did with any consistency; I was blogging just for fun. But after my diagnosis, my blog suddenly had a purpose. It was a place for me to record my low-carb experiments, to note what worked and what didn't, and to share my ideas with other people. As I slowly gained confidence, I began to understand how these new ingredients behaved and how to adjust recipes accordingly. It wasn't long before I was taking conventional high-carb recipes and attempting to make them over with ketogenic ingredients. And then I began dreaming up all-new recipe ideas and heading to the kitchen to see if I could bring them to fruition. I had a lot of success, with a few outright failures thrown in to keep me humble.

I will be the first to admit that cutting carbs from my diet and gaining control of my blood sugar wasn't a walk in the park. Because I didn't need to lose any weight, I didn't follow a set plan or diet. I simply "ate to my meter," as we say in diabetes-speak. I cut out breads and most grains, legumes, and starches. I avoided refined sugars at all costs. And then I tested after everything I ate, seeing what worked and what didn't. I cut back on carbs rather slowly at first because I struggled to give things up cold turkey. The more I cut back, the better my glucose control, until I finally found that sweet spot of fat, carbs, and protein that really worked for me. I didn't know at the time that this "sweet spot" was considered a ketogenic diet!

I also immersed myself in the world of alternative nutrition, reading as much as I could find about carb-restricted diets. The more I read, the more I came to see how backward we've had it for decades; the culprit behind obesity and many illnesses is not saturated fats, but sugars and excess carbohydrates. This blew my mind, but it also made me incredibly happy. I spent the first seven years of my life on a beef cattle farm just north of Toronto, and I'd always loved a good fatty steak with a pat of butter melting on top. Suddenly being given the green light to eat these foods without guilt was a joyous revelation.

So that's my story, and I'm sticking to it. I stumbled into the ketogenic lifestyle almost by accident without really knowing what I was doing or where it would take me. But here I am, seven years in, and I love it beyond comprehension. I also firmly believe that it is the path to better health for many people. My words to my father hold true: if my diabetes up and disappeared tomorrow, I still wouldn't change a thing.

I share my recipes because I want to make the keto diet as accessible and as delicious as possible. I want you to love it as much as I do, and I want you to reap the many health benefits that come with it. This isn't a fad or a short-term solution; it's a whole new, wonderful way of living. And it really is one you can do every day for the rest of your life.

Welcome to *The Everyday Ketogenic Kitchen*.

HOW TO USE THIS BOOK

Many people think that the ketogenic diet is simply a fad, a phase, or a short-term solution. After all, how can such a "restrictive" diet be sustainable in the long term? How can anyone follow it day in and day out for an extended period? With innovative low-carb, high-fat recipes and expert tips, *The Everyday Ketogenic Kitchen* seeks to change that perception. Through a love of food and good cooking, I want to inspire you to embrace this low-carb, high-fat lifestyle.

To make these delicious ketogenic recipes as accessible as possible, I have included many handy tips and other features throughout the book.

Chapter 1 takes you through the best ingredients and where to source them. The vast majority are everyday foods that you can find at your local grocery store, but a few are specialty items that make ketogenic living a little more fun. In Chapter 2, I discuss kitchen equipment and gadgets—all the necessary tools that you need for cooking success.

And because I love baking so much (and because it is more of an exact science than cooking), in Chapter 3, you will find all my best tips for making your low-carb baked goods really shine. In my baking recipes, I have even included weights in grams for key ingredients such as almond flour and coconut flour for greater accuracy. I find U.S. standard cup and tablespoon measurements to be very accurate in my recipes, but I always use the same brand, Bob's Red Mill. Different brands can vary somewhat in volume, so measuring by weight can help reduce these differences in low-carb baking.

For each recipe, you will also find the following information.

Nutritional Information:

Each recipe lists the number of calories and the fat, protein, carbohydrate, and fiber contents in grams. For sweetened recipes, I have listed the erythritol in grams separately from the total carb count. Erythritol is a sugar alcohol and a useful non-nutritive, low-carb sweetener. It actually contains about the same amount of carbs per serving as sugar, but it has no effect on blood glucose levels in most people. However, some special diet plans require this information for calculating carb counts.

All the nutritional information was calculated using MacGourmet, a software program that relies on the USDA Nutritional Database. While I strive to be as precise as possible, these numbers are often only estimates based on the average size of certain ingredients. Produce, cuts of meat, and even brands of nut flour can vary in size, density, and fat and protein content. People with serious medical conditions should calculate their own nutritional information before relying on these numbers.

Swaps and Substitutions:

While I recommend following the recipes as written, I understand that food allergies, intolerances, and ingredient availability might require the occasional substitution. I have done my best to recommend swaps wherever possible, but keep in mind that the nutritional information was calculated using the ingredients listed. Swapping one ingredient for another might change the counts, so be sure to calculate them independently.

For more on standard swaps and substitutions, check out the chart on page 37.

Quick Reference Icons:

For folks with food allergies or intolerances, I have noted which recipes are free of dairy, nuts, and eggs. I have also noted which recipes have options to make them free of these potential allergens; look for the Everyday Swaps at the ends of those recipes.

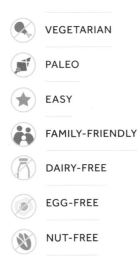

VEGETARIAN

PALEO

EASY

FAMILY-FRIENDLY

DAIRY-FREE

EGG-FREE

NUT-FREE

I have also included icons to designate vegetarian, Paleo, easy, and family-friendly recipes. In the interest of full disclosure, "family friendly" means that my kids liked it. They are my toughest critics, so if they enjoyed it, chances are your family will, too.

Finally, to illustrate what a low-carb, high-fat diet actually looks like, I have included a personal week-long food journal in Chapter 4, "An Everyday Ketogenic Diet." I am not in the habit of keeping such a detailed account of my own food consumption, but I wanted you to see how delicious and enjoyable this lifestyle can be. It really is something you can do every day for the rest of your life.

To learn more about the ketogenic lifestyle, be sure to check out the additional resources on page 365.

THE KETO

REVOLUTION

What if you took everything you ever knew about diet and nutrition and turned it on its head? That, in a nutshell, is the ketogenic diet. In essence, it takes the current standard nutritional advice and inverts it. Remember that old food pyramid with its broad base of bread, cereal, and pasta at the bottom and slim little triangle of meats, cheeses, and fats at the top? Go ahead and turn it upside down. Now, instead of trying to reduce your intake of fat, it becomes the most important macronutrient. And what about those whole grains that are supposed to be so good for you? Just throw them away, because they have no place here. Any carbohydrates you consume will be in the form of vegetables, nuts, and seeds, with a few fruits thrown in for good measure. Supplement this with a moderate amount of protein, and there you have it: the ketogenic diet.

The science of nutrition really is undergoing something of a revolution. After decades of low-fat advocacy that only made us fatter and sicker, nutrition experts are being forced to capitulate. Study after study now supports the idea that fat—including saturated fat—isn't so bad for you. In fact, it might actually be good for you, offering protective benefits against neurological disorders and heart disease. Many other studies have implicated sugars and excess carbohydrates as the real causes of weight gain, heart disease, and, of course, diabetes.

Still, this is a slow-moving revolution at times. The low-fat dogma has become so institutionalized that changing people's minds can be an uphill battle. But it does make you wonder why those high-carb, low-fat guidelines have led to more obesity, more heart disease, and more diabetes. Is it just because we all lack the willpower to follow them properly? Or is it because the guidelines themselves are based on flawed science? Increasingly, it appears to be the latter. The evidence is piling up, and it's getting harder to deny that we've had it backwards and we've done some serious damage along the way.

I am not a nutrition expert, and I don't play one on TV. So I will refer you to those with more credentials than I have on the subject. For a detailed look at the history of nutrition and how we got to where we are today, I highly recommend the book *The Big Fat Surprise: Why Butter, Meat and Cheese Belong in a Healthy Diet* by Nina Teicholz. It's incredibly eye-opening to understand the combination of poor scientific methods and serious ego that led Ancel Keys to push his flawed diet-heart hypothesis, which became the foundation of the low-fat movement.

SO HOW DOES IT ACTUALLY WORK?

To really see the benefits of a ketogenic diet, it's important to have at least a rudimentary understanding of how ketosis works. For decades, we've been told that the most important source of fuel for energy is glucose, but it turns out that this isn't necessarily true. Our bodies are kind of like hybrid cars and can utilize two very different types of fuel. When glucose is readily available, the body will use it preferentially because it's easier to access. However, during times of scarce food and/or carbohydrate restriction, the liver will convert fat into small molecules called ketone bodies. Ketones, as they are often referred to, can fuel our bodies and brains just as well as—and arguably better than—glucose. Whereas the body can store enough glucose to last only a few days, it can store fat in almost unlimited amounts. When the body is in a state of ketosis, it accesses those fat stores and turns them into energy.

This "flex-fuel" system provides an adaptive advantage in times of scarcity, and without it, our species likely would not have survived. Times were tough back in the caves, and many foods were available only seasonally. Naturally, there were stretches of time when food was hard to come by and human bodies would have to turn to ketones for enough energy for daily life. However, the good news is that you don't have to be in starvation mode to access this other fuel. By eating a diet that is low in carbohydrates and high in fat, you can achieve what's known as "nutritional ketosis" (to distinguish it from the starvation variety).

Becoming a fat-burner isn't instantaneous; it can take weeks for your body to adapt to this new fuel source, particularly if it has been accustomed to burning glucose. And, like any lifestyle change, it's not one-size-fits-all. There really is no single right way to follow a ketogenic diet, and everybody tolerates and processes things a little differently. How much fat, protein, and carbs each individual needs to get into and stay in ketosis can depend on a variety of factors, including age, gender, body weight, and activity level. However, most experts agree on a basic formula of macronutrients:

FAT: 60 to 85 percent   **PROTEIN: 15 to 30 percent**   **CARBS: 5 to 20 percent**

From these relatively wide ranges, you can surmise that the formula is by no means exact. Your job, should you choose to accept it, is to tinker with these numbers, adjusting and fine-tuning, until you have a diet that works for you. For most people, it's worth the effort. And once your body is fully adapted, it becomes easier and easier to stick with it. Cravings will diminish and you will have more energy than ever before.

Note that fat is by far the largest source of nutrition and calories in the ketogenic diet, while protein intake is moderate. It can be a little scary to make that leap into high-fat eating if you've never done it before. There are several great resources that can guide you through the process of starting and maintaining a balanced ketogenic diet. The book *Keto Clarity* by Jimmy Moore and Eric Westman, MD, is a good place to start. *Diet Doctor,* the website of Dr. Andreas Eenfeldt, is also wonderfully informative for keto newbies (go to www.dietdoctor.com). And if you're looking for something a little more technologically advanced, I recommend KetoDietApp for tracking your macronutrients (or "macros") on mobile devices.

HEALTH BENEFITS: IT'S NOT JUST FOR WEIGHT LOSS

With its newfound popularity, the ketogenic diet might seem like a newcomer on the health scene, but it's not. It's actually been around since the 1920s, not as a weight-loss tool, but as a therapeutic method for managing epilepsy and other neurological seizure disorders.

More recently, a growing number of studies indicate that ketogenic diets have many other health benefits, from slowing the growth of cancer to helping with Alzheimer's disease and Parkinson's disease. The keto diet is also helpful for managing diabetes and other metabolic disorders.

Let that news sink in for a moment. A low-carb, high-fat, moderate-protein diet is good for both the body and the brain. We are just beginning to scratch the surface on all the illnesses and complaints that may be treated or managed by ketogenic diets, but the list thus far is impressive:

Alzheimer's disease	Inflammation
Cancer	Irritable bowel syndrome
Cardiovascular disease	Migraines
Epilepsy	Parkinson's disease
Hashimoto's thyroiditis	Polycystic ovarian syndrome
Hypertension	Type 2 diabetes

Clearly, nutritional ketosis is so much more than a weight-loss tool, and it's incredibly exciting. But if weight loss or diabetes management is your ultimate goal, then you are most certainly on the right path. Again, I refer you to the experts for a more detailed look at the health benefits of a keto diet; you can find a list of resources on page 365.

KETO AND DIABETES

I am one of those enviable people who never had to struggle with her weight. Okay, so in college, I gained a few extra pounds just like everyone around me. However, once I hit my stride, the weight came off easily and never came back. I say this not to make anyone feel bad about their own weight struggles but because it helps to illustrate my point. Being slender and active didn't keep me from developing gestational diabetes, and it didn't help me later as my blood sugar began to rise again. Even though I'd cut out most sugar from my diet and was getting plenty of exercise, my numbers were creeping upward.

I am by no means an expert on all things diabetes, but I am an intelligent woman and I can spot a problem when I see it. I am continually horrified by the standard nutritional advice put forth by various medical and diabetes associations, which recommends whole grains, lean meats, limited fats, and plenty of carbohydrates. It was the same advice I received when I was pregnant, and even back then, I could see that it wasn't working. I had to work really hard to stay within those guidelines, taking a walk after every meal to lower my glucose levels. I managed to stay off diabetes medications for my entire pregnancy, but just barely. It was a struggle every single day.

This advice makes very little sense when you think about it. You don't tell someone who is lactose intolerant to consume dairy. Why would you tell someone who can't tolerate carbs to make sure they get plenty of carbs? I am truly thankful that there are doctors and other medical professionals who are speaking out against the party line and making their voices heard in favor of low-carb and ketogenic diets. There are some amazing thought leaders out there, doctors Richard Bernstein, William Davis, Jason Fung, and Ron Rosedale among them. (Again, check out the resources on page 365.)

COMMON MISCONCEPTIONS

As with any lifestyle choice, there are plenty of myths and misconceptions about ketogenic diets. Low-fat eating has become so widely accepted that it's hard to shift the collective mindset to accept such a radically different approach to health and weight loss. You're bound to hear any number of interesting comments when you tell people that you have adopted a low-carb, high-fat lifestyle. You might also find that you don't get a lot of support from friends and family.

While it's not your job to change their minds, it does help to arm yourself with a few solid pieces of information. I urge you to do your own research so that, at the very least, you are confident in your choices and can ignore the naysayers. But don't believe everything you read on the Internet; these days, anyone can pose as an expert and dole out nutrition advice. I like to find well-researched articles that cite at least a few peer-reviewed studies. I often check out the links to the actual studies as well.

Here are a few of the misconceptions you might find yourself discussing with well-meaning people.

LOW-CARB, NOT NO-CARB

One reason people balk at the idea of a ketogenic diet is that they perceive it as cutting out all carbohydrates. This is patently false, and I know of no low-carb experts who advocate for this kind of extreme dieting. Plenty of non-starchy vegetables and a few well-chosen fruits are a mainstay of any healthy diet, including the keto diet. And I actually eat more of them now than I did when I was following a "healthy" standard American diet.

This misconception perhaps stems from the fact that keto diets do eliminate all grains. Heretofore, we've been taught to consider grains as essential to our health and well-being. How can a diet that eliminates an "essential" group of foods possibly be healthy? Well, chew on this for a moment: For hundreds of thousands of years, the human species did pretty well without any grains at all. Grains became a significant part of the human diet only with the domestication of plants and animals, roughly 10,000 to 12,000 years ago. Prior to that, the seeds of tall grasses, such as wheat, barley, and rice, were small and hard to harvest and did not contribute much to the diet of hunter-gatherers. Because anatomically modern humans have been around for 200,000 years, that represents a good 190,000 years of grain-free living.

Back when I was a graduate student in anthropology, I wrote a research paper on the health of ancient hunter-gatherer groups compared to that of early agricultural societies that relied heavily on grains. It was an eye-opener at the time. While the hunter-gatherer societies had recurrent periods of food scarcity and sometimes starvation, they had fewer overall signs of disease and malnutrition than the agricultural societies. Domesticated grains are easy to store and can feed a great many more people, but at what cost to overall nutrition?

The wonder of it all is that I never applied this knowledge to my own diet until I developed diabetes. You wouldn't think a woman with a master of arts in paleoanthropology would be quite so thick! While grains and grain-based foods are still being heavily promoted as integral to a healthy diet, a significant body of evidence suggests otherwise. Studies indicate that grain consumption can exacerbate inflammatory conditions, such as arthritis, autoimmune disorders, leaky gut, and irritable bowel syndrome. And don't get me started on diabetes. As someone who tests her blood glucose, I can tell you that even a small amount of whole grains spikes my blood sugar. By far the best resources on the potential health issues caused by grains are the books *Wheat Belly* by William Davis, MD, and *Grain Brain* by David Perlmutter, MD.

KETOSIS IS NOT THE SAME THING AS KETOACIDOSIS

When I first read that people were *trying* to get themselves into ketosis, I was horrified. Why? Because my endocrinologist had lectured me extensively on avoiding *ketoacidosis* at all costs. It is not uncommon for laypeople to confuse these two terms; in fact, many medical professionals do as well.

So what's the difference? Both are states in which an individual has elevated ketone levels. However, ketoacidosis is a life-threatening condition that occurs in people whose bodies make virtually no insulin of their own (mostly people with type 1 diabetes, but occasionally some individuals with type 2). When diabetes is uncontrolled and the body doesn't make enough insulin to transfer glucose from the bloodstream to the cells, the body thinks it is starving. In essence, it panics and begins producing ketones at an alarming rate in an effort to provide fuel...even while the bloodstream is full of glucose. Ketones rise to a toxic level, and the individual might become extremely ill and possibly even fall into a coma.

The symptoms of ketoacidosis, such as dizziness, nausea, extreme thirst, and constant urination, are often the first signs of type 1 diabetes in an undiagnosed individual. Blood tests will show both high glucose levels and extremely high ketone levels at the same time.

Nutritional ketosis, on the other hand, occurs in the presence of both insulin and normal blood sugar. The body doesn't panic, and it produces ketones at a much more moderate and healthy rate. Insulin keeps ketone production under control. And most people— even those with type 2 diabetes, such as myself—make enough insulin to keep ketones at healthy levels. Type 1 diabetics who choose to follow a ketogenic diet sometimes find their need to take insulin much reduced.

It's a fascinating and complex system, and I urge you to read up on it. Two great sources of information include the books *Keto Clarity* by Jimmy Moore and Eric Westman, MD, and *Dr. Bernstein's Diabetes Solution* by Richard K. Bernstein.

IF YOU EXERCISE, YOU NEED CARBS

Exercise is a subject about which I am very passionate. I saw the power of exercise firsthand when I was pregnant and struggling to control my blood sugar. Whenever it ventured too high, I went for a walk, and my glucose level would drop by up to 60 points. It didn't seem to matter how slowly I moved. Even when I was heavily pregnant and waddling along the Charles River during my lunch hour, I could get back into my target range. I was sold, and I vowed to commit to regular exercise after the baby was born.

There are any number of misconceptions about exercise and ketogenic diets. The most common is that you absolutely need carbohydrates for energy during exercise. In fact, if you were to Google "do you need carbs for exercise?" you would find an overwhelming number of websites and articles stating that you do. My body, and the bodies of many other keto dieters and athletes, seem to state otherwise. In fact, I ran my best half-marathon fueled on only a two-egg omelet with cheese, and I didn't need anything but water during the whole 13.1 miles. That, of course, is purely anecdotal evidence, but bear with me for a moment.

Consider the fact that, as a society, we have been eating a high-carb diet for decades, even centuries. Thus the majority of studies done on the energy requirements for athletic performance are, by default, done on people who are carb-adapted (that is, their bodies rely on carbohydrates for energy). Therefore, the results are automatically going to show that carbs are essential for fuel. However, pioneering studies by people like doctors Stephen Phinney and Jeff Volek have shown that once individuals become keto-adapted, their athletic performance does not suffer; in fact, it might even improve.

Becoming keto-adapted is important here. If you are already a regular exerciser and you suddenly switch to a low-carb, high-fat diet, you will indeed see your performance suffer at first. For a few weeks at least, you might feel like you don't have the energy for your standard routine. But I speak from personal experience when I say that it does come back. And when it does, you will feel better than ever.

Another misconception is that you don't actually need to exercise on a ketogenic diet—that being low-carb and high-fat is all you need for good health. Thunk! My head just hit the table. This is a nasty little rumor, and it's one I'd like to address. I believe it stems from studies indicating that diet is the most important factor when it comes to weight loss. But weight loss and optimal health are not at all the same thing. Our bodies were designed to move, not sit at desks all day or lounge on couches watching TV all evening.

If weight loss is your only goal, that's fine. If good health is important to you, you have to get moving. I'm not saying you have to run 10 miles or hit the gym hard every day. But barring serious physical limitations, physical activity should be a part of your day. It hardly matters whether you're walking, running, cycling, dancing, or waddling along the river when you are nine months pregnant. Movement: it does a body good.

KETO IS NOT
A "RESTRICTED DIET"

Make no mistake: the keto diet is not a diet of deprivation or starvation. There are so many delicious, satisfying foods to eat and so many creative ways to prepare them. In fact, choosing to eat this way has widened my food horizons rather than narrowed them. When you enter the world of low-carb cooking and baking, you find yourself introduced to new ingredients you've never heard of before, as well as using familiar ingredients in brand-new ways. And filling up on real, nutrient-dense food keeps you satiated longer. You never have to go hungry on a keto diet.

One of my goals in writing this cookbook is to help shift the mindset from seeing this as a special diet to viewing it as an everyday lifestyle. I have come to the conclusion that, with a little ingenuity, I can make a keto version of almost anything. Of course, I can't magically make apples, pasta, or bread low-carb, but I can make things that taste like apples or behave like pasta or bread—and that's good enough for me. Knowing that it's healthier and doesn't send my blood glucose soaring adds a little extra appeal to each dish. The absence of guilt tastes really, really good sometimes.

Admittedly, shifting your diet away from carbs and toward fat does take some getting used to. You likely will feel a little strange at first, and you may experience what is often called the "keto flu" as your body adjusts to burning ketones instead of glucose for energy. Headaches, achiness, and lethargy are common symptoms. I distinctly remember the feeling of weakness, like my blood sugar was low, even when my glucometer was telling me that everything was normal. You can help mitigate these symptoms by drinking plenty of fluids and making sure you are getting enough electrolytes.

TIPS FOR EVERYDAY KETO DIET SUCCESS

There's a pretty simple formula for sticking with any special diet; it all comes down to loving what you eat. If you're brand-new to keto, you might think that it's not so simple. After all, you're giving up so much of what you love, including bread, pizza, and cake—all those comfort foods that get you through a tough day.

Except you're not really giving these things up. You can still have bread, pizza, and cake on a ketogenic diet. Are the keto versions exactly the same? No. Are they just as delicious, or possibly even more so? I certainly think so, and I have a few hundred thousand blog readers who would agree with me.

Beyond that, there are a few other tips and tricks for sticking with the keto diet and enjoying all it has to offer, from delicious foods to amazing health benefits.

1

As the Boy Scout motto says: Be Prepared. This might be the most important element of keto diet success. Having the right foods on hand and having some easy meals prepped ahead of time means that you will be less likely to succumb to temptation. Many keto dieters set aside one day a week to make meals and snacks so they can stay the course all week long.

Your freezer is your friend when it comes to prepping ahead. Many low-carb meals and baked goods can be frozen for future emergencies. I often make a double batch of grab-and-go foods like muffins so that I can put some away for days when I am short on time (which, let's face it, is almost every morning!). If you're the only one in your household on a low-carb diet, try freezing individual portions.

2

Find a support network. The benefits here are twofold: support and accountability. Sometimes we stink at making promises to ourselves. Those promises are only in our heads, after all, so it's pretty easy to pretend that we never made them in the first place. But when you say it out loud to a friend or a support group, a promise seems that much harder to break.

In this day and age, there's no excuse for not having someone to make promises to. Even if you don't have any real-life friends or family who support your low-carb lifestyle, there are numerous online groups and forums. People who have been at this for a while are usually incredibly supportive and helpful, and they have amazing ideas to help you stay the course.

3

Keep a food journal, at least some of the time. Tracking everything you eat in a day can be time-consuming, but it's also eye-opening. It can help you identify what works and what doesn't. Because there is no set formula for a ketogenic diet, this step can be critical. I don't keep a journal very frequently anymore, but I certainly did at the beginning. I had to know which foods were spiking my blood sugar and which foods were "safe." An added benefit is that tracking your food makes you a more conscious eater. The very act of putting it down on paper makes you stick with the program a little better.

4

Chew the fat. When you're new to keto, it can be tricky to increase your fats without also increasing your proteins. You might be reaching for bacon and eggs, which are certainly good choices, but eat too much of them and you may find that you've inadvertently consumed a lot of protein, too.

This is where high-fat snacks like fat bombs and butter coffee come in handy. Because they are mostly fat with very little in the way of carbs or protein, they can really help you feel full and stay on track.

Also, be sure to choose the fattiest cuts of meat that you can. Choose skin-on chicken thighs over skinless chicken breasts, chops with a good rind of fat on them, and nicely marbled steaks and roasts. Add fat to your meals wherever you can. I always put butter on my steak, and because it's so satisfying that way, I find that I can eat only half the meat. Bonus: I get two meals out of one steak!

5

Beat boredom eating. I don't know about you, but boredom eating is my potential downfall. I work from home, and when I am not particularly engaged in what I'm doing, I find myself wandering aimlessly into the kitchen. Here are a few strategies to beat that 3 p.m. snack attack:

- Find other things to do with your mouth, like sipping sparkling water, herbal tea, or warm bone broth.

- Get up and get moving. A little action, even a 10-minute walk, can reset your mental state.

- Drink a glass of water. So often, that "hunger" you feel is actually thirst. Once you've downed the water, you will no longer feel the urge to eat.

- Eat fat bombs! When it comes to fatty snacks, just a little helps satisfy and curb those cravings. Check out the White Chocolate Raspberry Cups recipe on page 312 and the Salted Chocolate Macadamia Nut Fat Bombs recipe on page 314.

6

Get excited about recipes and cooking. Remember, this is not meant to be a diet of deprivation. I really believe that there is a low-carb version of almost everything. Just knowing that you can enjoy some of your old favorites, albeit in newer and healthier forms, can be reassuring. And exploring new recipes and techniques can be incredibly exciting. Keep a list of the dishes you want to make, save them to your recipe files, and get ready to enjoy yourself.

7

If you cheat—if you succumb to temptation and fall off the wagon—do not, under any circumstances, beat yourself up. I participate in many forums for low-carb and keto diets, and there are always people flagellating themselves for cheating, for failing, for not having the willpower to stick it out. Well, guess what? We all fail at this sometimes. Let's face it, we live in a sugar- and gluten-filled world. Unless we are hermits who never leave the house, we are faced with temptation daily—at work, at social functions, on television, and on the Internet. Temptation is all around us; the wonder of it all is that we don't give in more often!

Be kind to yourself. You wouldn't berate a friend or loved one who slipped, would you? Then why on earth do you talk to yourself that way? It really doesn't help, and the guilt can send you into a downward spiral. So take a deep breath and repeat after me: "I am human. I had a moment of failure. And I will probably fail again. That's okay. What's important is that I keep trying."

CHAPTER 1
EVERYDAY KETO
INGREDIENTS

You will be happy to hear that low-carb, high-fat cooking really isn't any harder than conventional cooking. In fact, in many ways it's easier because it employs fresh, whole-food ingredients and straightforward cooking techniques. There really is no magic, hocus-pocus, or strange ketogenic voodoo to it. Granted, you can't just reach for a prepackaged meal and toss it into the microwave. But that's why you're here, after all: because you no longer want to rely on unhealthy convenience foods full of sugar and starches. You care too much about your health for that, and so do I. Thankfully, you will find that most of the recipes in this book rely on familiar ingredients and cooking methods—with a few fun little twists to keep you on your toes.

Ketogenic baking is another matter altogether. For the uninitiated, I liken it to entering an alternate universe or falling down the rabbit hole into Wonderland. Nothing behaves quite the way you think it should. Nut meals and coconut flour might look a lot like wheat flour, but they sure don't bake like it. That means direct substitutions almost inevitably result in failure. Gluten is something of a magical substance in conventional baking, providing structure and helping baked goods to rise and hold together properly. In its absence, you must compensate for these magical properties or you might end up with something that looks and tastes like a hockey puck.

Not to fear, however. Low-carb, high-fat baking is my favorite topic in the whole wide world. I've always loved to bake, long before diabetes came along and I had to make all my muffins, breads, and cookies from scratch. However, I think I love baking even more now than I did before going keto. Baking with alternative ingredients has challenged my creativity and pushed me to experiment—and nothing makes me happier than re-creating old favorites with ketogenic ingredients. My enthusiasm for the subject knows no bounds, and I have made it my mission to pass on my knowledge and expertise to you.

I believe that a well-stocked kitchen is a key to success for the ketogenic lifestyle. Having the ingredients and tools you need at your fingertips makes it much easier to whip up your favorite dishes at a moment's notice, which, in turn, makes you much less likely to succumb to high-carb temptation. My husband and kids don t always eat keto, so we often have some higher-carb foods in the house. But as long as I have my own low-carb goodies on hand, I rarely feel the urge to cheat.

EVERYDAY INGREDIENTS

Going keto will inevitably introduce you to some interesting foods you might not have heard of, though the vast majority are everyday ingredients that you are likely already familiar with. Stocking up on healthy fats and oils, rich proteins, non-starchy vegetables, nuts, and seeds will put you well on your way to low-carb, high-fat success.

HEALTHY FATS AND OILS

Notice I said "healthy" fats and oils here. We hear that term a lot these days, bandied about by various factions. The ketogenic concept of healthy fats is very different from that of, say, the American Heart Association's. While the AHA promotes the use of unsaturated vegetable oils, the keto diet focuses on healthy sources of saturated fats, as well as monounsaturated fats and natural polyunsaturated fats.

Not all oils and fats are created equal. At this point, we are well aware that hydrogenated oils and trans fats aren't good for us, but many of the oils we have heretofore been told were good for us might not be. Keto experts generally agree that soybean oil, canola oil, corn oil, safflower oil, and sunflower oil should be avoided because they are highly refined and, in some cases, even man-made.

Good Keto Oils and Fats

BUTTER

GHEE (clarified butter)

HEAVY CREAM

CHEESES OF ALL KINDS

CREAM CHEESE

GREEK YOGURT
(whole milk, unsweetened)

SOUR CREAM

FULL-FAT COCONUT MILK
(the canned variety)

AVOCADO OIL
(I love Primal Kitchen brand)

COCONUT OIL

NUT OILS (almond, hazelnut,
macadamia nut, walnut)

OLIVE OIL (use light olive oil for
frying and high-heat cooking)

BACON FAT

DUCK FAT

LARD

MAYONNAISE (made with avocado
oil if you can find it, such as Primal
Kitchen brand, or make your own—
see page 65)

RICH PROTEINS

Because protein consumption is supposed to be moderate on a keto diet, it's important to choose your proteins wisely. Look for fatty cuts of beef and pork and opt for skin-on dark meat poultry whenever possible. Some recipes are better suited to skinless white meat, but you can always add more fat to those dishes.

Good Rich Proteins

EGGS	LAMB	POULTRY	BACON	SHELLFISH
BEEF	PORK	SAUSAGE	FISH	BROTHS

VEGETABLES

When I first went low-carb, I was surprised to discover which vegetables are higher or lower in carbs. I knew to avoid potatoes and other tubers, but I was startled by how many carbs an onion contains. The moral of the story is to do your research before you eat. I still use onions in my recipes, but in small quantities as a flavoring element or garnish. The veggies below are some of your best options for a keto diet.

Good Vegetable Choices

ARTICHOKES	CABBAGE	GREEN BEANS	SPAGHETTI SQUASH
ASPARAGUS	CAULIFLOWER	JICAMA	SUGAR SNAP PEAS (the whole pod)
BELL PEPPERS	CHILE PEPPERS	LEAFY GREENS (spinach, lettuce, endive, kale, chard)	
BOK CHOY	CUCUMBERS		SUMMER SQUASH
BROCCOLI	EGGPLANT	MUSHROOMS	ZUCCHINI
BRUSSELS SPROUTS	GARLIC	RADISHES	FRESH HERBS
		RHUBARB	

FRUIT

You don't have to avoid fruit altogether, but it should be eaten sparingly. Again, you might be surprised by which fruits are higher or lower in carbs. Tropical fruits, such as bananas, pineapples, and mangoes, are very high in carbs, while sweet summer berries are surprisingly low in carbs.

Good Fruit Choices

AVOCADOS	BLACKBERRIES	CRANBERRIES	STRAWBERRIES
TOMATOES	BLUEBERRIES	RASPBERRIES	LEMONS AND LIMES

NUTS AND SEEDS

Most nuts and seeds have a high fat content and are great for low-carb snacking. I always keep some on me while traveling so I can avoid the high-carb airplane food. However, cashews and pistachios are much higher in carbs than other nuts and seeds, so limit or avoid them altogether.

Good Nut and Seed Choices

ALMONDS	PEANUTS (not really a nut, but let's just go with it!)	WALNUTS	PUMPKIN SEEDS (pepitas)
HAZELNUTS		CHIA SEEDS	SUNFLOWER SEEDS
MACADAMIA NUTS	PECANS	HEMP SEEDS	COCONUT
	PINE NUTS		

SOME NOT-SO-EVERYDAY INGREDIENTS

While almost all keto diet staples are available at your neighborhood grocery store, there are a few not-as-common ingredients that you might want to consider for your pantry. I don't even think of many of these items as "specialized" because they are quite commonplace in Paleo, low-carb, and gluten-free circles. Some have become so popular that many major grocery chains now carry them. Others can be a little harder to source and are best purchased online or from specialty food stores.

COCONUT AMINOS

Many people in the low-carb and Paleo communities steer clear of soy because it is often genetically modified and heavily processed, and it might have adverse effects on endocrine function. However, soy sauce is an integral ingredient in many Asian dishes and lends a distinct umami taste. Fortunately, coconut aminos—the aged sap from coconut trees—mimics the flavor of soy sauce and contains only 1 gram of carbs per teaspoon. It's become so popular that it's now available in many grocery stores. It's readily available online.

GRASS-FED GELATIN AND COLLAGEN

Gelatin and collagen are the new darlings of the health-food world. Rich in amino acids and other nutrients, they are said to improve bone and joint health, as well as the appearance of skin, hair, and nails. Bone broth is so popular because it contains a significant amount of collagen. When those bones have simmered for ages and the broth becomes gelatinous as it cools, you know you've got the good stuff.

I keep powdered grass-fed gelatin and collagen in my pantry because they are useful in the kitchen. Gelatin helps to set no-bake desserts, such as panna cotta, and collagen makes butter coffee and hot chocolate (page 172) rich and frothy.

XANTHAN GUM AND GUAR GUM

Xanthan gum is a common ingredient in gluten-free recipes because it acts as a binder in the absence of gluten. I don't use it much in baking anymore because I have found other ways to compensate. However, xanthan gum is also useful as a thickening agent for custards, puddings, and sauces. And because it inhibits the formation of ice crystals, it helps give sugar-free ice cream a smoother, creamier mouthfeel.

Guar gum works similarly to xanthan gum. However, I find that it makes foods more "gummy," so I suggest using only about half as much guar gum. I recently mixed up the two when making a chicken dish and used guar gum instead of xanthan gum. My children joked that that sauce was like Flubber. It wasn't particularly appetizing, I have to admit.

Some people object to these gums on various grounds, but research indicates that they are generally safe as food additives. They are both naturally derived; xanthan gum is made by fermenting glucose with *Xanthromonas campestris* bacteria, and guar gum is harvested from the guar bean. Of course, being all natural is no guarantee of safety, but I personally feel very comfortable using them on occasion as thickeners and emulsifiers.

Some studies indicate that both gums can have a significant laxative effect at high doses (15g—1 tablespoon—or more per day). Given that I use ¼ teaspoon of xanthan gum in a recipe that serves four or more people, there is very little xanthan gum per serving (0.3g or less). However, you may omit the xanthan gum from any of these recipes. Just be aware that the consistency of the dish might be somewhat different.

CACAO BUTTER

Cacao butter, or cocoa butter, is the fat extracted from the cacao bean. I've found it to be a very useful keto ingredient. Unlike other fats and oils, it is completely solid at room temperature, so it can help firm up low-carb candies and other confections. It also has a distinct "white chocolate" flavor, which makes for delicious treats. It's just icing on the white chocolate cake that cacao butter is also quite good for you. It fits well into the ketogenic diet because it's full of antioxidants and vegetable-based saturated fats.

Despite its popularity as a health food, cacao butter is still not widely available in stores, so it's best purchased online. Be sure to purchase food-grade cacao butter, as it's also used for making soaps and cosmetics. I like to buy the kind that comes in smaller chips or discs, such as Wild Foods brand, because it's easier to measure out. Chipping an ounce of cacao butter from a big block is not my idea of a good time!

PORK RINDS

Pork rinds are nothing new, of course, but they have become a popular ingredient in ketogenic cooking. People are using them in a number of creative ways. I've seen them used as croutons, nachos, and even cereal. Crushed up finely, they make a great breading for chicken or fish. There is even a company called Bacon's Heir that sells precrushed pork rinds, which it calls "pork dust."

EXTRACTS AND FLAVORINGS

Being the bakeaholic that I am, I always have a number of extracts and flavorings spilling out of my pantry. They are an easy and inexpensive way to make keto baked goods and treats that taste like their high-carb counterparts; banana extract can replace bananas to give a baked good a banana flavor, for example. I always advocate for natural flavors over imitation extracts, if you can find them. The basics, such as vanilla, almond, orange, and lemon, are usually available at any grocery store. Maple extract is always in my pantry, too, because maple syrup is out of the question on a ketogenic diet. Fruit flavors, such as apple, pineapple, and cherry, are useful as well, but those often need to be purchased online.

MY EVERYDAY BAKING PANTRY

Because baking is essential to my very existence, I have a well-stocked baking cabinet. Or perhaps I should say overstocked, because it's usually spilling over into the rest of my pantry. Alternative flours and sweeteners are increasingly available at regular grocery stores, often in the gluten-free or natural foods aisles. Many of us consider these alternative flours to be everyday ingredients. Here are the items I always have on hand for when the urge to bake strikes. You can find more information about these ingredients and how to use them in the sections following the list.

ALMOND FLOUR

COCONUT FLOUR

PROTEIN POWDER

COCOA POWDER (unsweetened)

UNSWEETENED CHOCOLATE

SUGAR-FREE DARK CHOCOLATE

SWEETENERS

SPICES

BAKING POWDER

BAKING SODA

VANILLA EXTRACT

And of course, I always have the holy trinity of low-carb baking on hand:

BUTTER

EGGS (LARGE)

HEAVY CREAM

NUT AND SEED FLOURS

Almond flour is perhaps the most widely recognized alternative to wheat flour, and I think it is one of the most versatile low-carb ingredients. Different brands of almond flour can vary greatly, so you need to know what to look for. The finest almond flours are made from blanched almonds and have no darker specks of almond skin. The finer the grind of the flour, the finer the consistency of your baked goods. Bob's Red Mill produces a finely milled almond flour that is available in many supermarkets, as well as online. Honeyville is another good brand; it is sold online and at Costco.

Almond "meal" is often not nearly as finely ground, and it might or might not contain the husks of the almonds. It also tends to be less expensive and is still useful in recipes that don't require as fine a texture, such as muffins. However, I recommend blanched almond flour for most recipes.

If you're not a fan of almonds or have an almond or tree nut allergy, there are plenty of other nut and seed flours and meals out there. In my experience, very few of them are as finely ground as good almond flour, but they can make for some truly delicious baked goods. Sunflower seed flour is a great nut-free replacement for almond flour. You can actually grind your own quite easily; check out my recipe on page 84.

COCONUT FLOUR

Coconut flour is a different beast altogether from almond flour. It is actually the by-product of coconut milk production. After the milk has been extracted, the leftover coconut meat is dried at low temperatures for a long time and then ground. The result is a finely powdered substance that resembles wheat flour in texture, although it smells distinctly of coconut. But don't try to treat it like wheat flour, or you will end up with a few tasteless hockey pucks and a stress headache. Because it's so absorbent, coconut flour requires a lot of eggs, as well as quite a bit of oil and other liquids, to bake properly.

Even if you don't enjoy the taste of coconut, you might want to try baking with coconut flour because the coconut taste can often be masked by other strong flavors. Vanilla, chocolate, and cocoa powder work well for sweet recipes. For savory items, try adding a little garlic or onion powder.

As with nut flours, different brands of coconut flour can vary greatly. Some flours seem to absorb more liquid than others, and your end result can be overly soggy. I use Bob's Red Mill brand coconut flour in my recipes because it produces the most consistent results.

PROTEIN POWDER

Perhaps the question I receive most frequently on my blog is, "Why do you use protein powder in your baked goods? Is it to add more protein to your diet? What can I replace it with?" That's actually three questions, but you get the picture. Adding protein powder to a recipe for cake or muffins might seem strange if you are used to conventional wheat-and-sugar baking, but it all comes down to the science of gluten-free baking.

Many people don't realize that gluten is actually a set of proteins found in wheat, rye, and barley. These proteins have important properties that help baked goods rise and hold their shape. In the absence of gluten, you need to compensate for these properties so that your baked goods don't sink or crumble to pieces. After a great deal of experimentation, I have found that adding a small amount of unflavored whey protein powder goes a long way toward getting the right texture and consistency.

We've already established that a proper ketogenic diet should be moderate in protein, so adding protein powder to recipes is certainly not about getting in more protein. I'd much rather get my protein from meat and eggs. Rest assured that the added protein powder usually contributes only about 2 grams of protein per serving.

If you want your results to be absolutely stellar, there really isn't a good replacement for protein powder. That said, you don't have to use whey protein; I've also used egg white protein with great success. Hemp protein and pea protein work, too, but they are both green in color, and I recommend them only for chocolate baked goods. I like to use Tera's Whey grass-fed protein powder or Paleo Protein Egg White Powder; I usually use the unflavored variety. The flavored varieties tend to contain sweeteners that throw off the sweetness of my baked goods.

UNSWEETENED CHOCOLATE AND COCOA POWDER

If you're a chocolate lover like me, you will want to load up on good-quality unsweetened chocolate and cocoa powder. As far as I am concerned, they are absolute musts for any keto baking cupboard. Unsweetened chocolate can be tricky to work with because it can seize and become clumpy and grainy when subjected to too much heat or any additional liquids. I usually go for better-quality brands, such as Ghirardelli or Dagoba, and I stock up when I see a sale.

SUGAR-FREE CHOCOLATE AND CHOCOLATE CHIPS

Sugar-free is a popular industry these days, and many companies are getting in on the act. However, not all sugar-free chocolate is created equal. I recommend steering clear of brands that are sweetened with maltitol or sorbitol because they tend to spike blood sugar as much as sugar does (and they are tough on the tummy!). I am not a fan of artificial sweeteners, either, like sucralose and aspartame. Personally, I stick with brands

Unsweetened Chocolate vs. Sugar-Free Chocolate

Note that "unsweetened" chocolate and "sugar-free" chocolate are not the same thing. Unsweetened chocolate or "baking" chocolate is 100 percent cacao and isn't sweetened with anything at all. Sugar-free chocolate, on the other hand, contains some sort of alternative sweetener and comes in many varieties, from milk chocolate to dark chocolate to flavored versions. When a recipe calls for one or the other, don't try to swap them. Sugar-free chocolate has a lower fiber content, which can affect the consistency of your desserts.

like Lily's and ChocoPerfection, both of which are sweetened with erythritol and stevia. (See the section "Low-Carb Sweeteners" on page 35 for more on the different types.)

While sugar-free chocolate and chocolate chips are really useful in low-carb baking, there's no question that they are a bit spendy. They are a luxury item for many people, so I often recommend using very dark chocolate (85 percent cacao or higher) in their stead. Lindt 90 percent is a good choice and can stand in for chocolate chips when chopped up. I've also included a recipe for making your own sugar-free dark chocolate and chocolate chips on page 322.

LEAVENING AGENTS

Baking powder and baking soda are standard in any baker's arsenal, of course. Baking soda is simply sodium bicarbonate and requires the addition of an acidic ingredient to produce carbon dioxide. It is this reaction between base and acid that helps baked goods rise. Baking powder is really just baking soda with a couple of additives. It contains a dry acid, such as cream of tartar, and a stabilizer, such as cornstarch, so that it will begin to react only when it comes in contact with a liquid.

I keep both on hand, but I use baking powder much more frequently. I find it easier to work with because it reacts more slowly than baking soda. This means I don't have to rush quite so much to get things into the oven. Hain Baking Powder is a good choice because it is both aluminum-free and made with potato starch rather than cornstarch (the starches add little to no carbohydrate to a recipe).

SALT

I have about four varieties of salt in my kitchen at any given moment. Adding salt to a recipe, savory or sweet, enhances the flavor. But the type you use is also of great importance, in part because the crystal size can make a difference in how salty the result is—the smaller the particles, the more sodium you are adding. A tablespoon of finely ground salt contains more sodium than a tablespoon of coarse salt simply because it's more compact.

For almost all of my recipes, I use fine sea salt or regular table salt. But I often use the coarser kosher salt for seasoning meats and in spice rubs, and I use large-flake sea salt when I want the crystals to show up on the finished product.

LOW-CARB SWEETENERS

Everyone has opinions about which low-carb sweeteners are best for a ketogenic diet, and I am no exception. However, the best sweetener for *you* depends as much on personal preference as anything else. I am not a purist, and I am not going to tell you that you can't use sucralose if that's what you like best. That said, the different types of sweeteners behave a little differently in cooking and baking, and some are better for certain applications than others. It's important to understand their unique properties and how these qualities might affect your results.

Artificial High-Intensity Sweeteners

These artificial sweeteners include sucralose (Splenda), aspartame, and saccharin, among others, and they contain little or no calories or carbohydrates. They have the distinct advantage of being relatively inexpensive and widely available in most grocery stores. In their basic form, they are much, much sweeter than sugar, so you often need very little to sweeten an entire recipe. Many manufacturers combine them with other food additives, such as maltodextrin, so that they can be measured cup for cup like sugar. Be forewarned, however, because these additives can raise the carb count.

The biggest issue with these high-intensity sweeteners is that they don't have much volume; even the granulated versions are so light and powdery that they don't add much besides sweetness. These sweeteners also won't help your recipe brown or caramelize with heat, so the final product might be much paler than one made with another sweetener.

I steer clear of these sweeteners because I don't think they bake very well. Also, to my palate, they have a strong chemical aftertaste. Should you choose to use them, just know that the lack of bulk and caramelization might affect the outcome of some of the recipes in this book.

Stevia Extract and Monk Fruit Extract

Stevia and monk fruit sweeteners are similar to artificial high-intensity sweeteners in that they are much sweeter than sugar and have little bulk on their own. Stevia is a naturally occurring zero-carb sweetener derived from the *Stevia rebaudiana* plant, which is native to South America. Monk fruit is a small gourd found in Southeast Asia, the extract of which is intensely sweet. Both stevia and monk fruit extracts come in liquid and powder form, and you need only a small amount of either form to replace a cup of sugar. A few manufacturers combine these sweeteners with bulking agents like maltodextrin to make a "baking blend" that measures more like sugar. Again, these baking blends can add to the carb count of a recipe.

Stevia has a distinct aftertaste similar to licorice. Though not necessarily unpleasant, it doesn't always combine well with other flavors. Some people find stevia quite bitter when used on its own, but combining it with other sweeteners can lessen this effect. I sometimes use a combination of Swerve (an erythritol blend; see page 35) and liquid stevia extract in my recipes. However, my son seems to have developed an intolerance (stevia is related to ragweed), so I don't use it as often anymore.

Sugar Alcohols

Sugar alcohols, such as xylitol and erythritol, are popular low-carb sweeteners because they have significantly less effect on blood glucose levels than sugar does. (Other sugar alcohols, such as sorbitol and maltitol, might raise blood sugar.) They are naturally occurring substances found in fruits and fermented foods, and they have a crystalline structure similar to sugar. Because these sweeteners contain bulk, they are useful for achieving the right texture in low-carb baked goods.

Sugar alcohols don't always stay in solution and tend to settle out of liquids, making it more difficult to sweeten drinks and sauces. Erythritol in particular tends to revert to a crystalline state and can produce a grainy mouthfeel in some foods. One distinct advantage to erythritol, however, is that it will caramelize when you apply heat to it. Erythritol also tends not to cause the gastrointestinal upset that many other sugar alcohols are known for causing.

Erythritol Blends

Because erythritol is only about 70 percent as sweet as sugar, many manufacturers combine it with other ingredients and sweeteners. There are several brands available nowadays, and each of them is formulated a little differently. Some are combined with stevia, some with monk fruit extract, and others with sweet-tasting fibers such as inulin. Some are made to be just as sweet as sugar, and others are more concentrated, making them two or three times as sweet.

I use Swerve brand sweetener almost exclusively because it is formulated to measure cup for cup with sugar, and I find that it produces the best results. It is an all-natural blend of erythritol and oligosaccharides (a prebiotic fiber), both from non-GMO fruit and vegetable sources. Swerve has little to no effect on blood glucose or insulin levels. I've tested this on myself repeatedly, so I feel confident using it. Swerve comes in both granulated and powdered (confectioner's-style) form, so it's useful for cakes, cookies, frostings, beverages, and more.

One thing to note about erythritol-based sweeteners is that they do contain carbohydrates. It can be a little shocking for a first-timer to pick up a bag of zero-calorie sweetener and see that it contains as many carbs as sugar does. However, erythritol-based sweeteners are metabolized completely differently, and the erythritol carbs are excreted directly into the urine without ever entering the bloodstream. Like many of you, I was skeptical at first, but I have seen it to hold true when I've tested my blood sugar. I can eat a large slice of chocolate cake made with almond flour and Swerve and it barely moves the needle. Astonishing!

Low-Carb Sweeteners and Their Properties

The recipes in this book were tested using Swerve. While I recognize that everyone has their own tastes and preferences, substituting another sweetener might change the results of a recipe. Wherever possible, I have noted those recipes in which substitutions can be made; I've also noted the best choices when making substitutions. Also keep in mind that erythritol blends are not all made to measure the same way. Be sure to check how your preferred sweetener measures against sugar and adjust the amount accordingly.

SWEETENER	INGREDIENT(S)	EQUIVALENT TO 1 CUP OF SUGAR	PROPERTIES
EZ-SWEETZ (liquid sucralose)	Sucralose	24 drops (less than ¼ teaspoon)	Has no bulk, man-made, may have a chemical aftertaste
POWDERED STEVIA EXTRACT	Stevia	½ to 1 teaspoon	Has no bulk, may have a strong aftertaste
LIQUID STEVIA EXTRACT	Stevia, water, vegetable glycerin	1 to 2 teaspoons	Has no bulk, may have a strong aftertaste
SPLENDA PACKETS	Dextrose, maltodextrin, sucralose	24 packets	Has no bulk, man-made, may have a chemical aftertaste
TRIM HEALTHY MAMA SUPER SWEET BLEND	Stevia, erythritol	3 tablespoons	Has some bulk, but much sweeter than sugar so less is needed
TRIM HEALTHY MAMA GENTLE SWEET BLEND	Xylitol, erythritol, stevia	¼ cup plus 2 tablespoons	Has some bulk, somewhat sweeter than sugar
PYURE	Erythritol, stevia	½ cup	Has some bulk, somewhat sweeter than sugar
LAKANTO	Erythritol, monk fruit extract	1 cup	Has bulk, as sweet as sugar, will caramelize
SPLENDA GRANULATED	Maltodextrin, sucralose	1 cup	Has bulk, but is light and powdery so may affect results, as sweet as sugar, won't caramelize, man-made, may have a chemical aftertaste
SWERVE	Erythritol, oligosaccharides	1 cup	Has bulk, as sweet as sugar, will caramelize
XYLOSWEET	Xylitol	1 cup	Has bulk, as sweet as sugar, may cause stomach upset in higher quantities
ZSWEET	Erythritol, stevia	1 cup	Has bulk, as sweet as sugar, will caramelize
SUKRIN	Erythritol	1⅓ cups	Has bulk, less sweet than sugar so more is needed, may caramelize
WHOLESOME ORGANIC ZERO	Erythritol	1⅓ cups	Has bulk, less sweet than sugar, may caramelize

Other Sweeteners

On occasion, I use small amounts of molasses or coconut sugar. Although these sweeteners are high in carbs, they help achieve a "brown sugar" appearance and flavor. I try to keep the amounts so little as to not raise the carb count per serving by more than 1 gram. You may omit them or replace them with a lower-carb sweetener if you prefer.

EVERYDAY SWAPS AND SUBSTITUTIONS

In many cases, swapping one similar ingredient for another makes very little difference in the outcome of a recipe. In other cases, particularly in baking, it can mean the difference between success and failure. For example, substituting coconut oil for butter in a pan-fried dish doesn't really change anything except the flavor. But swapping coconut flour for almond flour might end in a kitchen disaster. However, there are some standard substitutions that I recommend. Whether it's for dietary intolerances or just personal preference, here are a few that you can substitute cup for cup.

BUTTER

- Coconut oil (in baking, reduce the amount by 1 or 2 tablespoons because coconut oil tends to be greasier than butter)

- Avocado oil (a good substitute for melted butter)

WHIPPED CREAM

- Whipped coconut cream (there are many great articles on how to make coconut whipped cream online)

BAKING POWDER

- One-quarter the amount of baking soda plus one-half the amount of cream of tartar

UNSWEETENED CHOCOLATE

- Per ounce, use 3 tablespoons cocoa powder and ½ ounce cacao butter or 1 tablespoon coconut oil

HEAVY CREAM

- Whipping cream

- Full-fat coconut milk (the canned variety) or coconut cream (a thicker version of coconut milk, with less water)

ALMOND FLOUR

- Sunflower seed flour plus 1 tablespoon vinegar or lemon juice (sunflower seed flour tends to turn baked goods green, but the addition of vinegar or lemon juice offsets that reaction)

- Other nut meals (they won't be as finely ground, which could affect the outcome)

- Crushed pork rinds (as a breading or filler for meatballs and meatloaf, but not useful in baking)

WHEY PROTEIN POWDER

- Egg white protein powder

What's the difference between heavy cream and whipping cream?

I think that heavy cream and whipping cream can be used almost interchangeably. They function in very much the same way, both whipping into beautiful peaks for toppings and frostings (and eating with a spoon!). However, heavy cream has a higher fat content, with 36 percent or more milk fat, whereas whipping cream can be anywhere between 30 and 36 percent. Heavy cream is the obvious choice for keto, but whipping cream will work in most recipes. Many brands market heavy cream as "heavy whipping cream." I use Organic Valley Heavy Whipping Cream in almost all my recipes.

CHAPTER 2

TOOLS OF
THE TRADE

Just as having a well-stocked low-carb pantry is a key to ketogenic success, so is having the right tools with which to cook. You don't have to outfit your kitchen with every gadget on the market. It's much more important to have good-quality basic equipment that can stand up to a fair bit of abuse. Invest in tools that have multiple functions to save both money and kitchen space. Take it from someone whose drawers are full to bursting with unique but rarely used gadgets—you really don't need all that to be an everyday ketogenic cook.

EVERYDAY KITCHEN EQUIPMENT

These are the must-have tools for any good ketogenic kitchen.

COOKWARE

Chances are you probably already have a few pots and pans in your kitchen. Whenever possible, aim for quality over quantity. A small saucepan (1 to 2 quarts), a large saucepan (3 to 4 quarts), a few skillets of different sizes (8, 10, and 12 inches), plus a good large stockpot will put you well on your way to keto kitchen success.

The quality of a saucepan or skillet can make a significant difference to the outcome of your recipes. Good-quality pans distribute heat more evenly over the cooking surface, which allows for better cooking. Poor-quality pans tend to have hotspots that cause some of the food to cook too quickly before the rest is done. When choosing cookware, look for durable pans that have a copper or aluminum core. They should have some heft to them and not feel light as a feather in your hand. I also like the metal handles that are riveted to the pans so that the pans can go straight from the stovetop to the oven.

Cast iron is all the rage these days—and I do love my cast-iron pans—but they are not a requirement for low-carb cooking. They're heavy and require some TLC to stay in good shape. I also have a selection of good stainless-steel pans and some environmentally friendly nonstick cookware; both do a great job in most situations.

BAKEWARE

My mother once asked me if I owned every piece of bakeware known to man, and I had to admit that it wasn't outside the realm of possibility. However, the reality is that I could get by with a lot less, and so can you. A few good pans will go a long way, especially if you take good care of them by hand-washing them with warm soapy water and a soft cloth. I suggest having a 9 by 5-inch loaf pan, a standard 12-cup muffin pan, a 9-inch or 8-inch square pan, and a few good rimmed baking sheets (17 by 12 inches and 18 by 13 inches are common sizes for home baking). A 9-inch springform pan is a must for cheesecake.

Ceramic or glass bakeware is also useful. Consider investing in a pie or tart pan, a 13 by 9-inch casserole dish, and some 4-ounce and 8-ounce ramekins.

KNIVES

Once again, quality matters. Good stainless-steel knives help you slice and dice more efficiently. I suggest having a chef's knife and a small paring knife, plus one with a serrated edge for slicing keto breads and tomatoes. I've also become a big fan of Santoku knives for slicing cooked and raw meats. Good, well-known brands include Wüsthof, J.A. Henckels, and Cutco. Look for knives with sturdy handles that are riveted or welded to the blade, and be sure to keep your knives well sharpened. Dull knives require more force to cut through food, and you're more likely to cut yourself if your hand slips.

BLENDER OR FOOD PROCESSOR

You heard it here first: a good blender can do almost as much as a food processor, and sometimes more. I've had a series of mediocre blenders in my life, but when I finally made the leap to a Blendtec, I was astonished at the difference. My food processor doesn't get much play anymore because the blender purees, mixes, and blends far better. I make smoothies, nut butters, soups, cauliflower rice (yes, cauliflower rice!), pancake batter, muffin batter, and even chocolate mousse in my blender. How's that for multi-purpose?

If you don't want to invest in a high-powered blender, a food processor is a great alternative. You can really use the two interchangeably for most purposes, and certainly for the recipes in this book. Regular blenders often aren't up to the task of grinding nuts or chopping hard veggies like cauliflower.

HAND MIXER OR STAND MIXER

You don't need a big, fancy stand mixer, although it certainly does help. But you at least need a hand mixer for creaming butter, beating eggs, and whipping cream. Have you ever tried to whip cream by hand? It's good exercise, but it gets old very fast.

KITCHEN SCALE

While most cooks measure ingredients using standard American cups and tablespoons, an accurate kitchen scale is a must. Some ingredients just don't lend themselves well to being measured by volume, so it's imperative to know their weight. Because low-carb baking can be an exact science, I've provided measurements in both weight and volume for baking ingredients, such as almond flour and coconut flour.

For best results, whenever you see gram weights included for baking ingredients, I urge you to weigh those ingredients with a kitchen scale—at least at first as you get used to these low-carb ingredients. If you don't own a kitchen scale, measure the ingredients by volume using the scoop-and-level method described on page 45.

INSTANT-READ THERMOMETER

Don't just guess when your meat is properly cooked...measure the temperature with an instant-read thermometer! A good thermometer is also useful for making custards and ice creams so you can be sure that your egg yolks are fully cooked.

PARCHMENT PAPER

How on earth did I live before parchment paper? I'm not sure I could bake without it now. You can use parchment paper for everything from lining cookie sheets to rolling out sticky gluten-free dough. Nonstick parchment paper cupcake liners are handy, too; baked goods practically fall right out of them.

SILICONE BAKING MATS AND MUFFIN CUPS

Reusable silicone mats are wonderful for lining cookie sheets and for rolling out doughs. They also offer an added level of insulation so that the bottoms of your baked goods don't brown too quickly against the hot pan. I've also become a convert to silicone muffin cups. They are just as good as parchment paper liners, and nothing sticks to them. They wash easily in hot soapy water, so cleanup is a snap.

DRY AND LIQUID MEASURING CUPS

Yes, you need some of both because they are designed very differently. Dry measuring cups are made so that you can scoop ingredients into them and level them off, which allows for more accuracy. Liquid measuring cups are transparent so that you can see exactly where the liquid hits the line. If you fill a dry measuring cup with liquic, you might underfill it while trying to prevent spillage.

GRATERS AND ZESTERS

If you have a box grater, it likely has large and small holes and can be used for both grating cheese and zesting citrus. However, I love my little hardheld microplane zester for getting all the zest off a lemon or lime.

OFFSET SPATULAS

In a kitchen full of expensive cooking utensils, would you believe that the item I find most useful costs about $5? Seriously, my little offset spatula from Ateco, which is about 4 inches long, gets the most use. Ostensibly, it's for spreading frosting, but it's also good for spreading thick low-carb batter in pans because it can get into the corners. It's also useful for wiggling under rolled-out dough to help lift the dough without cracking. I have two, and I find myself reaching for them constantly.

NOT-SO-EVERYDAY KITCHEN EQUIPMENT

These tools and gadgets may not be necessities for a ketogenic kitchen, but they do make life a little easier and a lot more fun.

SPIRAL VEGETABLE SLICER

Spiral slicers are so commonplace now that I rather think they should go in the "Everyday Kitchen Equipment" section of this chapter. I'd love to tell you that this tool is not a requirement for a keto lifestyle, but part of me thinks that it is. If you want to turn veggies into noodles, you really do need a spiral slicer. They aren't all that expensive, so it's a purchase you won't regret.

ICE CREAM MAKER

You can get by in the low-carb world without an ice cream maker, but it's really lovely to have one. There aren't many truly healthy low-carb ice creams on the market, and it's so nice to dig into something creamy and cold on a hot day. I use mine year-round, and the basic Cuisinart model costs only about $50. However, there are ways to make ice cream without an ice cream maker. Check out my No-Churn Strawberry Sour Cream Ice Cream on page 338.

ICE POP MOLD

An ice pop mold is an inexpensive way to make keto frozen treats. You can take any low-carb ice cream base and pour it into an ice pop mold if you don't want to purchase an ice cream maker. There's no real standardization for ice pop molds; they come in a variety of shapes and sizes. I like the ones that look like old-fashioned Popsicles and hold about 3 ounces in each cavity.

SLOW COOKER

It's so nice to dump ingredients into a slow cooker and come back to a meal; I am tempted to put this item under the "almost required" category. You don't have to shell out for the most expensive brand. I have a $60 Hamilton Beach 6-quart slow cooker that works like a dream!

COFFEE GRINDER

No, I am not about to lecture you on how important it is to grind your coffee every morning. I really don't care how you make your coffee, or if you even drink coffee. I use my coffee grinder for grinding sunflower seeds to make sunflower seed flour (page 84), which is a great nut-free alternative to almond flour. Seeds like sunflower and chia are too small for food processors to catch and grind properly, and high-powered blenders often turn them into butter. A coffee grinder really does the trick. Some of my readers also use their coffee grinders to turn granulated sweeteners into powdered ones. And a coffee grinder is great for grinding whole spices like cardamom or coriander seed should you be so inclined.

PIPING BAGS AND DECORATING TIPS

If you want to get all fancy with low-carb cakes and desserts, you need a piping bag and some decorating tips. I am not very good at cake decorating. It's finicky, and I have neither the inclination nor the patience to spend much time on it. But I still keep some disposable piping bags and a few fun star-shaped tips around. You can always spread frosting with a knife or spoon mousse into dessert cups, and it's just as delicious that way, but piping the frosting onto the cake or piping the mousse into the cups can make your dessert look a little more polished.

CHAPTER 3

THE JOY OF
LOW-CARB BAKING:
TIPS & TRICKS

Baking is my happy place, and I know I am not alone in that sentiment. For people who love to bake, it is not simply a means to an end. As much as I love the treats that come out of the oven when the timer goes off—and I really do—it's the process itself that is so enjoyable to me. Baking is burrowing into the kitchen, slowly mixing, measuring, tasting, and adjusting. Baking is the warmth of the preheated oven and the delightful smells that waft through the house. Baking is coziness and comfort and memories of being surrounded by family and friends. It's just a lucky break that it happens to end in something delicious.

Ketogenic baking can be a little daunting, particularly if you're used to conventional flour-and-sugar recipes. It isn't just a matter of swapping in low-carb ingredients for high-carb ones; these ingredients don't behave in the same manner at all. However, ketogenic baking is worth the effort, and it doesn't take long to adjust to this new world, I promise. I've gathered my best tips to help you master the art of low-carb, grain-free baking from the start.

Use properly softened butter and cream cheese.

For seasoned bakers, this goes without saying. This advice is certainly not specific to ketogenic baking, but it can make a big difference to the end result. If your butter and cream cheese are too cold, they will clump up in your batter or dough and won't get evenly distributed.

Properly softened butter and cream cheese dent easily when you press them, but they still maintain their overall shape without squishing all over the place. If your house is quite cool, you might need to help them soften a bit. Ten seconds in the microwave is often enough. I sometimes put butter in a bowl and place it near one of my heating vents.

Let eggs and liquids come to room temperature unless otherwise specified.

It's tempting just to grab these items from the fridge and dump them in, but that properly softened butter will be for naught if you do. Cold eggs and cream will make it all clump up again.

Don't pack your ingredients unless specified.

When measuring almond flour or other low-carb flours, I always use the scoop-and-level method. I simply use my measuring cup to scoop the flour out of the bag, and then I level it off with a knife. Pressing the ingredients down into the measuring cup can significantly change the amount and throw off the proportions.

For even greater accuracy, use a kitchen scale to measure flour. For the most part, I find that using U.S. measuring cups works well for my recipes; however, I also have included gram weights for low-carb flours. Measuring by weight is more accurate and makes my recipes more accessible to people living in countries where dry ingredients are typically measured by weight rather than volume.

Liberally grease your baking pans.

Because ketogenic recipes lack gluten, they sometimes stick a little bit more. I often double-grease my pans, first with a coat of butter and then with coconut oil spray.

Use unsalted butter.

Unsalted butter is the standard for baking, so use unsalted unless the recipe states otherwise. The amount of salt in a stick of butter can vary from one brand to another, which can affect the flavor of your baked goods. It's better to add the amount of salt called for in the recipe than to rely on butter to add a salty flavor. Personally, I sometimes use salted butter in my baked goods, but I have a high tolerance for salty flavors.

Use large eggs.

Large eggs are the standard for baking; I rarely, if ever, see a recipe that calls for any other size. I always specify large eggs in my recipes.

Oven and stovetop temperatures vary.

The thermostat on your oven might not be entirely accurate; many ovens run a little hot or cold. For this reason, baking and cooking times should be considered guidelines, not hard-and-fast rules. Use the visual and tactile cues outlined in the recipes to determine when a food is done cooking. I always set my oven timer for about ten minutes less than the recipe states. That way, I can start checking on the food early to ensure that it doesn't overcook.

Similarly, medium heat on my gas stovetop might not be the same as medium on your electric or induction cooktop. Again, use the visual and tactile cues to know when to move on to the next step in a recipe.

Low-carb batters are often thicker than conventional batters.

Resist the urge to add liquid to thin them; otherwise, you might end up with a goopy mess that won't cook through. As long as you can spread the batter easily in the pan, it should be fine. If the batter is too thick to spread, then something went wrong!

Coconut flour is a bit of a wild card for low-carb baking because it can vary a lot from brand to brand. Because some brands are more absorbent and some are less so, your batter might end up too thick or too thin. After you've worked with coconut flour for a while, you'll gain a gut instinct for whether your batter is right or not. If the batter is really thin, try adding another tablespoon or two of coconut flour. Adding a few tablespoons of liquid can help if the batter is so thick that you can hardly stir it.

A slower rise helps.

Many of my recipes require an oven temperature of no more than 325°F. I noticed early on in my keto baking exploits that a slower rise helps recipes made with almond flour and coconut flour cook through properly and maintain their shape.

Grain-free requires more leavening agent.

Don't be surprised if you see a low-carb recipe that requires a full tablespoon of baking powder. Nut flours and other keto ingredients need a little more encouragement to rise properly.

No, you can't substitute coconut flour for almond flour.

Well, you can, but you'd have to change the rest of the recipe, too (less coconut flour, more eggs, more oil, and more liquid). Swapping flours completely changes a recipe. In my opinion, there is no good formula for substituting one for the other.

Let foods cool properly.

I know, I know, it can be really hard to resist cutting into that cake or grabbing a cookie when it's still warm from the oven. However, aside from the risk of burning your tongue, the goodies in question might fall to pieces if you dig in too soon. Low-carb and grain-free items continue to firm up or crisp up as they cool. If the instructions say to let something cool in the pan for fifteen minutes or to let it cool completely, you're better off following those instructions to the letter.

Always melt chocolate double boiler style.

I am guilty of being lazy at times and trying to melt my chocolate directly in the pan. However, I always regret it when I do. Chocolate is prone to seizing when it's subjected to too much heat, and you can end up with a gloppy mess. Chocolate melts more easily and smoothly with gentle heat. Simply set a heatproof bowl over a pan of barely simmering water. The bottom of the bowl should not be touching the water.

You can rescue seized chocolate.

Melted chocolate also can seize when you introduce a liquid, such as water, cream, or even vanilla extract. Don't panic if your chocolate goes all grainy and clumpy, because it's often salvageable. The funny part is that you add more liquid to fix the problem.

Simply keep the chocolate over low, gentle heat and add lukewarm liquid (water, cream, coffee, whatever) a teaspoon or so at a time. Whisk continuously as you add the liquid until the chocolate becomes smooth again.

Adding more liquid doesn't always work, but I find that it helps more often than not. Because of the additional liquid, the seized chocolate might not be appropriate for the intended recipe, but at least you won't have to toss out the whole thing! Just pour it into some fun molds and refrigerate for a sweet snack.

CHAPTER 4

AN EVERYDAY KETOGENIC DIET

A ketogenic diet sounds pretty good in theory, doesn't it? But what does an everyday ketogenic diet actually look like? I am frequently asked about my daily food consumption and whether I really eat all the things I make. I do, but I certainly don't eat it all at once! Plus, I have a family of five with a very tall, very hungry husband and three rapidly growing children. I have to share with them sometimes.

I crave variety, and I don't like to eat the same thing day to day. I don't track my macronutrients (fat, protein, and carbohydrates) much anymore, either, because I've been eating this way long enough to go by how I feel. I keep an eye on my carbs and try to listen to my body. I ask myself whether I'm actually hungry or I'm just bored. Boredom eating is a hard habit for many of us to break. Thankfully, keto diets have ways and means to deal with that.

However, to share with you what a real keto diet looks like, I kept a food diary for a week. A couple of patterns stand out: I love to eat dinner leftovers for breakfast the next day, and I always finish my day with a little dessert. While some people feel the need to avoid sweets completely when they go keto, having a little treat helps me stay on track. To each his own on that matter, but I try to save my sweets for the end of the day so that they feel like a treat to cap off my day. Unless I am recipe testing, in which case I must have at least a few tastes!

You'll notice that I don't count calories in the diary that follows. While calories are not entirely irrelevant on a low-carb diet, focusing on them can be misleading. The premise behind the ketogenic lifestyle is that you fill up mostly on fat, and thus you are more easily satiated. You shouldn't need to count those pesky calories because portion control becomes almost automatic. If you do go overboard (and who among us doesn't do that once in a while?), you'll feel it pretty quickly. Counting the macronutrients of fat, protein, and carbs gives you a much better sense of how to portion out your day.

Activity level plays a significant role in how much food you can and should consume. Keep in mind that I am quite active, running three times a week and doing CrossFit two or three times a week, too. On my off days, I try to go for at least a short walk to keep the old bod moving. On heavy-lifting CrossFit days, I can tolerate more protein and a little more carbohydrate. I find myself craving fatty meats, such as chicken thighs or steak, after a tough workout. I've included my fitness activities in my diary so that you can see how exercise affected my appetite.

However, I am also in my forties and approaching menopause, so at times, my metabolism seems sluggish no matter what I do. During these times I have very little appetite, and when I do eat, I feel full within a few bites. When that happens, I sometimes do what I call "super keto," where I try to eat mostly fat with a little protein and very few carbs. After two or three days of that approach, I feel myself getting back on track: I feel less bloated and uncomfortable and more energized.

DAY 1

5 a.m.	Black coffee (half-decaf)
7 a.m.	Leftover roasted broccoli and a fried egg (12g fat, 8g protein, 5g carbs)
8 a.m.	CrossFit
10 a.m.	Leftover Pan-Seared Chicken Thigh with Creamy Rosemary Mushrooms (page 240) and espresso with 1 tablespoon heavy cream (28g fat, 24g protein, 5g carbs)
1 p.m.	2 Bacon-Wrapped Halloumi Fries (page 162) dipped in Spicy Cajun Mayonnaise (page 66) and 1 Coconut Oil Brownie (page 330) with 1 tablespoon peanut butter (40g fat, 22g protein, 7g carbs)
4 p.m.	1 ounce cheddar cheese and ¼ avocado (16g fat, 8g protein, 4g carbs)
6 p.m.	4 ounces filet mignon with butter and fresh veggies (¼ red bell pepper, 6 cucumber slices, and 6 jicama sticks) (26g fat, 32g protein, 11g carbs)
7 p.m.	¼ cup Browned Butter Ice Cream (page 340) (17g fat, 2g protein, 1g carbs)
MACROS:	70 percent fat, 22 percent protein, 8 percent carbs

DAY 2

5 a.m.	Black coffee (half-decaf)
7 a.m.	1 cup low-carb cheeseburger soup (a weird breakfast, but warm and comforting) (25g fat, 25g protein, 5g carbs)
9 a.m.	2-mile walk
10 a.m.	1 Duck Fat Chocolate Chip Cookie (page 324) spread with 1 tablespoon peanut butter and espresso with 1 tablespoon heavy cream (24g fat, 6g protein, 6g carbs)
1 p.m.	1 ounce salami, 1 ounce Brie, 8 sugar snap peas, ½ avocado, and 2 Chocolate Truffles (page 318) (36g fat, 17g protein, 11g carbs)
6:30 p.m.	Restaurant dinner: 6 chicken wings, salad with ranch dressing, and a glass of wine (17g fat, 30g protein, 10g carbs)
8 p.m.	½ Tiramisu Mousse Cup (page 348) (18g fat, 2g protein, 4g carbs)
MACROS:	70 percent fat, 21 percent protein, 9 percent carbs

DAY 3

6 a.m.	Butter coffee (coffee with 1 tablespoon butter) (12g fat, 0g protein, 0g carbs)
8:30 a.m.	Leftover chicken with ranch cream sauce and a low-carb muffin (31g fat, 25g protein, 8g carbs)
9:30 a.m.	4.5-mile run
12:30 p.m.	2 ounces smoked salmon, ½ cup roasted broccoli and cauliflower, and an Easy Peanut Butter Cup (page 310) (28g fat, 17g protein, 11g carbs)
4 p.m.	1 Coconut Flour Pancake (page 106) with 1 tablespoon butter (19g fat, 3g protein, 3g carbs)
6:30 p.m.	½ cup carnitas with ½ cup cauliflower rice, ¼ avocado, ½ ounce shredded cheese, 8 sugar snap peas, and 2 ounces jicama (36g fat, 34g protein, 12g carbs)
7:30 p.m.	½ Tiramisu Mousse Cup (page 348) (18g fat, 2g protein, 4g carbs)
MACROS:	73 percent fat, 18 percent protein, 9 percent carbs

DAY 4

5 a.m.	Black coffee (half-decaf)
6:30 a.m.	Low-carb muffin with 1 tablespoon peanut butter (25g fat, 10g protein, 12g carbs)
8 a.m.	CrossFit
9:30 a.m.	Cappuccino with 2 tablespoons heavy cream (12g fat, 0g protein, 0g carbs)
10:45 a.m.	Leftover veggie stir-fry, a fried egg, and a Salted Chocolate Macadamia Nut Fat Bomb (page 314) (29g fat, 9g protein, 10g carbs)
1:15 p.m.	1 ounce beef jerky and ¼ cup truffled almonds (22g fat, 16g protein, 7g carbs)
5:30 p.m.	4 ounces grilled salmon, a thick slice of eggplant caprese, 2 ounces jicama, and ½ cup cucumber slices (23g fat, 44g protein, 14g carbs)
6:30 p.m.	⅓ cup Super-Simple Vanilla Ice Cream (page 336) with Chocolate Sauce (page 320) (37g fat, 3g protein, 5g carbs)
MACROS:	71 percent fat, 18 percent protein, 11 percent carbs

DAY 5

5:30 a.m.	Black coffee (half-decaf)
8:30 a.m.	3 ounces leftover salmon and ½ cup Brussels sprouts (12g fat, 35g protein, 7g carbs)
11 a.m.	Large salad with cheese, 2 tablespoons guacamole, and ranch dressing and a Butter Pecan Cookie (page 328) (28g fat, 13g protein, 12g carbs)
3 p.m.	1 ounce salami, 1 ounce cheddar cheese, and green tea (18g fat, 13g protein, 0g carbs)
6:30 p.m.	6 ounces steak with butter and mushrooms, roasted cauliflower, and a glass of red wine (47g fat, 47g protein, 5g carbs)
MACROS:	64 percent fat, 30 percent protein, 6 percent carbs

DAY 6

5:30 a.m.	Black coffee (half-decaf)
7 a.m.	Rich and Creamy Hot Chocolate (page 172) (23g fat, 8g protein, 4g carbs)
8:30 a.m.	5-mile run
10:30 a.m.	Fried egg, 3 strips bacon, and ½ avocado (26g fat, 11g protein, 6g carbs)
1 p.m.	Dry Rub Fall-Off-the-Bone Ribs (page 226), celery, and a small slice of Zucchini Spice Sheet Cake (page 360) (42g fat, 28g protein, 6g carbs)
3:30 p.m.	Freeze-dried cheese snacks and pumpkin seeds (14g fat, 9g protein, 4g carbs)
6 p.m.	6 ounces pan-fried shrimp, 3 ounces shirataki noodles, asparagus, peppers, and cucumbers (12g fat, 25g protein, 12g carbs)
8 p.m.	⅓ cup Super-Simple Vanilla Ice Cream (page 336) with Chocolate Sauce (page 320) (37g fat, 3g protein, 5g carbs)
MACROS:	74 percent fat, 18 percent protein, 8 percent carbs

DAY 7

5 a.m.	Black coffee (half-decaf)
7 a.m.	⅓ cup low-carb "granola" (nuts, coconut flakes, sunflower seeds, etc.) with 2 tablespoons heavy cream (33g fat, 7g protein, 10g carbs)
8 a.m.	CrossFit
9:30 a.m.	Fried egg over ½ cup cauliflower rice, and cappuccino with heavy cream (17g fat, 8g protein, 6g carbs)
12 p.m.	1 ounce salami, 1 ounce cheddar cheese, 4 Basic Almond Flour Crackers (page 142), and 2 sticks celery (25g fat, 19g protein, 7g carbs)
2 p.m.	2 ounces Lily's Dark Chocolate with 1 tablespoon peanut butter (10g fat, 5g protein, 11g carbs)
6:30 p.m.	Restaurant dinner: deviled eggs, lamb chops, steamed veggies, and a glass of red wine (32g fat, 51g protein, 14g carbs—estimated)
8 p.m.	2 low-carb Thin Mints (10g fat, 3g protein, 7g carbs)
MACROS:	65 percent fat, 21 percent protein, 14 percent carbs

As you can see, my percentages of fat, protein, and carbs fall well within the macronutrient recommendations of most ketogenic experts (see the section "So How Does It Actually Work?" on page 14), all without really trying. I didn't plan out these meals or these numbers; I simply ate when I was hungry and recorded what I consumed. That level of comfort with the low-carb, high-fat lifestyle comes with time, and I've had plenty of time to get comfortable with it. I have keto foods around at all times, so I am never at a loss for what to eat.

You can certainly use this food diary as a rough guide for your own diet, but keep in mind that your mileage may—indeed, will—vary. You might need more or less food than I do, depending on both your lifestyle and your ultimate goals. Are you active or sedentary? Are you male or female, younger or older? Are you eating keto to lose weight, to manage your blood sugar, or simply to get healthy? All these factors will play a large role in your specific dietary needs.

If you are new to keto and looking for more guidance on diet and menu planning, there are a number of great resources listed on page 365.

RECIPES

SLOW COOKER CHICKEN BROTH

This isn't technically bone broth because I usually use the leftover carcass of a roasted chicken instead of fresh chicken parts. But it sure beats store-bought canned broth. I also use any little ends of veggies I have in the fridge: part of an onion, a few stalks of celery, whatever needs to be used up. I keep the salt to a minimum so I can control the saltiness and other flavors later on in soups and other recipes.

YIELD: 8 cups (1 cup per serving)   **PREP TIME:** 5 minutes   **COOK TIME:** 13+ hours

1 to 2 pounds leftover chicken carcass (bones, skin, and any remaining flesh)

2 stalks celery, coarsely chopped

½ onion, coarsely chopped

10 cups water

1 tablespoon apple cider vinegar

1 teaspoon salt

1. Place the chicken and vegetables in a large slow cooker (5 quarts or larger). Add the water, vinegar, and salt.

2. Cover and cook on high for 1 hour, then cook on low for 12 or more hours.

3. Scoop out as many of the solids as possible using a slotted spoon, then strain the broth through a fine-mesh sieve.

4. Divide into glass jars and store in the refrigerator for up to 5 days. The broth can also be frozen.

EVERYDAY TIPS:

A slow cooker is ideal for broth because it needs to simmer for a very long time. This way, you don't need to have your stove on overnight or when you are away from home.

If you're freezing the broth, use freezer-safe jars and leave 1 inch of space at the top of the jar. Freeze without the lids on to avoid breakage. Once the broth is frozen, you can lightly screw on the lids.

NUTRITIONAL INFORMATION:
CALORIES: 11 | FAT: 0g | PROTEIN: 1g | CARBS: 0.8g | FIBER: 0g

STEAK MARINADE

Fish sauce may sound like an unusual ingredient for a steak marinade, but believe me, it really works! It's great for tenderizing all sorts of inexpensive cuts of meat, such as chuck steak or London broil.

YIELD: ¼ cup (enough for 1 to 2 pounds of meat) PREP TIME: 2 minutes
COOK TIME: —

2 tablespoons fresh lime juice

2 tablespoons fish sauce

2 cloves garlic, minced

1 teaspoon ground cumin

½ teaspoon ginger powder

1. Combine the lime juice, fish sauce, garlic, cumin, and ginger in a bowl.

2. Pour over steak or other meat and marinate in the refrigerator for at least 1 hour or up to 4 hours.

EVERYDAY TIP:
The marinade can be made up to 2 days ahead.

NUTRITIONAL INFORMATION:
CALORIES: 6 | FAT: 0g | PROTEIN: 0.6g | CARBS: 0.9g | FIBER: 0g

SPICE RUBS AND SEASONINGS

Store-bought rubs and seasonings often contain sugar and other additives like maltodextrin and cornstarch. But it's so easy to make your own at home with just the classic spices. My husband and I use the basic rub on everything from chicken to my favorite dry-rub ribs—and with a few small changes, you have taco seasoning or Cajun seasoning. If stored in an airtight container away from light and heat, homemade spice blends will keep for up to 3 months.

PREP TIME: **2 minutes** COOK TIME: —

BASIC SPICE RUB

1 tablespoon chili powder

1 tablespoon paprika

1 tablespoon kosher salt or flake sea salt

1 tablespoon black pepper

1 teaspoon garlic powder

1 teaspoon onion powder

1 teaspoon dried oregano leaves

¼ teaspoon cayenne pepper

YIELD: About 5 tablespoons (7 servings)

In a small bowl, stir together the chili powder, paprika, salt, black pepper, garlic powder, onion powder, oregano, and cayenne.

NUTRITIONAL INFORMATION:
CALORIES: 11 | FAT: 0.3g | PROTEIN: 0.6g | CARBS: 2.5g | FIBER: 1.2g

---

CAJUN SEASONING

2 tablespoons paprika

1 tablespoon coarse salt

1 tablespoon black pepper

2 teaspoons garlic powder

1 teaspoon onion powder

1 teaspoon cayenne pepper

1 teaspoon dried oregano leaves

1 teaspoon dried thyme leaves

Great for blackened chicken and fish. I also love to mix it into mayo for a spicy dipping sauce (see page 66).

YIELD: 6 tablespoons (about 9 servings)

In a small bowl, stir together the paprika, salt, black pepper, garlic powder, onion powder, cayenne, oregano, and thyme.

NUTRITIONAL INFORMATION:
CALORIES: 10 | FAT: 0.2g | PROTEIN: 0.5g | CARBS: 2.3g | FIBER: 1g

TACO SEASONING

2 tablespoons chili powder

1 tablespoon paprika

1 tablespoon coarse salt

1 tablespoon black pepper

2 teaspoons ground cumin

1 teaspoon garlic powder

1 teaspoon onion powder

1 teaspoon dried oregano leaves

¼ to ½ teaspoon cayenne pepper

The perfect seasoning for my Easy Taco Pie (page 218).

YIELD: About 7 tablespoons (about 10 servings)

In a small bowl, stir together the chili powder, paprika, salt, black pepper, cumin, garlic powder, onion powder, oregano, and cayenne. Use ¼ teaspoon of cayenne if you prefer a milder seasoning, or ½ teaspoon for a bolder one.

NUTRITIONAL INFORMATION:
CALORIES: 11 | FAT: 0.4g | PROTEIN: 0.6g | CARBS: 2.4g | FIBER: 1.2g

BASIC SPICE RUB   CAJUN SEASONING   TACO SEASONING

BLENDER HOLLANDAISE SAUCE

Hollandaise is the ultimate in ketogenic sauces, and it's a great way to boost the fat content of a meal without increasing carbs or protein. It's so easy to make, and you can pour it over everything, from veggies to steak to eggs.

YIELD: ½ cup (4 servings) PREP TIME: 2 minutes COOK TIME: —

2 large egg yolks

2 teaspoons fresh lemon juice

¼ teaspoon salt

¼ cup (½ stick) unsalted butter, melted

⅛ teaspoon cayenne pepper

1. Place the egg yolks, lemon juice, and salt in a blender. Blend on high for 15 seconds.

2. Remove the blender lid insert and place a small funnel with a narrow stem in the hole. With the blender running on high, slowly pour in the melted butter until the hollandaise is creamy and thickened.

3. Add the cayenne and blend briefly. Add more salt to taste. Use immediately.

EVERYDAY TIPS:
Putting a funnel in the top of the blender allows you to drizzle the melted butter in slowly, which is the key to success with hollandaise.

Hollandaise should be used the day it's made. It doesn't reheat well, but you can make it up to an hour ahead of time. Reheat it gently in a heatproof bowl over barely simmering water. If it thickens too much, add a little water and whisk until it thins out.

NUTRITIONAL INFORMATION:
CALORIES: 129 | FAT: 12.9g | PROTEIN: 1.5g | CARBS: 0.5g | FIBER: 0g

AVOCADO OIL MAYONNAISE

Although it's gotten a bad rap over the years, mayonnaise can be quite a healthy condiment—assuming, of course, that it's not made with soybean or canola oil. Avocado oil is a perfect choice for a creamy, tangy homemade mayo.

YIELD: About ¾ cup (6 servings) PREP TIME: 1 minute COOK TIME: —

1 large egg yolk

2 teaspoons fresh lemon juice

1 teaspoon apple cider vinegar

¼ teaspoon dry mustard

¼ teaspoon salt

½ cup avocado oil

1. Place the egg yolk, lemon juice, vinegar, mustard, and salt in a blender. Blend on high for 15 seconds.

2. Remove the blender lid insert and place a small funnel with a narrow stem in the hole. With the blender running on low, slowly pour in the avocado oil and continue blending until the mayonnaise is thick and creamy. Store in an airtight container in the refrigerator and use within 3 days.

EVERYDAY TIPS:
Because homemade mayonnaise contains raw egg yolks, it needs to be used within 3 days. If you're looking for a store-bought avocado oil–based mayo, I highly recommend Primal Kitchen brand.

NUTRITIONAL INFORMATION:
CALORIES: 96 | FAT: 19.4g | PROTEIN: 0.5g | CARBS: 0.3g | FIBER: 0g

SPICY CAJUN MAYONNAISE

Tired of plain mayo? Give it a little kick with some Cajun seasoning and a dash of hot sauce.

YIELD: ¼ cup (4 servings) PREP TIME: **2 minutes** COOK TIME: —

¼ cup avocado oil mayonnaise, store-bought or homemade (page 65)

1 tablespoon Cajun seasoning (page 62)

½ to 1 teaspoon hot sauce

1. In a small bowl, whisk together the mayonnaise, Cajun seasoning, and ½ teaspoon of the hot sauce.

2. Taste and add more hot sauce if desired. Keeps for up to 3 days if made with homemade mayo, or for several weeks if made with store-bought mayo.

NUTRITIONAL INFORMATION:
CALORIES: 56 | FAT: 9.7g | PROTEIN: 0.3g | CARBS: 1.8g | FIBER: 0.8g

DIJON VINAIGRETTE

A classic vinaigrette that goes with almost any salad.

YIELD: 10 tablespoons (5 servings) **PREP TIME:** 5 minutes **COOK TIME:** —

¼ cup avocado oil or extra-virgin olive oil

¼ cup apple cider vinegar

1 tablespoon balsamic vinegar

1 tablespoon Dijon mustard

1 clove garlic, minced

¾ teaspoon salt

½ teaspoon black pepper

½ teaspoon dried oregano leaves

1. Place all the ingredients in a jar with a lid. Cover and shake vigorously until well combined.

2. Adjust the seasonings to taste. Store in the refrigerator for up to a month.

EASY RANCH DRESSING

Seriously, ranch dressing is so easy to make, there's almost no excuse to buy it at the store.

¼ cup avocado oil mayonnaise, store-bought or homemade (page 65)

¼ cup unsweetened almond milk

2 cloves garlic, minced

1 teaspoon dried dill weed

½ teaspoon dried parsley

½ teaspoon salt

YIELD: About ½ cup (4 servings) **PREP TIME:** 2 minutes **COOK TIME:** —

1. Place all the ingredients in a glass jar with a lid. Shake vigorously to combine.

2. Adjust the seasonings to taste. Store in the refrigerator; it will keep for up to 3 days if made with homemade mayo or for up to 2 weeks if made with store-bought mayo.

EVERYDAY TIP:
I like my ranch really thick, and this dressing thickens as it sits. If you want a thinner dressing, add another tablespoon or two of almond milk.

NUTRITIONAL INFORMATION:
CALORIES: 107 | FAT: 11.3g | PROTEIN: 0.2g | CARBS: 0.8g | FIBER: 0.2g

CHIPOTLE BACON RANCH DRESSING

A spicy and flavorful twist on classic ranch dressing.

YIELD: **About ½ cup (4 servings)**   PREP TIME: **2 minutes**   COOK TIME: **—**

¼ cup avocado oil mayonnaise, store-bought or homemade (page 65)

¼ cup unsweetened almond milk

2 tablespoons finely minced chipotle peppers in adobo sauce

4 slices bacon, cooked crisp and crumbled

2 cloves garlic, minced

1 teaspoon dried dill weed

½ teaspoon dried parsley

½ teaspoon salt

½ teaspoon black pepper

1. Place all the ingredients in a glass jar with a lid. Shake vigorously to combine.

2. Adjust the seasonings to taste. Store in the refrigerator; it will keep for up to 3 days if made with homemade mayo or for up to 2 weeks if made with store-bought mayo.

NUTRITIONAL INFORMATION:
CALORIES: 130 | FAT: 12.1g | PROTEIN: 2.1g | CARBS: 1.4g | F BER: 0.6g

CREAMY CILANTRO DRESSING

Cilantro drives me nuts because it comes in big bunches at the grocery store, and you need only a few tablespoons for most recipes. I began making this dressing as a way to use it up before it went bad. It has become one of my favorite dressing recipes.

YIELD: About ¾ cup (6 servings) PREP TIME: 5 minutes COOK TIME: —

¾ cup loosely packed fresh cilantro leaves

⅓ cup unsweetened almond milk

¼ cup avocado oil mayonnaise, store-bought or homemade (page 65)

2 cloves garlic, coarsely chopped

½ teaspoon salt

¼ teaspoon black pepper

⅛ teaspoon chipotle powder or cayenne pepper

1. Place all the ingredients in a food processor or blender. Blend until smooth.

2. Adjust the salt and pepper to taste. Store in the refrigerator; it will keep for up to 3 days if made with homemade mayo or for up to 2 weeks if made with store-bought mayo.

NUTRITIONAL INFORMATION:
CALORIES: 72 | FAT: 7.6g | PROTEIN: 0.2g | CARBS: 0.6g | FIBER: 0.2g

PESTO

Sending up my thanks to the person who invented this garlicky basil concoction. My family loves it on everything, from fish to chicken to pizza.

2 packed cups fresh basil leaves

½ ounce Parmesan cheese, grated (about ½ cup)

⅓ cup extra-virgin olive oil

¼ cup pine nuts, lightly toasted

2 cloves garlic, coarsely chopped

1 tablespoon fresh lemon juice

¾ teaspoon salt

½ teaspoon black pepper

1. Place all the ingredients in a blender or food processor and blend until smooth, scraping down the sides with a rubber spatula as necessary.

2. Add more salt and pepper to taste. Use within 24 hours or store in the freezer.

EVERYDAY TIP:

Basil tends to brown really quickly when it's chopped and exposed to the air. If I make a big batch of pesto and know it won't get used right away, I store it in glass jars and press plastic wrap flush to the surface to keep the air out. I also freeze it this way.

NUTRITIONAL INFORMATION:

CALORIES: 157 | FAT: 15.6g | PROTEIN: 2g | CARBS: 1.7g | FIBER: 0.4g

CHIMICHURRI SAUCE

Traditionally, this Argentinian parsley sauce is served over steak, but it goes with almost anything, from fish to chicken to veggies. It's even great over eggs.

YIELD: ¾ cup (about 6 servings) PREP TIME: 5 minutes COOK TIME: —

¼ cup chopped red onions

¼ cup avocado oil

¼ cup apple cider vinegar

2 cloves garlic

½ teaspoon salt

½ teaspoon black pepper

¼ teaspoon red pepper flakes

2 loosely packed cups fresh parsley leaves

1. Combine the onions, avocado oil, vinegar, garlic, salt, black pepper, and red pepper flakes in a food processor or blender. Pulse to chop and combine.

2. Add the parsley leaves and process on low to puree. Adjust the seasonings to taste. Store in the refrigerator for up to a week.

EVERYDAY TIP:
Because of the vinegar, this sauce lasts longer than something like pesto (page 71), and it stays nice and green.

NUTRITIONAL INFORMATION:
CALORIES: 56 | FAT: 9.6g | PROTEIN: 0.8g | CARBS: 2.5g | FIBER: 0.9g

LOW-CARB BBQ SAUCE

Everyone needs a good sugar-free BBQ sauce in their low-carb arsenal.

YIELD: **1 cup (16 servings)**   PREP TIME: **2 minutes**   COOK TIME: **20 minutes**

1 (15-ounce) can pureed tomatoes

⅓ cup apple cider vinegar

3 tablespoons powdered erythritol sweetener

2 teaspoons yacón syrup or blackstrap molasses (optional)

1 teaspoon liquid smoke

1 teaspoon chili powder

1 teaspoon garlic powder

1 teaspoon salt

½ teaspoon chipotle powder (or more chili powder)

½ teaspoon onion powder

½ teaspoon black pepper

⅛ teaspoon cayenne pepper

⅛ teaspoon xanthan gum

1. In a medium skillet over medium heat, whisk together the tomatoes, vinegar, sweetener, yacón syrup (if using), liquid smoke, chili powder, garlic powder, salt, chipotle powder, onion powder, black pepper, and cayenne. Bring to a boil.

2. Turn the heat to low and simmer until the mixture is reduced by about half, 15 to 20 minutes. Sprinkle the surface with the xanthan gum and whisk briskly to combine.

3. Store in an airtight container in the refrigerator for up to a week.

EVERYDAY TIPS:
Cooking this sauce in a skillet rather than a deeper saucepan allows the liquids to evaporate more quickly.

You can freeze this sauce if you aren't going to use it all up within a week.

EVERYDAY SWAP:
You can use any sweetener you like in this sauce. Use the equivalent of 3 tablespoons of sugar.

NUTRITIONAL INFORMATION:
CALORIES: 9 | FAT: 0.1g | PROTEIN: 0.4g | CARBS: 2g | FIBER: 0.5g | ERYTHRITOL: 2.8g

TERIYAKI SAUCE

This makes a great stir-fry sauce or glaze for chicken.

YIELD: **About 6 tablespoons (6 servings)** PREP TIME: **2 minutes**
COOK TIME: **10 minutes**

¼ cup coconut aminos or soy sauce

¼ cup water

2 tablespoons apple cider vinegar

2 cloves garlic, minced

½ teaspoon ginger powder

½ teaspoon hot sauce

3 tablespoons powdered erythritol sweetener

¼ teaspoon xanthan gum

1. In a medium saucepan over medium heat, combine the coconut aminos, water, vinegar, garlic, ginger, and hot sauce. Bring to a boil, then reduce the heat and simmer for 5 minutes.

2. Remove from the heat and whisk in the sweetener. Sprinkle the surface with the xanthan gum and whisk briskly to combine. Let cool to thicken. Keeps for up to a week in the refrigerator.

NUTRITIONAL INFORMATION:
CALORIES: 14 | FAT: 0g | PROTEIN: 0g | CARBS: 2.5g | FIBER: 0g | ERYTHRITOL: 7.5g

PICO DE GALLO

Fresh pico de gallo is hands-down my favorite salsa.

YIELD: **About 2 cups (8 servings)** PREP TIME: **10 minutes** COOK TIME: **—**

¾ pound tomatoes, seeded and chopped

1 large jalapeño pepper, minced (leave the seeds in if you like it more spicy)

2 packed tablespoons coarsely chopped cilantro leaves

2 tablespoons fresh lime juice

2 tablespoons minced onions

2 cloves garlic, minced

1 teaspoon salt

1. In a large bowl, combine the tomatoes, jalapeño, cilantro, lime juice, onions, and garlic. Mix well.

2. Add the salt just before serving. Store leftovers in the refrigerator for up to 3 days.

EVERYDAY TIP:
Because salt draws the moisture out of the vegetables, it's best to add it just before serving to prevent water from pooling at the bottom of the bowl.

NUTRITIONAL INFORMATION:
CALORIES: 11 | FAT: 0g | PROTEIN: 0.5g | CARBS: 2.6g | FIBER: 0.6g

ROASTED TOMATO CREAM SAUCE

This rich and creamy tomato sauce is pure magic over zucchini noodles (see page 274) or paired with chicken or fish. It also makes a wonderful low-carb replacement for ketchup.

OPTION

YIELD: About 1 cup (4 servings) PREP TIME: 5 minutes COOK TIME: 30 minutes

¾ pound fresh tomatoes, coarsely chopped

1 tablespoon avocado oil or light olive oil

¾ teaspoon salt

½ teaspoon black pepper

1 clove garlic, coarsely chopped

Dash of red pepper flakes

⅓ cup heavy cream

1. Preheat the oven to 400°F.

2. Place the tomatoes in a single layer in a glass or ceramic baking dish. Drizzle with the oil and sprinkle with the salt and pepper. Toss to combine.

3. Roast the tomatoes until they are caramelized and browned in spots, about 30 minutes. Transfer to a food processor or blender and add the garlic and red pepper flakes. Puree until smooth.

4. Add the cream and continue to blend until smooth and well combined. Adjust the seasonings to taste. This sauce is best served the day it's made but can be refrigerated for up to 3 days.

EVERYDAY SWAP:
For a dairy-free version, try substituting full-fat coconut milk for the cream.

NUTRITIONAL INFORMATION:
CALORIES: 102 | FAT: 10.6g | PROTEIN: 1.3g | CARBS: 4.7g | FIBER: 1.3g

WILD BLUEBERRY SYRUP

This is my favorite low-carb pancake topping. It's also delicious over ice cream or cheesecake!

YIELD: About 1 cup (8 servings) **PREP TIME:** 2 minutes, plus time to cool
COOK TIME: 8 minutes

1 cup frozen wild blueberries

¼ cup water

¼ cup powdered erythritol sweetener

1 tablespoon fresh lemon juice

¼ teaspoon xanthan gum

1. In a medium saucepan over medium heat, combine the blueberries and water. Bring to a boil, then reduce the heat and simmer for 5 minutes.

2. Remove the pan from the heat and stir in the sweetener and lemon juice.

3. Sprinkle the surface with the xanthan gum and whisk briskly to combine. Let cool to room temperature to thicken. Store leftovers in the refrigerator for up to 3 days.

EVERYDAY TIP:
You can make this sauce with any berry you like, but the carb count will vary. I like to make it with frozen raspberries for my New York–Style Cheesecake (page 334).

NUTRITIONAL INFORMATION:
CALORIES: 16 | FAT: 0.1g | PROTEIN: 0.1g | CARBS: 3.6g | FIBER: 0.8g | ERYTHRITOL: 7.5g

EASY PRESS-IN PIE CRUST— TWO WAYS

This simple crust recipe is easily adapted for savory or sweet recipes. To make a savory version, simply replace the sweetener with a smaller amount of garlic powder. You can prebake the crust and use it for a no-bake filling like custard, or par-bake it for 10 minutes, fill it, and return it to the oven to make baked pies or tarts like lemon meringue or quiche. Instructions for prebaking and par-baking the crust are below.

YIELD: One 9-inch pie crust or one 9- or 10-inch tart crust   **PREP TIME:** 15 minutes
COOK TIME: 10 to 12 minutes (for par-baked crust), or 20 minutes (for prebaked crust)

SWEET PIE CRUST:

1½ cups (150g) blanched almond flour

¼ cup granulated erythritol sweetener

¼ teaspoon salt

¼ cup (½ stick) unsalted butter, melted

SAVORY PIE CRUST:

1½ cups (150g) blanched almond flour

½ teaspoon garlic powder

¼ teaspoon salt

¼ cup (½ stick) unsalted butter, melted

1. Preheat the oven to 325°F.

2. In a medium bowl, whisk together the flour, sweetener or garlic powder, and salt. Stir in the melted butter until the dough resembles coarse crumbs.

3. Turn the loose dough out into a 9-inch glass or ceramic pie pan or a 9- or 10-inch tart pan. Press it firmly into the bottom and up the sides of the pan. Use a flat-bottomed glass or measuring cup to even out the bottom of the crust. Crimp the edges and prick the bottom all over with a fork.

4. To prebake the crust, place the crust in the oven and bake until the edges are golden brown, 20 to 25 minutes. Allow to cool before filling.

5. To par-bake the crust, place the crust in the oven and bake for 10 to 12 minutes, until just slightly puffed and not yet browned. Allow to cool before filling. Return the filled pie to the oven and bake according to the recipe you are making. You may need to cover the edges with foil to avoid overbrowning.

NUTRITIONAL INFORMATION:
CALORIES: 137 | FAT: 12.7g | PROTEIN: 3.7g | CARBS: 3.6g | FIBER: 1.8g | ERYTHRITOL: 6g (sweet version only)

MAGIC MOZZARELLA DOUGH

This stuff really is magic. It's astonishing how the melted mozzarella creates a stretchy dough similar to pizza dough. It's so versatile, and I am constantly coming up with new uses for it. Besides using it to make keto pizza, you can use it to make Spanakopita Hand Pies (page 164), Pesto Twists (page 128), or Prosciutto and Arugula Flatbread (page 126). And with some slight tweaks (see the variation, opposite), it's great in sweet recipes, too. Check out the keto cinnamon rolls on page 130!

YIELD: **One 12-inch pizza crust**   PREP TIME: **2 minutes**   COOK TIME: **10 minutes**

6 ounces preshredded part-skim mozzarella cheese (about 1½ cups) (see Tips)

5 tablespoons unsalted butter

½ cup (50g) blanched almond flour

¼ cup (27g) coconut flour

2 teaspoons baking powder

½ teaspoon garlic powder

¼ teaspoon salt

1 large egg

1. Sprinkle a large piece of parchment paper or a silicone baking mat with almond flour.

2. In a large saucepan, melt the cheese and butter over low heat until they can be stirred together.

3. Remove from the heat and add the almond flour, coconut flour, baking powder, garlic powder, and salt. Add the egg and stir everything together until a cohesive dough forms. Use a rubber spatula to really knead the dough in the pan. It may still contain some streaks of cheese.

4. Turn the dough out onto the floured work surface and knead until uniform. This will take only a little kneading. If, after kneading for about 1 minute, your dough is still very sticky, add a tablespoon or two more almond flour and work it in. Use the dough to make pizza (see below) or another recipe in this book.

HOW TO MAKE MAGIC MOZZARELLA DOUGH PIZZA

To make a pizza crust, sprinkle the parchment paper or silicone baking mat with a little more almond flour to prevent sticking. Place the dough on the floured work surface and place another piece of parchment paper on top of the dough. Roll it out into a 12-inch circle. Remove the top piece of parchment and crimp the edges of the dough a bit to create a crust. Transfer the bottom piece of parchment or the silicone baking mat to a baking sheet or pizza stone. Bake at 350°F for 10 to 15 minutes, until golden, then add your favorite toppings and bake for another 10 minutes or so.

NUTRITIONAL INFORMATION:
CALORIES: 247 | FAT: 20.1g | PROTEIN: 9.7g | CARBS: 6g | FIBER: 2.7g | ERYTHRITOL: 10g (sweet version only)

VARIATION:
Sweet Mozzarella Dough. Replace the garlic powder with 1 teaspoon of vanilla extract. Add ¼ cup of powdered erythritol sweetener along with the almond flour in Step 3.

EVERYDAY TIPS:
The best mozzarella for this dough is the preshredded part-skim kind because it contains some anti-coagulating agents that help the consistency. Yes, it adds a tiny bit of starch, but it makes a difference and contributes almost nothing to the overall carb count. I often use the Whole Foods brand because it contains potato starch rather than cornstarch.

I almost always weigh the mozzarella for this recipe. Shredded mozzarella can get packed down and pressed together, and measuring by volume rather than weight can impact the outcome of your dough.

SUNFLOWER SEED FLOUR

This homemade sunflower seed flour makes a great nut-free replacement for almond flour and can be substituted cup for cup in most recipes. I have a video showing just how easy it is to make on my website, *All Day I Dream About Food.*

YIELD: **1¼ cups (5 servings)** PREP TIME:**15 minutes** COOK TIME: —

1 cup raw, unsalted sunflower seeds

1. Set a mesh colander over a medium bowl.

2. Pour the sunflower seeds into a coffee grinder and grind for 10 to 20 seconds. Don't grind too long, or you may end up with sunflower seed butter.

3. Pour the ground seeds into the colander and shake vigorously, then return any remaining seed pieces to the coffee grinder. Repeat three or four times, until almost all the sunflower seeds have been sieved.

4. Store in an airtight bag or container in the refrigerator or freezer until ready to use.

EVERYDAY TIPS:
The perfect tool to sieve the ground seeds is a mesh colander, or open-mesh sieve, which has holes about 1 mm in size. A fine-mesh sieve is too fine for the job, and the holes in a typical colander are way too large.

If you don't have a coffee grinder, you can use a food processor instead. Do more than 1 cup of seeds at a time because food processors have a hard time grinding small amounts properly.

Sunflower seeds can react with leavening agents like baking powder and baking soda to create a funny green color in the baked good. It's not bad for you; it just doesn't look very appetizing. You can offset this reaction with a tablespoon or two of acid, such as lemon juice or apple cider vinegar. For chocolate recipes, the dark color of the chocolate will mask any green.

NUTRITIONAL INFORMATION:
CALORIES: 165 | FAT: 14.6g | PROTEIN: 4.6g | CARBS: 5.5g | FIBER: 3.1g

BAKED DENVER OMELET

A fully loaded omelet that feeds a crowd and appeals to just about everyone? Sign me up. This also makes a great breakfast-for-dinner dish.

YIELD: **8 servings** PREP TIME: **15 minutes** COOK TIME: **about 45 minutes**

2 tablespoons salted butter

½ pound ham, diced

1 medium green bell pepper, chopped

1 medium red bell pepper, chopped

½ cup diced onions

1 cup shredded cheddar cheese (about 4 ounces), divided

10 large eggs

½ cup heavy cream

¾ teaspoon salt

½ teaspoon black pepper

1. Preheat the oven to 350°F and grease a 1½- to 2-quart oval baker or a 9 by 13-inch baking dish.

2. Melt the butter in a large skillet over medium heat. Once hot, add the ham and sauté until browned and crispy, about 2 minutes.

3. Add the bell peppers and onions and continue to cook, stirring frequently, until tender, 3 to 4 more minutes. Spread the ham and vegetables in the greased baking dish. Sprinkle with half of the cheddar cheese.

4. In a large bowl, whisk together the eggs, cream, salt, and pepper. Pour the egg mixture over the ham and vegetables in the baking dish. Sprinkle the top with the remaining cheese.

5. Bake for 35 to 40 minutes, until the center is cooked through. Remove from the oven and let cool for 5 minutes before serving.

SERVING SUGGESTION:
The Western flavors of this omelet pair well with a garnish of sour cream and avocado.

EVERYDAY TIP:
Store leftovers in the fridge for an easy grab-and-go breakfast. It will keep for up to 4 days.

NUTRITIONAL INFORMATION:
CALORIES: 281 | FAT: 19.8g | PROTEIN: 16.7g | CARBS: 4.8g | FIBER: 1.1g

CAPRESE OMELET ROLL

Omelet rolls look impressive but are remarkably easy to make. I love the fresh flavors of a caprese salad, and those same festive colors make this a perfect dish for a special brunch.

YIELD: **6 servings**   PREP TIME: **10 minutes**   COOK TIME: **22 to 25 minutes**

7 large eggs

⅓ cup heavy cream

2 ounces cream cheese (¼ cup), softened

1 clove garlic, minced

¾ teaspoon salt

½ teaspoon black pepper

6 ounces fresh mozzarella, finely chopped

1 cup finely chopped grape tomatoes, divided

¼ cup chopped fresh basil

1. Preheat the oven to 350°F and line a 12 by 17-inch rimmed baking sheet with parchment paper, leaving an overhang for easy removal. Grease the parchment.

2. In a blender, combine the eggs, cream, cream cheese, garlic, salt, and pepper. Blend until smooth. Pour the mixture into the prepared baking sheet and spread to the edges. Bake for 12 to 15 minutes, until the omelet is just cooked through.

3. Sprinkle the omelet with the mozzarella and about two-thirds of the chopped tomatoes. Working from one of the shorter ends and using the parchment paper to help you lift the omelet, roll the omelet up tightly. Return it to the oven for another 10 minutes to melt the cheese.

4. Remove from the oven and sprinkle with the chopped basil and the remaining tomatoes. Slice and serve.

EVERYDAY TIP:
Make sure to chop the mozzarella and tomatoes finely. This makes it much easier to roll up, slice, and serve the omelet without all the fillings spilling out.

NUTRITIONAL INFORMATION:
CALORIES: 252 | FAT: 18.3g | PROTEIN: 14.8g | CARBS: 3.3g | FIBER: 0.4g

SMOKED SALMON SCRAMBLED EGGS

8 large eggs

¼ cup heavy cream

½ teaspoon salt

¼ teaspoon black pepper

1 tablespoon salted butter

4 ounces cold-smoked salmon, such as Nova lox, coarsely chopped

4 ounces cream cheese (½ cup), cut into small chunks

2 tablespoons chopped fresh dill, for garnish

I've often said that if I had to choose only one food to eat for the rest of my life, it would be smoked salmon. Yes, even over chocolate and peanut butter, I would choose smoked salmon. Nutrient dense and naturally high in fat, it's a perfect keto food.

YIELD: **4 servings**   PREP TIME: **10 minutes**   COOK TIME: **10 minutes**

1. In a large bowl, whisk the eggs with the cream, salt, and pepper until well combined and smooth.

2. Heat a 12-inch skillet over medium-low heat. Add the butter and let it melt, then swirl the pan to coat it with the melted butter.

3. Pour the egg mixture into the skillet and cook without disturbing until it just begins to set around the edges. Using a rubber spatula, gently lift and turn the curds from the edge of the pan toward the center, allowing the uncooked eggs to run back out to the edges. Continue to lift and turn until the eggs are just barely set.

4. Remove the pan from the heat and quickly add the smoked salmon and cream cheese. Gently fold the salmon and cream cheese into the curds to combine.

5. Divide among 4 plates and sprinkle with the dill.

EVERYDAY TIP:
Scrambling eggs slowly over lower heat will keep them from drying out and create very tender curds. (By the way, my husband is a scrambled egg master, and I owe everything I know about cooking perfect scrambled eggs to him.)

NUTRITIONAL INFORMATION:
CALORIES: 349 | FAT: 14.1g | PROTEIN: 19.8g | CARBS: 2.4g | FIBER: 0g

SAUSAGE AND EGG CUPS

OPTION · OPTION

These little cups are a fun and delicious way to start your morning. Drizzle them with hollandaise for a special brunch treat.

YIELD: **8 cups (1 per serving)** PREP TIME: **10 minutes** COOK TIME: **25 minutes**

12 ounces bulk breakfast sausage, store-bought or homemade (page 98), or uncooked breakfast sausage links, casings removed

8 large eggs

Salt and black pepper

1 batch Blender Hollandaise Sauce (page 64) (optional)

Smoked paprika, for garnish

2 tablespoons coarsely chopped fresh parsley or cilantro, for garnish

1. Preheat the oven to 350°F and lightly grease eight 4-ounce ramekins. Place the ramekins on a rimmed baking sheet.

2. Divide the sausage into 8 equal portions. Form each portion into a thin, flat patty (as thin as you can make it) and press into the bottom and partway up the sides of a ramekin.

3. Bake until the sausage is cooked through, about 15 minutes. Remove the ramekins from the oven and carefully drain any liquid that has accumulated.

4. Break an egg into each sausage cup and season with salt and pepper. Bake for another 10 minutes for set whites and still-runny yolks; bake longer if you prefer set yolks.

5. Let cool for a few minutes, then run a sharp knife around the edges to loosen and lift the cups out onto a plate.

6. Drizzle with hollandaise, if using, and sprinkle with smoked paprika and chopped parsley or cilantro. Serve immediately.

EVERYDAY TIPS:
The sausage cups can be prepped a day or two ahead. Just follow the directions through Step 2 and refrigerate. Then start at Step 3 when you're ready to complete the recipe.

Store leftovers in the refrigerator for up to 3 days and rewarm gently in the oven. If you don't want leftovers, it's easy to make a half batch of this recipe.

EVERYDAY SWAP:
Leave off the hollandaise for a dairy-free, Paleo breakfast.

NUTRITIONAL INFORMATION (including hollandaise):
CALORIES: 274 | FAT: 21.6g | PROTEIN: 14.9g | CARBS: 1.2g | FIBER: 0g

CHORIZO GRAVY

This is a spicy take on traditional sausage gravy. It's delicious spooned over Cheddar Zucchini Drop Scones (page 138)—a low-carb version of biscuits and gravy!

YIELD: **6 servings**   PREP TIME: **5 minutes**   COOK TIME: **20 minutes**

8 ounces fresh (raw) chorizo, casings removed

¼ medium white onion, finely chopped

½ teaspoon salt

1 cup heavy cream

¼ teaspoon xanthan gum

1. Heat a large skillet over medium heat. Add the chorizo and cook until browned, about 10 minutes, stirring frequently to break up any clumps. Remove with a slotted spoon and set on a paper towel–lined plate to drain.

2. Reduce the heat to medium-low, add the onion to the pan, and sprinkle with the salt. Cook, stirring frequently, until the onion is translucent, about 5 minutes.

3. Add the cream and bring to a simmer. Cook until the cream is reduced by about one-third, then whisk in the xanthan gum. Add the cooked chorizo and stir to combine. Cook for 1 more minute, until the chorizo is warmed through, then serve.

EVERYDAY SWAP:
Feel free to substitute regular breakfast sausage (page 98) for the chorizo for a more conventional sausage gravy.

NUTRITIONAL INFORMATION:
CALORIES: 310 | FAT: 27.6g | PROTEIN: 10g | CARBS: 2.2g | FIBER: 0g

HOMEMADE BREAKFAST SAUSAGE

Store-bought breakfast sausage often contains sugar or (ugh!) corn syrup. But making your own is easy, and you can adjust the seasonings to suit your palate.

**YIELD: 8 small patties (2 patties per serving) PREP TIME: 5 minutes
COOK TIME: 16 minutes**

1 pound ground pork

1 to 2 tablespoons granulated erythritol sweetener

1 teaspoon fennel seeds, crushed

1 teaspoon garlic powder

1 teaspoon dried ground sage

1 teaspoon salt

½ teaspoon black pepper

½ teaspoon paprika

⅛ teaspoon cayenne pepper

2 tablespoons avocado oil or coconut oil, divided, for the pan

1. In a large bowl, combine the ground pork, sweetener, fennel seeds, garlic powder, sage, salt, black pepper, paprika, and cayenne. Mix until well combined. Shape by hand into 8 small patties, each about ½ inch thick.

2. In a large skillet, heat half of the oil over medium heat until shimmering. Add half of the sausage patties and cook for about 4 minutes per side, until the patties are nicely browned and the internal temperature registers 165°F.

3. Repeat with the remaining oil and sausage patties.

SERVING SUGGESTION:
My favorite way to eat these is with some sliced or mashed avocado on top. It's my version of the ubiquitous avocado toast.

EVERYDAY TIP:
The patties can be shaped and frozen ahead of time. Make sure to thaw them properly before cooking.

NUTRITIONAL INFORMATION:

CALORIES: 290 | FAT: 24.8g | PROTEIN: 17.7g | CARBS: 1.3g | FIBER: 0.5g | ERYTHRITOL: 7.5g

SALMON CAULIFLOWER HASH

It's not always easy to find egg-free ketogenic breakfast options. This recipe was inspired by my love of eating leftover salmon for breakfast the next day.

OPTION   OPTION

YIELD: 4 servings   **PREP TIME:** 5 minutes   **COOK TIME:** 10 minutes

3 tablespoons salted butter

¼ cup chopped onions

1 medium head cauliflower, chopped into ½-inch pieces

2 tablespoons water

1 tablespoon fresh lemon juice

¾ teaspoon salt

½ teaspoon black pepper

½ pound leftover cooked salmon, broken into small pieces

1. In a large skillet, melt the butter over medium-high heat. Add the onions and sauté until just translucent, about 4 minutes. Add the cauliflower in a single layer and cook without disturbing for 2 to 3 minutes, until the pieces are beginning to brown.

2. Add the water, lemon juice, salt, and pepper and stir a few times to combine. Cover the pan and cook for another 3 minutes, until the cauliflower is just tender.

3. Add the salmon and stir gently to combine. Cook just until the salmon is warmed through, 1 to 2 more minutes.

SERVING SUGGESTIONS:
Serve with some chopped fresh dill and a squeeze of lemon. A dollop of crème fraîche would also be divine.

EVERYDAY TIP:
Because salmon is fragile and easily overcooked, you want to add it at the very end and toss it *lightly* with the cauliflower. Then cook it only until it's warmed through.

EVERYDAY SWAP:
Use coconut oil or avocado oil in place of the butter for a dairy-free, Paleo hash.

NUTRITIONAL INFORMATION:
CALORIES: 184 | FAT: 10.6g | PROTEIN: 13.4g | CARBS: 8.7g | FIBER: 3.2g

SAVORY BREAKFAST COOKIES

Weekday mornings are seriously chaotic in my house. If I want my kids to eat a good breakfast, I have to have something ready to go. These savory breakfast cookies are a nice change from sweet muffins.

YIELD: **8 cookies**   PREP TIME: **10 minutes** (not including time to cook sausage and bacon)   COOK TIME: **20 to 25 minutes**

1 (8-ounce) package cream cheese, softened

3 large eggs, room temperature

¼ cup plus 2 tablespoons (41g) coconut flour

2 teaspoons baking powder

¾ teaspoon salt

½ teaspoon black pepper

½ teaspoon garlic powder

¼ pound breakfast sausage, store-bought or homemade (page 98), cooked and crumbled

6 slices Canadian bacon, cooked and chopped

1 cup shredded cheddar cheese (about 4 ounces)

1. Preheat the oven to 350°F and line a baking sheet with parchment paper or a silicone baking mat.

2. In a large bowl, using an electric mixer, beat the cream cheese with the eggs until smooth. Add the coconut flour, baking powder, salt, pepper, and garlic powder and beat until well combined.

3. Stir in the sausage, Canadian bacon, and cheese. Spoon the mixture into 8 mounds on the lined baking sheet. Using wet hands, press the mounds down to a thickness of about 1 inch.

4. Bake for 20 to 25 minutes, until golden brown and firm to the touch. Let cool on the pan for 15 minutes before serving. Store leftovers in the refrigerator for up to a week.

EVERYDAY TIP:
These cookies store well in the fridge, so you can make a batch for the week. They taste best when gently warmed.

EVERYDAY SWAP:
You can easily swap in regular bacon or ham for the Canadian bacon.

NUTRITIONAL INFORMATION:
CALORIES: 245 | FAT: 17.1g | PROTEIN: 12.7g | CARBS: 5.4g | FIBER: 1.9g

RASPBERRY RICOTTA BREAKFAST CAKE

What's the difference between a breakfast cake and a regular cake? Not much, if I am being perfectly honest. I conceived of this recipe as a cross between a coffee cake and a cheesecake—something you could enjoy with your morning coffee. It's a lovely way to start the day.

**YIELD: 10 servings   PREP TIME: 10 minutes, plus 2 to 3 hours to chill
COOK TIME: 50 to 60 minutes**

1 (15-ounce) container whole-milk ricotta cheese

⅔ cup granulated erythritol sweetener

3 large eggs

1½ teaspoons almond extract

1 cup (100 g) blanched almond flour

2 teaspoons baking powder

½ teaspoon salt

1 cup frozen raspberries

¼ cup sliced almonds

Powdered erythritol sweetener, for sprinkling

1. Preheat the oven to 325°F and generously grease a 9-inch springform pan.

2. In a blender or food processor, combine the ricotta, granulated sweetener, eggs, and almond extract. Blend until smooth, about 30 seconds. Add the almond flour, baking powder, and salt and blend until well combined.

3. Pour the batter into the greased pan. Arrange the raspberries in a single layer on top, then sprinkle with the sliced almonds. Bake for 50 to 60 minutes, until the cake is just barely set in the middle. Cover with foil for the last 20 minutes of baking if the top is browning too much.

4. Remove from the oven and let cool in the pan for 20 minutes. Run a sharp knife around the edges to loosen the cake from the pan, then release the sides. Refrigerate the cake for 2 to 3 hours. Sprinkle with powdered sweetener before serving.

5. Store leftovers covered with plastic wrap in the refrigerator for up to 5 days.

EVERYDAY SWAP:
If you aren't a fan of strong almond flavors, you can substitute vanilla extract for the almond extract.

NUTRITIONAL INFORMATION:
CALORIES: 182 | FAT: 13.2g | PROTEIN: 9.8g | CARBS: 6g | FIBER: 1.9g | ERYTHRITOL: 15.9g

COCONUT FLOUR PANCAKES

If you've never worked with coconut flour, pancakes are a great place to start. It's the strangest "flour" you will ever use, soaking up eggs and liquid like mad and still staying as thick as porridge. It takes some getting used to, but it makes fantastic low-carb pancakes. Use sparkling water to make the pancakes extra fluffy.

OPTION

YIELD: 12 pancakes (2 per serving) **PREP TIME:** about 10 minutes
COOK TIME: 20 minutes

½ cup (55g) coconut flour

3 tablespoons granulated erythritol sweetener

½ teaspoon baking powder

½ teaspoon salt

6 large eggs

¼ cup (½ stick) unsalted butter, melted but not hot

½ teaspoon vanilla extract

¾ cup sparkling water or regular water

Butter or oil, for the pan

1. In a large bowl, whisk together the coconut flour, sweetener, baking powder, and salt. Add the eggs, melted butter, and vanilla extract and stir to combine. Add the water and whisk until smooth. Let the batter rest for a few minutes to thicken. It won't be pourable like conventional pancake batter, but it should be easy to scoop into the pan.

2. Heat a large nonstick skillet over medium heat and lightly grease it with a little butter or oil. Use about 3 tablespoons of batter for each pancake and spread them into 4-inch circles. Cook the pancakes until bubbles begin to appear on the tops and the bottoms are set and golden brown, 2 to 3 minutes.

3. Carefully flip the pancakes and continue to cook until golden brown on the second side, another 2 to 3 minutes. Repeat with the remaining batter, adding more butter or oil to the pan as needed.

SERVING SUGGESTION:
Top the pancakes with butter and Wild Blueberry Syrup (page 78) or your favorite keto-friendly pancake syrup. I love them with a smear of peanut butter.

EVERYDAY TIPS:
These pancakes reheat really well, so you can make a big batch and store them in the refrigerator for up to a week. For my hungry family, I often make two batches on the weekend for easy breakfasts during the week.

Due to variations in coconut flour, your batter may be too thick or too thin after resting. If it's too thick, add another tablespoon or two of water. If it's too thin, whisk in another tablespoon of coconut flour.

Your pancakes may appear very flat when cooking on the first side, but they will puff up after being flipped.

EVERYDAY SWAP:
For dairy-free pancakes, use avocado oil or melted coconut oil in place of the melted butter in the batter and for the pan.

NUTRITIONAL INFORMATION:
CALORIES: 181 | FAT: 12.8g | PROTEIN: 7.7g | CARBS: 5.9g | FIBER: 3.3g | ERYTHRITOL: 7.5g

CREAM CHEESE WAFFLES

Crispy waffles are hard to achieve with low-carb ingredients, but these flourless waffles hit the mark. They come out of the waffle iron on the soft side but crisp up quickly.

YIELD: Ten 4-inch Belgian-style waffles (1 per serving) **PREP TIME:** 2 minutes
COOK TIME: about 20 minutes

1 (8-ounce) package cream cheese, softened

¼ cup (½ stick) unsalted butter, melted but not hot

3 large eggs

2 tablespoons heavy cream

1 tablespoon water

¾ cup unflavored whey protein powder

¼ cup plus 2 tablespoons granulated erythritol sweetener

2 teaspoons baking powder

1 teaspoon vanilla extract

¼ teaspoon salt

1. Preheat a waffle iron and grease it well.

2. In a blender or food processor, combine the cream cheese, melted butter, eggs, cream, and water. Blend on high for 30 seconds, then scrape down the sides with a rubber spatula.

3. Add the protein powder, sweetener, baking powder, vanilla extract, and salt and blend for another 30 seconds, until smooth.

4. Pour about ¼ cup of the batter into each section of the waffle iron and close the lid. Cook until the waffles are puffed and golden brown on both sides. The time will vary depending on your waffle iron.

5. Remove the waffles and repeat with the remaining batter. Store leftovers in the refrigerator for up to 5 days. The waffles can also be frozen for up to a month.

SERVING SUGGESTION:
Top with butter and Wild Blueberry Syrup (page 78) or any sugar-free pancake syrup.

EVERYDAY TIP:
The number of waffles you get and how long they take to cook will vary greatly depending on your type of waffle iron. Some, like mine, are very deep Belgian-style waffle makers; others are more shallow. My deep iron produces ten 4-inch square waffles. If your waffle iron makes regular waffles (not the thick Belgian style), you will end up with more waffles.

NUTRITIONAL INFORMATION:
CALORIES: 175 | FAT: 13g | PROTEIN: 8.5g | CARBS: 2.1g | FIBER: 0g | ERYTHRITOL: 9g

CHOCOLATE CREPES

I will be the first to admit that making crepes, especially low-carb crepes, is a bit tricky. You have to spread the batter quickly and flip the crepes very carefully. But they're so delicious, they're definitely worth the effort. I always make a big batch because my kids love them so much.

YIELD: **About 12 crepes (2 per serving)** PREP TIME: **5 minutes**
COOK TIME: **20 minutes**

⅓ cup (34g) blanched almond flour

⅓ cup Swerve confectioners'-style sweetener or equivalent powdered erythritol sweetener, plus extra for sprinkling

¼ cup cocoa powder

⅛ teaspoon xanthan gum

⅛ teaspoon salt

4 ounces cream cheese (½ cup), softened

4 large eggs

¼ cup unsweetened almond milk

½ teaspoon vanilla extract

Butter or oil, for the pan

1. In a blender, combine the almond flour, sweetener, cocoa powder, xanthan gum, and salt. Pulse a few times to combine.

2. Add the cream cheese, eggs, almond milk, and vanilla extract. Blend on high until smooth.

3. Heat a 10-inch nonstick skillet over low heat. Melt a scant ½ teaspoon of butter in the pan, then spread it around the pan. Add about 3 tablespoons of batter to the pan and quickly tilt the pan in a circular motion so that the batter spreads to the edges.

4. Cook until the top is mostly set and the edges are dry. Run a spatula around the edges to loosen and lift one edge. Grab the edge with your fingers and gently peel the crepe from the pan to flip it over.

5. Cook for another minute or so, then remove the crepe from the pan and lay it flat on a tea towel. Repeat with the remaining batter, greasing the pan only as necessary.

6. Fold into quarters and sprinkle with powdered erythritol, if desired.

SERVING SUGGESTION:
These crepes are dreamy with a little lightly sweetened whipped cream and some berries. But my family also loves them spread with peanut butter and rolled up for a quick-and-easy breakfast.

EVERYDAY TIPS:
A good nonstick pan is key to crepe-making success. I find that I don't have to regrease the pan after every crepe.

These crepes can be made ahead and stored in the refrigerator for up to 3 days. Reheat them gently in the microwave.

NUTRITIONAL INFORMATION:

CALORIES: 177 | FAT: 13.9g | PROTEIN: 7.4g | CARBS: 4.5g | FIBER: 2g | ERYTHRITOL: 12.5g

STRAWBERRY SMOOTHIES

I used to think that a store-bought smoothie was the epitome of healthy eating. Now I shudder to think of all the sugars and carbs I was unwittingly consuming. I find that using cream cheese is a great way to thicken a low-carb smoothie.

YIELD: **2 servings** PREP TIME: **5 minutes** COOK TIME: **—**

5 medium strawberries, chopped

3 ounces cream cheese
(6 tablespoons), softened

1 cup crushed ice

1 cup unsweetened almond milk

¼ cup heavy cream

2 tablespoons powdered erythritol
sweetener

1. In a blender, layer the strawberries, cream cheese, ice, almond milk, and cream. Add the sweetener and blend until smooth.

2. Add more sweetener to taste and divide between 2 glasses.

EVERYDAY TIP:
Layering the thicker and more fibrous ingredients toward the bottom of the blender helps ensure that they will blend properly.

EVERYDAY SWAP:
You can use any sweetener you prefer in place of the powdered erythritol. Stevia extract also works well.

NUTRITIONAL INFORMATION:
CALORIES: 275 | FAT: 24.2g | PROTEIN: 3.8g | CARBS: 5.4g | FIBER: 1.1g | ERYTHRITOL: 15g

CHAPTER 7

BREADS, MUFFINS & SCONES

FLOURLESS SUNFLOWER BREAD

I wanted a quick and easy bread recipe that wasn't overly sweet and would taste delicious toasted. It took me more than a few tries to get this one right! It even makes a pretty great grilled cheese sandwich.

YIELD: One 9 by 5-inch loaf (12 servings) **PREP TIME:** 10 minutes
COOK TIME: 25 minutes

1 cup sunflower seed butter (preferably unsweetened)

3 large eggs, room temperature

3 tablespoons water

2 tablespoons coconut oil, softened

1 tablespoon apple cider vinegar

½ cup unflavored egg white protein powder

1 tablespoon granulated erythritol sweetener

2 teaspoons baking powder

1 teaspoon salt

1. Preheat the oven to 350°F and generously grease a 9 by 5-inch loaf pan.

2. In a large bowl, stir together the sunflower seed butter, eggs, water, coconut oil, and vinegar until combined.

3. Add the protein powder, sweetener, baking powder, and salt. Mix with a rubber spatula until thoroughly combined.

4. Pour the batter into the greased baking pan and bake for about 25 minutes, until the edges are golden brown and the top is firm to the touch. Remove and let cool for 10 minutes, then flip out onto a wire rack to cool completely.

5. Store leftover bread in the refrigerator for up to 5 days.

EVERYDAY TIP:
This bread tends to be quite moist, so it's best to keep it in the refrigerator.

EVERYDAY SWAPS:
If you don't need this bread to be dairy-free, you can use butter in place of the coconut oil and whey protein powder in place of the egg white protein powder. You can also add more sweetener for a sweet quick bread. It's great with sugar-free chocolate chips! (See page 322 for my recipe.)

NUTRITIONAL INFORMATION:
CALORIES: 185 | FAT: 15g | PROTEIN: 8.1g | CARBS: 5.6g | FIBER: 1.2g | ERYTHRITOL: 1.3g

SKILLET CORNBREAD

I know, I know, you can't really call it cornbread if there's no corn in it. But there is something remarkably cornbread-esque about this lightly sweetened skillet bread. And that's good enough for me.

OPTION

YIELD: 10 servings **PREP TIME:** 10 minutes **COOK TIME:** 40 to 50 minutes

1 cup (110g) coconut flour

½ cup (50g) blanched almond flour

¼ cup granulated erythritol sweetener

1 tablespoon baking powder

½ teaspoon xanthan gum (optional)

½ teaspoon salt

6 large eggs, room temperature

½ cup (1 stick) unsalted butter, melted but not hot

1 cup unsweetened almond milk

½ teaspoon vanilla extract

1. Preheat the oven to 350°F and generously grease a 10-inch ovenproof skillet.

2. In a large bowl, whisk together the coconut flour, almond flour, sweetener, baking powder, xanthan gum (if using), and salt. Stir in the eggs, melted butter, almond milk, and vanilla extract until well combined.

3. Spread the batter in the greased skillet and smooth the top. Bake for 40 to 50 minutes, until the edges are golden and the center is firm to the touch. Let cool in the pan for 15 minutes before slicing.

4. Wrap leftover bread tightly in foil and store on the counter for up to 2 days or in the refrigerator for up to a week. The bread can also be frozen for several months.

SERVING SUGGESTION:
Serve warm with a pat of butter melting on top for a delicious cornbread experience.

EVERYDAY TIP:
You don't need to use a cast-iron pan, but a skillet is much better than a baking dish. It helps crisp up the edges and gives the bread a real cornbread texture.

EVERYDAY SWAP:
For a dairy-free version, substitute a neutral-tasting oil like avocado oil for the melted butter. Coconut oil has too strong a flavor for this delicate bread.

NUTRITIONAL INFORMATION:
CALORIES: 210 | FAT: 15.8g | PROTEIN: 6.8g | CARBS: 8.3g | FIBER: 4.7g | ERYTHRITOL: 6g

FOCACCIA

I clearly remember the first time I was served focaccia with olive oil at a restaurant. I'd always been a butter girl, but dipping warm rosemary-flecked bread into olive oil and salt was a flavor revelation. It was an experience that I was eager to repeat time and again. With my keto focaccia, I still get to enjoy that experience, just without the resulting blood sugar spike.

OPTION   OPTION

YIELD: 12 servings   **PREP TIME:** 10 minutes   **COOK TIME:** 20 to 25 minutes

1 cup (100 g) blanched almond flour

⅓ cup (35 g) coconut flour

⅓ cup unflavored whey protein powder

2 tablespoons chopped fresh rosemary

1 tablespoon baking powder

¾ teaspoon salt

½ teaspoon garlic powder

½ cup extra-virgin olive oil, plus extra for the pan

½ cup water

2 large whole eggs

2 large egg whites

Coarse sea salt, for sprinkling

Fresh rosemary leaves, for sprinkling

1. Preheat the oven to 325°F and line a baking sheet with parchment paper. Grease the parchment paper.

2. In a large bowl, whisk together the almond flour, coconut flour, protein powder, rosemary, baking powder, salt, and garlic powder. Add the olive oil, water, whole eggs, and egg whites and mix until a sticky dough forms.

3. Turn the dough out onto the prepared baking sheet and use wet hands to spread it into a 9 by 12-inch rectangle. Use your fingertips to dimple the surface lightly. Sprinkle with coarse salt and rosemary leaves.

4. Bake for 20 to 25 minutes, until the bread is just golden on the edges and firm to the touch. Let cool for 10 minutes before slicing and serving.

5. Wrap leftover focaccia tightly in foil and store on the counter for up to 3 days or in the refrigerator for up to a week. It can also be frozen for several months.

EVERYDAY SWAP:
To make this focaccia dairy-free and Paleo, use unflavored egg white protein powder in place of the whey protein powder.

NUTRITIONAL INFORMATION:
CALORIES: 174 | FAT: 14.8g | PROTEIN: 6g | CARBS: 5g | FIBER: 2.5g

HAMBURGER BUNS

These keto hamburger buns don't contain any almond flour or coconut flour, and they really stand up to your juiciest burgers. I also like to turn them into tuna melts for the kids.

YIELD: **4 buns (1 per serving)** PREP TIME: **5 minutes**
COOK TIME: **18 to 22 minutes**

4 ounces cream cheese (½ cup), softened

1 large egg

2 tablespoons avocado oil or melted unsalted butter

1 tablespoon water

½ cup unflavored whey protein powder

1 teaspoon baking powder

½ teaspoon garlic powder

¼ teaspoon salt

1 tablespoon sesame seeds or poppyseeds

1. Preheat the oven to 350°F and generously grease four 4-inch ramekins or 4-inch round cake pans.

2. In a blender or food processor, combine the cream cheese, egg, avocado oil, and water. Blend until smooth. Add the protein powder, baking powder, garlic powder, and salt and blend until well combined.

3. Divide the batter evenly among the prepared ramekins. Sprinkle each with sesame seeds and press lightly to adhere. Bake for 18 to 22 minutes, until the tops are cracked and the edges are light golden brown.

4. Let the buns cool in the ramekins for at least 15 minutes, then run a sharp knife around the edge of each ramekin and transfer the buns to a wire rack to cool completely.

5. Store on the counter for up to 3 days.

EVERYDAY TIP:
This recipe relies on whey protein powder to work properly. I tried substituting egg white protein powder and ended up with strange, rubbery discs. I really don't recommend it!

NUTRITIONAL INFORMATION:
CALORIES: 213 | FAT: 18.5g | PROTEIN: 12.4g | CARBS: 3.4g | FIBER: 0.5g

LEMON POPPYSEED QUICK BREAD

OPTION

I challenge Starbucks to make a better-tasting lemon loaf!

YIELD: One 9 by 5-inch loaf (12 servings) PREP TIME: 10 minutes, plus time to cool COOK TIME: 50 to 60 minutes

BREAD:

3 cups (300g) blanched almond flour

½ cup granulated erythritol sweetener

⅓ cup unflavored whey protein powder

3 tablespoons poppyseeds

1 tablespoon grated lemon zest

2 teaspoons baking powder

½ teaspoon salt

⅔ cup unsweetened almond milk

½ cup (1 stick) unsalted butter, melted but not hot

3 large eggs

½ teaspoon lemon extract

GLAZE:

3 tablespoons powdered erythritol sweetener

1½ to 2 tablespoons fresh lemon juice

TO MAKE THE BREAD:

1. Preheat the oven to 325°F and generously grease a 9 by 5-inch loaf pan.

2. In a large bowl, whisk together the almond flour, granulated sweetener, protein powder, poppyseeds, lemon zest, baking powder, and salt. Break up any clumps with the back of a fork.

3. Stir in the almond milk, melted butter, eggs, and lemon extract until well combined. Transfer the batter to the greased baking pan and smooth the top.

4. Bake for 50 to 60 minutes, until the sides and top are golden brown and the bread is firm to the touch. A toothpick inserted in the center should come out clean.

5. Let cool in the pan for 20 minutes, then flip out onto a wire rack to cool completely.

TO MAKE THE GLAZE:

1. In a small bowl, whisk together the powdered sweetener and lemon juice until smooth.

2. Drizzle the glaze over the cooled bread. Store wrapped in foil on the counter for up to 3 days or in the refrigerator for up to a week.

EVERYDAY SWAPS:
This recipe is easy to make dairy-free. Use ⅓ cup of coconut oil in place of the ½ cup of melted butter and egg white protein powder in place of the whey protein powder.

NUTRITIONAL INFORMATION:
CALORIES: 272 | FAT: 23.3g | PROTEIN: 10g | CARBS: 7.5g | FIBER: 3.6g | ERYTHRITOL: 13.8g

PROSCIUTTO AND ARUGULA FLATBREAD

With a thin, crispy crust topped with salty prosciutto and fresh arugula, this flatbread is a perfect side for soup or salad.

YIELD: **One 12-inch square flatbread (9 servings)** PREP TIME: **10 minutes (not including time to make dough)** COOK TIME: **17 to 25 minutes**

1 recipe Magic Mozzarella Dough (page 82)

2 tablespoons extra-virgin olive oil or avocado oil

2 cloves garlic, minced

½ teaspoon coarse sea salt

½ teaspoon coarsely ground black pepper

4 ounces prosciutto, coarsely chopped

½ cup shredded mozzarella cheese (about 2 ounces)

1 ounce shaved Parmesan cheese

1 ounce fresh arugula

1. Preheat the oven to 325°F. If using a pizza stone, place it in the oven to preheat.

2. Place a large piece of parchment paper or a silicone baking mat on a work surface and sprinkle it lightly with almond flour. Place the mozzarella dough on the floured paper or mat and pat it into a rough square. Top the dough with a piece of parchment paper or waxed paper and roll it out to a 12-inch square.

3. In a small bowl, whisk together the oil, garlic, salt, and pepper. Brush the entire surface of the dough with the oil mixture.

4. Transfer the parchment paper or baking mat to the preheated pizza stone or a large baking sheet. Bake for 12 to 15 minutes, then remove from the oven and sprinkle with the prosciutto and mozzarella. Bake for another 5 to 10 minutes, until the cheese is melted and bubbly.

5. Remove from the oven and sprinkle with the Parmesan and arugula. Let sit for about 5 minutes to firm up, then cut into squares or triangles and serve.

6. Store leftover flatbread in the refrigerator for up to 3 days. Rewarm gently in an oven or toaster oven.

EVERYDAY TIP:
A pizza stone works well to get the crust nice and crisp. But never, ever put the dough directly on the pizza stone or it will stick like the dickens, as my mother used to say. Traditionally, cornmeal is sprinkled on the pizza stone to keep the dough from sticking. The keto solution is parchment paper or a silicone baking mat.

NUTRITIONAL INFORMATION:
CALORIES: 250 | FAT: 20.1g | PROTEIN: 19.8g | CARBS: 5.2g | FIBER: 1.9g

PESTO TWISTS

My kids go wild for these savory breadsticks. Enough said.

1 recipe Magic Mozzarella Dough
(page 82)

¼ cup pesto, store-bought or
homemade (page 71)

1 tablespoon melted salted butter

1 teaspoon flaked sea salt

YIELD: 10 twists (1 per serving) **PREP TIME:** 10 minutes (not including time to
make dough) **COOK TIME:** 15 minutes

1. Preheat the oven to 350°F and line a large baking sheet with
   parchment paper or a silicone baking mat.

2. Lightly dust a work surface with almond flour. Place the
   mozzarella dough on the floured work surface and pat it into a
   rough square. Top the dough with a piece of parchment paper or
   waxed paper and roll it out to a 10-inch square.

3. Spread the pesto all over the dough, then fold the dough carefully
   in half to form a 5 by 10-inch rectangle. Pinch to seal the seams.

4. Use a sharp knife to cut the dough crosswise into 10 strips. Hold
   both ends of a strip and twist gently in opposite directions two or
   three times; repeat with the remaining strips.

5. Lay the twists on the prepared baking sheet and brush with the
   melted butter. Sprinkle with the flaked salt and bake for about 15
   minutes, until golden brown and just firm to the touch. Remove
   from the oven and let cool on the pan.

6. Store leftover twists in the refrigerator for up to 3 days.

EVERYDAY TIP:
I find it easiest to manipulate the mozzarella dough when it is still
relatively warm. You don't have to hurry, but don't let it sit too long
before rolling it out and shaping it.

NUTRITIONAL INFORMATION:
CALORIES: 179 | FAT: 13.8g | PROTEIN: 6.2g | CARBS: 3.9g | FIBER: 1.7g

CINNAMON ROLLS

Who doesn't love a warm, gooey cinnamon roll right out of the oven? I think it's a primal desire in all of us, and we shouldn't have to forgo it simply because we've chosen to live a healthier lifestyle.

YIELD: 12 small rolls (2 per serving) **PREP TIME:** 15 minutes (not including time to make dough) **COOK TIME:** 20 to 25 minutes

ROLLS:

1 recipe Sweet Mozzarella Dough (page 83)

1 tablespoon unsalted butter, melted

2 tablespoons granulated erythritol sweetener

2 teaspoons ground cinnamon

CREAM CHEESE FROSTING:

2 ounces cream cheese (¼ cup), softened

2 tablespoons powdered erythritol sweetener

¼ cup heavy cream

½ teaspoon vanilla extract

TO MAKE THE ROLLS:

1. Preheat the oven to 350°F and lightly grease an 8-inch round cake pan.

2. Lay a large sheet of parchment paper or a silicone baking mat on a work surface. Sprinkle with almond flour to help prevent sticking. Place the mozzarella dough on the floured paper or mat and pat it into a rough square. Top the dough with a piece of parchment paper or waxed paper and roll it out to a 12-inch square. Brush the dough with the melted butter.

3. Mix together the granulated sweetener and cinnamon in a small bowl. Sprinkle this mixture over the dough.

4. Roll the dough up tightly and pinch the seam to seal. Use a sharp knife to cut the roll into 12 equal portions. Place the rolls in the greased cake pan, cut side up, leaving about 1 inch of space between them.

5. Bake the rolls for 20 to 25 minutes, until golden brown and just firm to the touch. Let cool slightly in the pan while you prepare the frosting.

TO MAKE THE FROSTING:

1. In a medium bowl, using an electric mixer, beat the cream cheese with the powdered sweetener until well combined. Beat in the cream and vanilla extract until smooth.

2. Spread the frosting over the warm rolls in the pan. Store leftovers in the refrigerator for up to 5 days.

EVERYDAY TIP:
The rolls can be prepped a day ahead and baked the next day. Simply cover the cake pan tightly in plastic wrap and refrigerate. Let the rolls come to room temperature before baking.

NUTRITIONAL INFORMATION:
CALORIES: 349 | FAT: 29.3g | PROTEIN: 11g | CARBS: 8.4g | FIBER: 3.2g | ERYTHRITOL: 20g

CHOCOLATE PECAN PIE MUFFINS

This may be one of the most beloved recipes on my website, *All Day I Dream About Food.* These are sweeter and denser than your average muffin, and they fall somewhere between pecan pie filling and chocolate chip cookies in flavor. You can see why they are such a hit.

YIELD: 12 muffins (1 per serving) PREP TIME: 10 minutes
COOK TIME: 26 to 30 minutes

¾ cup granulated erythritol sweetener

1 cup (100g) blanched almond flour

1 cup chopped pecans

½ teaspoon salt

½ cup (1 stick) unsalted butter, softened

2 large eggs, room temperature

2 teaspoons yacón syrup (optional, for color and flavor)

⅓ cup sugar-free chocolate chips or chunks, store-bought or homemade (page 322)

1. Preheat the oven to 325°F and line 12 standard-size muffin cups with parchment paper or silicone liners.

2. In a medium bowl, whisk together the sweetener, almond flour, pecans, and salt.

3. In a large bowl, beat the butter with the eggs and yacón syrup, if using, until smooth. Beat in the almond flour mixture until just combined. Stir in the chocolate chips.

4. Divide the batter among the prepared muffin cups, filling each about two-thirds full. Bake for 26 to 30 minutes, until golden brown and just set in the center. Let cool in the pan.

5. Store in the refrigerator for up to a week. The muffins can also be frozen for up to a month.

EVERYDAY TIPS:
These muffins won't rise at all, and they aren't supposed to. The best way to tell that they are done is to touch one in the center. It will be firm but still a bit tacky.

Because these are firm, dense muffins, they travel really well. I usually make a batch before a trip and take a few along in a container for snacking.

NUTRITIONAL INFORMATION:
CALORIES: 286 | FAT: 27.1g | PROTEIN: 4.4g | CARBS: 6.1g | FIBER: 2.6g | ERYTHRITOL: 15g

MAPLE BACON PANCAKE MUFFINS

Portable pancakes! These muffins combine the beloved flavors of maple and bacon in a grab-and-go breakfast treat.

YIELD: **8 muffins (1 per serving)** PREP TIME: **10 minutes**
COOK TIME: **22 to 25 minutes**

3 large eggs

¼ cup plus 2 tablespoons unsweetened almond milk

1½ teaspoons maple extract

3 tablespoons avocado oil

1 cup (100g) blanched almond flour

¼ cup (27g) coconut flour

¼ cup granulated erythritol sweetener

1½ teaspoons baking powder

¼ teaspoon salt

8 slices bacon, chopped and cooked crisp

1. Preheat the oven to 325°F and line 8 standard-size muffin cups with parchment paper or silicone liners.

2. Place the eggs, almond milk, maple extract, and avocado oil in a blender. Blend on high for 10 seconds to combine.

3. Add the almond flour, coconut flour, sweetener, baking powder, and salt and blend on high until the batter is smooth. Stir in about three-quarters of the cooked bacon.

4. Divide the batter evenly among the prepared muffin cups, filling each about three-quarters full. Sprinkle each muffin with a little of the remaining bacon. Bake for 22 to 25 minutes, until the muffins are golden brown and firm to the touch.

5. Let cool in the pan for 15 minutes, then transfer to a wire rack to cool completely. Store in the refrigerator for up to a week or in the freezer for up to a month.

EVERYDAY TIP:
Extracts and other flavorings are really useful in recipes like this. I used to love maple syrup, but let's be honest, it's just sugar in a different form. Using maple extract gives these muffins the maple flavor I love and helps me feel like I am not missing out.

EVERYDAY SWAP:
If you don't need these muffins to be dairy-free, there's no reason you can't use melted butter in place of the avocado oil.

NUTRITIONAL INFORMATION:
CALORIES: 193 | FAT: 17.6g | PROTEIN: 8.8g | CARBS: 5.5g | FIBER: 2.8g | ERYTHRITOL: 9.3g

APPLE CIDER DONUT BITES

Having lived in New England for almost twelve years, I can tell you that apple picking is practically a competitive sport there. These little muffins pay homage to the famous apple cider donuts sold at every apple farm.

YIELD: 24 donut bites (2 per serving) PREP TIME: 10 minutes
COOK TIME: 15 to 20 minutes

DONUT BITES:

2 cups (200g) blanched almond flour

½ cup granulated erythritol sweetener

¼ cup unflavored whey protein powder

2 teaspoons baking powder

½ teaspoon ground cinnamon

½ teaspoon salt

2 large eggs

⅓ cup water

¼ cup (½ stick) unsalted butter, melted

1½ tablespoons apple cider vinegar

1½ teaspoons apple extract or vanilla extract

CINNAMON "SUGAR" COATING:

¼ cup granulated erythritol sweetener

1½ teaspoons ground cinnamon

¼ cup (½ stick) unsalted butter, melted

TO MAKE THE DONUTS:

1. Preheat the oven to 325°F and generously grease a 24-well mini muffin pan.

2. In a large bowl, whisk together the almond flour, sweetener, protein powder, baking powder, cinnamon, and salt. Whisk in the eggs, water, melted butter, vinegar, and apple extract until well combined.

3. Divide the batter among the wells of the greased mini muffin pan, filling each to the top. Bake for 15 to 20 minutes, until the donuts are firm to the touch.

4. Let cool in the pan for 10 minutes, then transfer to a wire rack to cool completely.

TO MAKE THE CINNAMON "SUGAR" COATING:

1. In a small bowl, whisk together the sweetener and cinnamon.

2. Dip each donut into the melted butter, coating it completely. Then roll each donut in the cinnamon-sweetener mixture.

3. Store leftovers on the counter for up to 3 days or in the refrigerator for up to a week.

EVERYDAY TIP:
Apple extract helps give these donuts their apple cider flavor, but vanilla extract is a tasty substitute. I purchase apple extract online.

NUTRITIONAL INFORMATION:
CALORIES: 164 | FAT: 13.7g | PROTEIN: 6.5g | CARBS: 4.8g | FIBER: 2.2g | ERYTHRITOL: 15g

CHEDDAR ZUCCHINI DROP SCONES

Who says scones have to be sweet? These savory scones are a wonderful accompaniment to soup or salad. They make great breakfast sandwiches, too!

YIELD: 10 scones (1 per serving) PREP TIME: 15 minutes, plus 1 hour to drain zucchini COOK TIME: 20 to 22 minutes

2½ cups finely shredded zucchini (about 2 medium-small zucchini)

½ teaspoon salt

2 cups (200g) blanched almond flour

¼ cup (27g) coconut flour

1 tablespoon baking powder

½ teaspoon garlic powder

½ teaspoon salt

1 cup shredded sharp cheddar cheese (about 4 ounces), divided

2 large eggs

¼ cup unsalted butter, melted but not hot

1. Place the zucchini in a large sieve in the sink and sprinkle with the salt. Toss to coat and let drain for 1 hour, then wrap in a tea towel and squeeze out as much moisture as possible.

2. Preheat the oven to 325°F and line a large baking sheet with parchment paper or a silicone baking mat.

3. In a large bowl, whisk together the almond flour, coconut flour, baking powder, garlic powder, salt, and two-thirds of the cheese. Stir in the zucchini, eggs, and melted butter until the dough comes together.

4. Using about ¼ cup at a time, form the dough into balls, then press down to about 1 inch thick. Sprinkle each scone with some of the remaining cheese. Bake for 20 to 22 minutes, until the scones are golden brown and firm to the touch.

5. Let cool on the baking sheet for at least 10 minutes. Store leftovers in the refrigerator for up to a week. Rewarm in the microwave or toaster oven.

EVERYDAY TIP:
Be sure to squeeze that zucchini really well to reduce the moisture content before adding the zucchini to the flour mixture.

NUTRITIONAL INFORMATION:
CALORIES: 245 | FAT: 20.1g | PROTEIN: 9.5g | CARBS: 7.7g | FIBER: 3.6g

CHAPTER 8

APPETIZERS, SNACKS & BEVERAGES

BASIC ALMOND FLOUR CRACKERS

Back in my high-carb days, I loved making a meal out of crackers and cheese. So finding a way to make crackers keto-friendly was of the utmost importance.

OPTION   OPTION

YIELD: 30 to 40 crackers (10 servings)   PREP TIME: 15 minutes
COOK TIME: 35 to 40 minutes

DOUGH:

2 cups (200g) blanched almond flour

½ teaspoon salt

½ teaspoon baking powder

1 large egg

2 tablespoons unsalted butter, melted but not hot

TOPPING:

½ teaspoon coarse sea salt

1. Preheat the oven to 300°F.

2. In a large bowl, whisk together the almond flour, salt, and baking powder. Stir in the egg and melted butter until the dough comes together.

3. Turn the dough out onto a large piece of parchment paper and pat it into a rough rectangle. Top the dough with another piece of parchment and roll it out to a ⅛-inch thickness, as evenly as you can. Remove the top piece of parchment.

4. Using a sharp knife or pizza wheel, score the dough into 2-inch squares.

5. Sprinkle the scored cracker dough with the coarse sea salt and press lightly to adhere it to the dough.

6. Slide the piece of parchment paper onto a baking sheet. Bake for 35 to 40 minutes, until the edges are golden brown and the crackers are firm to the touch. Let cool completely on the baking sheet before breaking apart along the score lines.

7. Store in a covered container on the counter for up to 5 days.

EVERYDAY TIP:
Leave the crackers be until they are completely cool; they won't be entirely crisp if they are still warm. I find that they stay crisp as long as I leave them in a container on the counter. However, if you live in a very humid locale, it may be impossible to get them as crisp as traditional crackers.

EVERYDAY SWAP:
You can make these crackers dairy-free and Paleo by substituting avocado oil for the butter.

NUTRITIONAL INFORMATION:
CALORIES: 150 | FAT: 13.3g | PROTEIN: 5.2g | CARBS: 4.9g | FIBER: 2.4g

EVERYTHING BAGEL CRACKERS

Everybody's favorite bagel, now in a crispy low-carb cracker.

OPTION   OPTION

YIELD: 30 to 40 crackers (10 servings) PREP TIME: 15 minutes
COOK TIME: 35 to 40 minutes

1 recipe Basic Almond Flour
Crackers dough (page 142)

TOPPING:

1 tablespoon poppyseeds

1 tablespoon sesame seeds

1 teaspoon dried minced garlic

1 teaspoon dried minced onions

½ teaspoon crushed caraway seeds

½ teaspoon coarse sea salt

1. Preheat the oven to 300°F.

2. To make the cracker dough, complete Steps 2 through 4 of the Basic Almond Flour Crackers recipe.

3. In a small bowl, whisk together the poppyseeds, sesame seeds, garlic, onions, caraway seeds, and salt. Sprinkle the scored cracker dough with the seed mixture and press lightly to adhere it to the dough.

4. Slide the sheet of parchment paper onto a baking sheet. Bake for 35 to 40 minutes, until the edges are golden brown and the crackers are firm to the touch. Let cool completely on the baking sheet before breaking apart along the score lines.

5. Store in a covered container on the counter for up to 5 days.

EVERYDAY SWAP:
You can make these crackers dairy-free and Paleo by substituting avocado oil for the butter in the cracker dough.

NUTRITIONAL INFORMATION:
CALORIES: 163 | FAT: 14.4g | PROTEIN: 5.6g | CARBS: 5.7g | FIBER: 2.8g

CINNAMON GRAHAM CRACKERS

What child doesn't love snacking on slightly sweet, cinnamon-y graham crackers? These are a favorite in my house. My kiddos love them for breakfast with a smear of peanut butter.

Because these crackers have a little sweetener in them, I find that the best way to get them to crisp up without burning is to return them to a warm oven and let them sit inside.

YIELD: About 30 crackers (10 servings) PREP TIME: 15 minutes, plus 30 minutes to cool COOK TIME: 50 to 60 minutes

2 cups (200g) blanched almond flour

⅓ cup granulated erythritol sweetener

2 teaspoons ground cinnamon

1 teaspoon baking powder

⅛ teaspoon salt

1 large egg

2 tablespoons unsalted butter, melted but not hot

2 teaspoons yacón syrup (optional)

1 teaspoon vanilla extract

1. Preheat the oven to 300°F.

2. In a large bowl, whisk together the almond flour, sweetener, cinnamon, baking powder, and salt. Stir in the egg, melted butter, yacón syrup (if using), and vanilla extract until the dough comes together.

3. Turn the dough out onto a large piece of parchment paper or silicone baking mat and pat it into a rough rectangle. Top the dough with a piece of parchment and roll it out as evenly as possible to a ⅛- to ¼-inch thickness. Remove the top piece of parchment.

4. Use a sharp knife or pizza wheel to score the dough into 2-inch squares. Prick each cracker 2 or 3 times with a fork to make decorative indentations.

5. Slide the piece of parchment or baking mat onto a baking sheet. Bake for 20 to 30 minutes, until the crackers are just beginning to brown and firm up. Let cool for 30 minutes, then break the crackers apart along the score lines.

6. Return the baking sheet to the warm oven and let the crackers sit inside with the oven turned off for another 30 minutes. If your oven has cooled down too much, set the temperature to no higher than 200°F.

7. Remove the crackers from the oven and let cool completely on the baking sheet. Store in a covered container on the counter for up to 5 days.

NUTRITIONAL INFORMATION:

CALORIES: 156 | FAT: 13.4g | PROTEIN: 5.2g | CARBS: 6.2g | FIBER: 2.7g | ERYTHRITOL: 8g

NACHO CHIPS

A truly crispy, very-low-carb alternative to tortilla chips that stands up to dipping in salsa or guacamole. My kids ask for these chips all the time!

YIELD: 50 to 60 chips (6 servings) PREP TIME: 15 minutes COOK TIME: 40 minutes

2 large egg whites

¼ teaspoon salt

1½ cups finely crushed pork rinds

1 cup preshredded Mexican cheese blend or cheddar cheese (about 4 ounces)

1 tablespoon Taco Seasoning (page 63)

1. Preheat the oven to 300°F.

2. In a large bowl, whisk the egg whites with the salt until frothy. Stir in the pork rinds, cheese, and taco seasoning until well combined.

3. Turn the mixture out onto a large piece of parchment paper and pat it into a square. Top with another piece of parchment and roll out the mixture into a very thin square, about 12 inches. Remove the top piece of parchment and slide the bottom piece onto a large baking sheet.

4. Use a sharp knife to score the cheese mixture into 2-inch squares. Then score each square diagonally into 2 triangles. Bake for 20 minutes, until the chips are turning golden brown. Turn off the oven and let them sit inside until they are firm to the touch, about 20 minutes.

5. Remove from the oven and let cool completely on the baking sheet before breaking apart along the score lines. Store in a covered container on the counter for up to 3 days.

SERVING SUGGESTION:
These chips are great for scooping up Pico de Gallo (page 76).

EVERYDAY TIP:
You can crush pork rinds in several different ways, and you can even purchase precrushed "pork dust." To crush them at home, place them in a thick plastic bag and pound them with a rolling pin or kitchen mallet. You can also process them in a food processor. Be sure to crush them as finely as you can and measure them *after* crushing for accurate results.

NUTRITIONAL INFORMATION:
CALORIES: 146 | FAT: 9g | PROTEIN: 13g | CARBS: 0.6g | FIBER: 0.1g

CHEESY BROCCOLI TOTS

Cauliflower tots are all the rage as a replacement for tater tots, so I decided to apply the same principles to broccoli. These are tasty little nuggets!

YIELD: 36 tots (6 servings) PREP TIME: 10 minutes COOK TIME: 20 to 25 minutes

1 pound broccoli, cut into florets

1¼ cups shredded cheddar cheese (about 5 ounces)

2 large eggs

2 tablespoons (14g) coconut flour

1 teaspoon salt

½ teaspoon black pepper

½ teaspoon garlic powder

1. Fill a large saucepan with 1 inch of water and place a steamer basket inside. Bring the water to a boil over medium heat, then place the broccoli florets in the steamer basket. Reduce the heat to medium-low and steam for about 5 minutes, until the broccoli is just barely tender.

2. Transfer the broccoli to a food processor and pulse until it is chopped into small pieces. Add the cheese, eggs, coconut flour, salt, pepper, and garlic powder and continue to pulse until the broccoli is finely chopped and the mixture is well combined.

3. Preheat the oven to 350°F and line a large rimmed baking sheet with parchment paper. Grease the parchment.

4. Using your hands, roll the broccoli mixture into 1-inch balls and place them on the prepared baking sheet. Bake for 20 to 25 minutes, until golden brown and firm to the touch. Let cool slightly before serving.

SERVING SUGGESTION:
Serve these tots with Roasted Tomato Cream Sauce (page 77) for a delicious dipping experience.

EVERYDAY TIP:
You can easily cut this recipe in half to make a smaller amount of tots. The leftovers heat up nicely in the oven or microwave, but fresh tots taste best.

NUTRITIONAL INFORMATION:
CALORIES: 137 | FAT: 7.4g | PROTEIN: 9.2g | CARBS: 7g | FIBER: 2.9g

FRIED ARTICHOKES WITH SPICY CAJUN MAYO

I love finger foods, and I could really make dinner out of appetizers every night. These pan-fried artichokes are quick and easy to make, and everyone always gobbles them up.

YIELD: 4 servings (not including time to make mayo) **PREP TIME:** 5 minutes
COOK TIME: 6 to 8 minutes

12 ounces frozen artichoke hearts, thawed and drained

¼ cup avocado oil or light olive oil

Salt and black pepper

1 recipe Spicy Cajun Mayonnaise (page 66)

1. Cut the artichoke hearts into quarters, if not already quartered. Pat dry with paper towels or tea towels.

2. In a large skillet, heat the oil over medium-high heat until shimmering but not smoking. Add the artichoke hearts in a single layer and fry until nicely browned, 3 to 4 minutes per side.

3. Transfer the artichokes to a paper towel–lined plate and sprinkle immediately with salt and pepper.

4. Serve the artichokes warm with the spicy mayo on the side.

EVERYDAY SWAP:
You can also use marinated artichoke hearts. Just be sure to drain them well and be aware that the marinating liquid accounts for much of the total weight. Look for the dry weight on the can or jar so you know how much to use.

NUTRITIONAL INFORMATION (not including Spicy Cajun Mayo):
CALORIES: 93 | FAT: 14g | PROTEIN: 0g | CARBS: 5.7g | FIBER: 2.8g

GRILLED ZUCCHINI ROLLS WITH GOAT CHEESE AND PESTO

These little zucchini rolls are full of flavor and make a tasty appetizer or side dish.

YIELD: About 16 rolls (4 servings) **PREP TIME:** 15 minutes
COOK TIME: 6 to 10 minutes

3 medium zucchini, about 10 inches long

¾ teaspoon salt

¼ teaspoon black pepper

4 ounces fresh goat cheese

¼ cup pesto, store-bought or homemade (page 71)

FOR GARNISH (OPTIONAL):

Sliced fresh basil leaves

Toasted pine nuts

1. Preheat the grill to medium.

2. Trim the ends of the zucchini and cut each one lengthwise into ¼-inch-thick strips (you should get about 16 strips total). Lay the strips on the grill and cook until tender and grill marks appear, 3 to 5 minutes per side.

3. Transfer the grilled zucchini to a platter in a single layer. Sprinkle with the salt and pepper and let cool.

4. In a medium bowl, stir together the goat cheese and pesto until well combined. Spread each zucchini strip with about 2 teaspoons of the goat cheese mixture and roll up tightly.

5. For a pretty presentation, stand the zucchini rolls up on their ends and garnish with sliced basil leaves and toasted pine nuts, if desired. Serve cold or at room temperature.

EVERYDAY TIP:
Dry-grilling the zucchini helps keep it from getting soggy. If foods tend to stick to your grill, wipe the hot grates with a little oil rather than brushing the oil on the zucchini.

NUTRITIONAL INFORMATION:
CALORIES: 197 | FAT: 15.7g | PROTEIN: 8.2g | CARBS: 3.8g | FIBER: 1.2g

BAKED RICOTTA WITH MUSHROOMS AND THYME

Everyone loves a hot, gooey, cheesy dip on the appetizer table!

YIELD: 8 servings   PREP TIME: 5 minutes   COOK TIME: 20 minutes

BAKED RICOTTA:

1 (15-ounce) container whole-milk ricotta, room temperature

1 cup shredded mozzarella cheese (about 4 ounces)

½ ounce Parmesan cheese, grated (about ½ cup)

2 cloves garlic, minced

1 teaspoon chopped fresh thyme

1 teaspoon salt

½ teaspoon black pepper

MUSHROOM TOPPING:

3 tablespoons salted butter

1 clove garlic, minced

8 ounces cremini or button mushrooms, sliced

½ teaspoon salt

1 teaspoon chopped fresh thyme

TO MAKE THE BAKED RICOTTA:

1. Preheat the oven to 375°F.

2. In a medium bowl, whisk together the ricotta, mozzarella, Parmesan, garlic, thyme, salt, and pepper.

3. Spread the ricotta mixture in one 16-ounce baking dish or two 8-ounce baking dishes. Bake for about 20 minutes, until the cheese is melted and lightly browned on top.

TO MAKE THE MUSHROOM TOPPING:

1. In a large skillet over medium heat, melt the butter. Once melted and hot, add the garlic and sauté for 30 seconds.

2. Add the mushrooms and salt and cook, stirring frequently, until golden brown, about 5 minutes.

3. Sprinkle with the thyme and spoon the topping over the baked ricotta mixture.

4. Store leftovers in the refrigerator for up to 3 days. Reheat gently in the oven or microwave.

SERVING SUGGESTIONS:
Serve hot with fresh vegetables like celery sticks and endive leaves. Or make some Basic Almond Flour Crackers (page 142) for dipping. This dip is also delicious spread onto slices of Flourless Sunflower Bread (page 116).

NUTRITIONAL INFORMATION:
CALORIES: 203 | FAT: 14.8g | PROTEIN: 12g | CARBS: 3.9g | FIBER: 0.3g

BRIE AND CARAMELIZED ONION STUFFED MUSHROOMS

Onions are surprisingly high in carbs, but a little onion can go a long way. Caramelizing the onions brings out their natural sweetness, which offsets the tang of the Brie.

YIELD: 6 servings   PREP TIME: 10 minutes   COOK TIME: 32 to 35 minutes

2 tablespoons salted butter

½ large onion, thinly sliced

½ teaspoon salt

12 ounces cremini or button mushrooms (12 to 15 mushrooms)

2 tablespoons avocado oil

Salt and black pepper

4 ounces Brie cheese, cut into thin slices about 1 inch square

Chopped fresh herb of choice, for garnish (optional)

1. Melt the butter in a medium saucepan over medium-low heat. Add the onion slices and cook, stirring frequently, until translucent. Sprinkle with the salt and reduce the heat to low. Continue to cook, stirring frequently, until the onions are golden brown and caramelized, about 15 minutes.

2. Preheat the oven to 400°F and line a rimmed baking sheet with parchment paper or aluminum foil.

3. Remove the stems from the mushrooms and place the mushroom caps in a bowl. Drizzle with the avocado oil and season lightly with salt and pepper. Toss to coat.

4. Place the mushroom caps cavity side up on the lined baking sheet and divide the caramelized onions among them. Pack the onions into each cap.

5. Cover each mushroom cap with a piece of Brie. Bake for 12 to 15 minutes, until the mushrooms are softened and the Brie is melted. Garnish with fresh herbs, if using, and serve immediately.

EVERYDAY TIP:
You want to caramelize the onions *slowly* to bring out the best flavor. It takes a bit of time, but it's worth it.

NUTRITIONAL INFORMATION:
CALORIES: 132 | FAT: 13.2g | PROTEIN: 5.4g | CARBS: 2.8g | FIBER: 0.4g

BACON AND SUN-DRIED TOMATO TRUFFLES

These little bite-sized cheese balls make a delicious snack or party appetizer.

YIELD: 16 truffles (2 per serving) PREP TIME: 5 minutes, plus 30 minutes to chill COOK TIME: —

1 (8-ounce) package cream cheese, softened

2 tablespoons salted butter, softened

1 ounce oil-packed sun-dried tomatoes, drained and finely chopped

½ teaspoon salt

¼ teaspoon garlic powder

3 slices bacon, cooked crisp and finely chopped

1 tablespoon finely chopped fresh parsley

1. In a medium bowl, combine the cream cheese, butter, sun-dried tomatoes, salt, and garlic powder. Mix with a rubber spatula until well combined. Refrigerate the mixture until firm, about 30 minutes.

2. In another medium bowl, combine the bacon and parsley. Using wet hands, roll the cream cheese mixture into 1-inch balls, then roll each ball lightly in the bacon and parsley mixture to coat.

3. Keep the truffles chilled until ready to serve. They are best eaten within 2 days.

SERVING SUGGESTIONS:
Serve with toothpicks for eating on their own, or serve with Basic Almond Flour Crackers (page 142) or thick cucumber slices (as "crackers").

EVERYDAY TIP:
Wetting your hands every so often while rolling the cheese balls helps keep them from sticking.

NUTRITIONAL INFORMATION:
CALORIES: 148 | FAT: 12.2g | PROTEIN: 3.3g | CARBS: 3.3g | FIBER: 0.5g

BACON-WRAPPED HALLOUMI FRIES

Have you ever had halloumi? It's a very firm cheese from Cyprus that can stand up to grilling and frying without becoming a melty puddle. My kids love it. We call it squeaky cheese because of the noise it makes against your teeth when you eat it.

YIELD: **16 fries (4 servings)** PREP TIME: **10 minutes** COOK TIME: **7 minutes**

1 (7-ounce) package halloumi cheese

8 slices thin-sliced bacon

1. Starting at the short end of the brick, cut the halloumi crosswise into 8 even slices. Cut each slice in half to create 16 sticks.

2. Cut the bacon slices in half. Place one end of a half-slice of bacon over the end of a halloumi stick and then wind the bacon around, overlapping to cover as much of the halloumi as possible. Stretch the bacon slightly to make it fit and tuck in the ends. Repeat with the remaining bacon and halloumi sticks.

3. Heat a large skillet over medium heat and fry the bacon-wrapped halloumi sticks until golden on all sides, about 7 minutes.

SERVING SUGGESTIONS:
Serve with Spicy Cajun Mayonnaise (page 66) or Roasted Tomato Cream Sauce (page 77).

EVERYDAY TIP:
Do not use thick-cut bacon for this recipe. Thin-sliced bacon has a stretchy quality that allows you to wrap it tightly around the halloumi. As long as it's wrapped quite tightly, I find that it doesn't need to be secured with toothpicks.

NUTRITIONAL INFORMATION (not including dipping sauce):
CALORIES: 254 | FAT: 19.7g | PROTEIN: 16.3g | CARBS: 0.2g | FIBER: 0g

SPANAKOPITA HAND PIES

Conventional spanakopita is made with phyllo dough, which simply isn't keto-friendly. These hand pies have all the same Mediterranean flavor in a fun little package.

YIELD: 16 hand pies (1 per serving) **PREP TIME:** 15 minutes (not including time to make dough) **COOK TIME:** 20 minutes

6 ounces frozen spinach, thawed

1 cup crumbled feta cheese (about 4 ounces)

1 large egg

¼ cup finely chopped onions

1 clove garlic, minced

¾ teaspoon salt

½ teaspoon black pepper

1 recipe Magic Mozzarella Dough (page 82)

1. Preheat the oven to 350°F and line a rimmed baking sheet with parchment paper.

2. Place the spinach in a tea towel and squeeze out the excess moisture, then transfer to a large bowl. Add the feta, egg, onions, garlic, salt, and pepper and mix until well combined.

3. Sprinkle a work surface with 2 to 3 tablespoons of almond flour. Place the dough on the floured work surface and cover with a piece of parchment paper. Roll out the dough into a large square (about 16 inches). Using a sharp knife or pizza wheel, cut the dough into 16 squares.

4. Mound about 1 tablespoon of the spinach mixture in the center of each square. Fold the dough square diagonally over the filling to make a triangle-shaped pie and crimp the edges to seal. If the dough breaks or cracks as you're folding it, simply pinch it back together and shape it around the filling.

5. Place the triangles on the lined baking sheet and make a small slit in the top of each pie to allow steam to escape. Bake for 20 minutes, until golden brown. Let cool slightly on the baking sheet before serving.

6. Store leftovers in the refrigerator for up to 4 days. These pies reheat well in the oven or microwave.

EVERYDAY TIP:
If you end up with leftover filling, it's delicious in an omelet!

NUTRITIONAL INFORMATION:
CALORIES: 123 | FAT: 9.5g | PROTEIN: 5.7g | CARBS: 3.4g | FIBER: 1.5g

SMOKED SALMON PINWHEELS

My name is Carolyn, and I am a smoked salmon addict. These elegant little rolls are easy to make and require no bagels or crackers to eat them. I may or may not have made dinner out of them. I can neither confirm nor deny.

YIELD: **4 servings** PREP TIME: **10 minutes, plus 30 minutes to chill**
COOK TIME: —

8 ounces thinly sliced cold-smoked salmon

4 ounces cream cheese (½ cup), softened

¼ medium cucumber, cut into matchsticks

¼ cup finely chopped red onions

¼ cup capers, drained

½ lemon, thinly sliced

1. Lay a large piece of plastic wrap on a work surface. Arrange the slices of salmon in an overlapping fashion to create a rectangle about 6 inches wide by 12 inches long, with one of the long sides facing you.

2. Gently spread the cream cheese over the salmon, trying not to dislodge any of the pieces. Lay the cucumber matchsticks along one of the long sides of the rectangle, about ½ inch in from the edge.

3. Using the plastic wrap to guide you, roll the salmon up tightly around the cucumber sticks. Keep covered in the plastic wrap and refrigerate until firm, at least 30 minutes.

4. Using a sharp knife, cut the roll into ½-inch-thick slices. Sprinkle with the red onions and capers. Serve with lemon slices.

EVERYDAY TIP:
If you're serving these at a party, keep them refrigerated until the last minute. They hold together much better when they are chilled.

NUTRITIONAL INFORMATION:
CALORIES: 169 | FAT: 10.6g | PROTEIN: 12.4g | CARBS: 2.6g | FIBER: 0.5g

BBQ SLOW COOKER MEATBALLS

Party in a slow cooker! This is the keto appetizer that will have everyone asking for more. These meatballs are also tasty served over cauliflower rice (see page 278) as a full meal.

YIELD: About 36 meatballs (12 servings) PREP TIME: 20 minutes
COOK TIME: 3 to 4 hours

2 pounds ground beef (or 1 pound ground beef and 1 pound ground pork)

¾ cup crushed pork rinds (see Tip, page 148)

2 large eggs

2 cloves garlic, minced

1 teaspoon salt

1 teaspoon black pepper

2 tablespoons avocado oil, divided

1 recipe Low-Carb BBQ Sauce (page 73)

Chopped fresh parsley, for garnish (optional)

1. In a large bowl, combine the ground beef, pork rinds, eggs, garlic, salt, and pepper. Mix well and use your hands to form into 1-inch balls, about 36 total.

2. In a large skillet over medium heat, heat 1 tablespoon of the avocado oil until shimmering. Add half of the meatballs and brown on all sides, about 4 minutes. Transfer the meatballs to a large slow cooker. Repeat with the remaining oil and meatballs.

3. Pour the BBQ sauce over the meatballs and cook on low for 3 to 4 hours, until the meatballs reach an internal temperature of 165°F. Serve with the sauce from the slow cooker and garnish with parsley, if desired.

4. Store leftovers in the refrigerator for up to 3 days. They can be reheated in a saucepan on the stove or in the microwave.

EVERYDAY TIP:
Hand-formed meatballs are a labor of love, but they are well worth the trouble. You can always brown them ahead of time and freeze them after completing Step 2. Kept in a freezer bag or other airtight container, they should be good for up to a month. Be sure to thaw them thoroughly before proceeding to the slow cooker step, and make sure that they reach the proper internal temperature.

NUTRITIONAL INFORMATION:
CALORIES: 267 | FAT: 18g | PROTEIN: 24.9g | CARBS: 3.3g | FIBER: 0.8g

OLD BAY CHICKEN WINGS

I had Old Bay chicken wings at a restaurant in Ithaca, New York, and I fell hard and fast in love. I couldn't wait to find a way to make my own.

YIELD: 2 pounds (8 servings) PREP TIME: 5 minutes
COOK TIME: 55 to 65 minutes

2 pounds chicken wings

1 tablespoon baking powder

2 tablespoons salted butter

2 teaspoons Old Bay seasoning

Chopped fresh cilantro or parsley, for garnish

1. Preheat the oven to 250°F and place a baking rack over a rimmed baking sheet lined with foil. Brush the rack with oil to prevent sticking.

2. Pat the chicken wings very dry with paper towels and place in a large resealable plastic bag. Sprinkle with the baking powder and shake to coat the wings well.

3. Arrange the wings in a single layer on the prepared baking rack and bake in the lower third of the oven for 30 minutes.

4. Increase the oven temperature to 425°F and move the baking sheet to the upper third of the oven. Continue to bake for another 20 to 30 minutes, until the wings are crispy.

5. In a medium skillet over medium heat, cook the butter until it turns a deep amber color, 4 to 5 minutes. Watch carefully so it doesn't burn.

6. Transfer the wings to a bowl and pour the butter over them. Toss to coat. Sprinkle with the Old Bay seasoning and toss again. Sprinkle with cilantro or parsley and serve hot.

7. Store leftovers in the refrigerator for up to 3 days.

EVERYDAY TIPS:

It's imperative to use baking *powder*, not baking soda, to crisp up the wings.

Because both the baking powder and the Old Bay seasoning contain salt, don't add any extra. The wings will be plenty salty!

NUTRITIONAL INFORMATION:
CALORIES: 244 | FAT: 17.6g | PROTEIN: 19.9g | CARBS: 0.9g | FIBER: 0.1g

RICH AND CREAMY HOT CHOCOLATE

This rich hot chocolate is extra-frothy because it's blended with collagen. It's a great source of healthy fat, and it's filling enough to be a full meal. I find it to be a great post-workout treat on a chilly day.

OPTION OPTION   OPTION OPTION

YIELD: 2 servings   PREP TIME: 5 minutes   COOK TIME: 5 minutes

1 cup unsweetened almond milk or cashew milk

¼ cup heavy cream

2 tablespoons powdered erythritol sweetener, or more to taste

2 tablespoons cocoa powder

2 tablespoons grass-fed collagen powder (aka collagen peptides)

2 tablespoons unsalted butter

1. In a medium saucepan over medium heat, bring the milk and cream just to a simmer.

2. In a blender, combine the sweetener, cocoa powder, collagen powder, and butter. Pour in the heated milk mixture and blend on high for 30 seconds, until frothy.

3. Add more sweetener to taste, if desired.

EVERYDAY TIP:
If you're trying to keep your protein down, feel free to leave out the collagen powder. The hot chocolate will still be creamy and delicious without it.

EVERYDAY SWAPS:
To make this dairy-free and Paleo, use coconut milk in place of the heavy cream and coconut oil in place of the butter.

If you're looking for a nut-free hot chocolate, you can replace the almond or cashew milk with hemp milk or more coconut milk.

This recipe does not rely on erythritol for consistency, so you can use any sweetener you like. I find that this doesn't need to be sweetened very much to taste delicious! Use a Paleo-friendly sweetener like stevia for a Paleo version.

NUTRITIONAL INFORMATION:
CALORIES: 260 | FAT: 23.1g | PROTEIN: 8.3g | CARBS: 4.5g | FIBER: 2.5g | ERYTHRITOL: 15g

GREEN TEA FRAPPE

OPTION

2 cups crushed ice

1 cup unsweetened almond milk

¼ cup heavy cream

2 tablespoons powdered erythritol sweetener, or more to taste

2 teaspoons matcha green tea powder, plus extra for garnish (garnish optional)

¼ teaspoon vanilla extract

Lightly sweetened whipped cream, for topping (optional)

Fat bomb in a glass—that's what I call drinks like this. It's a great way to increase your daily fat intake without increasing your protein or carbs by very much.

YIELD: 2 servings PREP TIME: 5 minutes COOK TIME: —

1. Combine the ice, almond milk, cream, sweetener, green tea powder, and vanilla extract in a blender. Blend until smooth.

2. Add more sweetener to taste, if desired. Top with whipped cream, if using, and garnish with a sprinkle of green tea powder, if desired.

EVERYDAY TIP:
Matcha green tea powder is sold in many grocery stores now, but I often purchase it online.

EVERYDAY SWAPS:
This recipe can easily be made dairy-free by substituting coconut cream for the heavy cream and using whipped coconut cream for the optional topping.

NUTRITIONAL INFORMATION:
CALORIES: 244 | FAT: 23.3g | PROTEIN: 2.2g | CARBS: 2.8g | FIBER: 1g | ERYTHRITOL: 15g

SWEET TEA LEMONADE

This is by no means a high-fat recipe, but it sure is nice to have a refreshing glass of something cold and sweet on a hot summer day. Sugar-free, of course! The tea and the lemonade can also be served separately.

YIELD: About 8 cups (8 servings) **PREP TIME:** 5 minutes, plus time to steep tea **COOK TIME:** 5 minutes

SWEET TEA:

4 cups water, divided

3 bags black tea

¼ teaspoon baking soda

½ cup powdered erythritol sweetener

LEMONADE:

3¼ cups water

¾ cup fresh lemon juice

½ cup powdered erythritol sweetener

Ice, for serving

TO MAKE THE SWEET TEA:

1. In a medium saucepan over medium heat, bring 2 cups of the water to a boil. Remove from the heat and add the tea bags and baking soda.

2. Cover and let steep for 15 minutes, then remove the tea bags. Stir in the sweetener and remaining 2 cups of water until well combined.

TO MAKE THE LEMONADE:

Combine the water, lemon juice, and sweetener in a container. Stir to mix well and dissolve the sweetener.

TO SERVE:

1. Fill glasses with ice and add equal parts tea and lemonade. Alternatively, you can combine the tea and lemonade in a 2-quart pitcher and pour into glasses to serve.

2. Add more sweetener to taste, if desired.

EVERYDAY TIP:
Baking soda may be a funny thing to put in iced tea, but my research on sweet tea tells me that it helps reduce the tannins and thus the bitterness.

EVERYDAY SWAP:
You can use any sweetener you like here, and you can adjust the amount of sweetener to suit your tastes. Sweet tea is meant to be very sweet, but I don't find it to be as refreshing that way, so I just use the amounts called for in the recipe.

NUTRITIONAL INFORMATION:
CALORIES: 11 | FAT: 0g | PROTEIN: 0g | CARBS: 1.6g | ERYTHRITOL: 30g

CREAMY GOLDEN GAZPACHO

Nothing is more refreshing on a warm day than a bowl of gazpacho. This creamy version is no exception. It's a great way to enjoy the bounty of summer.

OPTION   OPTION OPTION

YIELD: 6 servings   **PREP TIME:** 15 minutes, plus at least 1 hour to chill
COOK TIME: —

1 pound yellow or orange tomatoes, chopped

1 medium cucumber, peeled, seeded, and chopped

1 medium-size orange bell pepper, chopped

½ medium jalapeño pepper, chopped (optional)

2 cloves garlic, chopped

2 tablespoons apple cider vinegar

1 teaspoon salt

½ teaspoon black pepper

½ cup heavy cream

Cooked, crumbled bacon, for garnish (optional)

1. Place the tomatoes, cucumber, bell pepper, jalapeño (if using), garlic, vinegar, salt, and pepper in a blender or food processor. Blend until smooth.

2. Stir in the cream and adjust the seasonings to taste. Chill for at least 1 hour before serving. Garnish each bowl with a little bacon, if desired.

EVERYDAY SWAPS:
Use full-fat coconut milk instead of cream for a dairy-free, Paleo version. Leave off the bacon garnish for a vegetarian gazpacho.

NUTRITIONAL INFORMATION:
CALORIES: 94 | FAT: 7.1g | PROTEIN: 1.6g | CARBS: 6g | FIBER: 1.7g

SPINACH ARTICHOKE SOUP

Everybody's favorite dip turned into a rich, satisfying keto soup.

YIELD: **6 servings** PREP TIME: **5 minutes** COOK TIME: **18 minutes**

2 tablespoons salted butter

8 ounces frozen artichoke hearts, thawed, drained, and chopped

4 cloves garlic, minced

¾ teaspoon salt

½ teaspoon black pepper

4 cups chicken broth, store-bought or homemade (page 58)

4 ounces cream cheese (½ cup), cubed

½ ounce Parmesan cheese, grated (about ½ cup), plus extra for garnish

6 ounces fresh spinach leaves, chopped

½ cup heavy cream

¼ teaspoon red pepper flakes (optional)

Cooked, crumbled bacon, for garnish

1. Melt the butter in a large saucepan over medium heat. Add the artichoke hearts, garlic, salt, and pepper and sauté for 2 minutes.

2. Stir in the chicken broth and bring to a simmer. Cook for 5 minutes. Add the cream cheese and Parmesan and stir until melted and smooth, about 8 minutes.

3. Stir in the spinach, cream, and red pepper flakes, if using. Continue to cook until the spinach is just wilted, about 2 more minutes. Adjust the seasonings to taste.

4. Sprinkle with bacon and Parmesan just before serving.

EVERYDAY TIPS:
Feel free to use marinated artichoke hearts here. Just be sure to drain them well.

To make this soup a full meal, try adding some diced cooked chicken.

NUTRITIONAL INFORMATION:
CALORIES: 209 | FAT: 16.7g | PROTEIN: 5.6g | CARBS: 6.4g | FIBER: 2g

THAI CHICKEN ZOODLE SOUP

I have a passion for Thai food. There is something about the combination of ginger, lemongrass, and hot peppers that delights my senses. This soup is light but still satisfying, with all that wonderful spicy Thai flavor.

YIELD: **8 servings**   PREP TIME: **10 minutes**   COOK TIME: **20 minutes**

1 tablespoon coconut oil

¼ medium onion, chopped

1 jalapeño pepper, chopped

1½ tablespoons Thai green curry paste

2 cloves garlic, minced

6 cups chicken broth, store-bought or homemade (page 58)

1 (15-ounce) can full-fat coconut milk

1 red bell pepper, thinly sliced

1 pound boneless, skinless chicken breasts or thighs, thinly sliced against the grain

2 tablespoons fish sauce

½ cup chopped fresh cilantro

2 medium zucchini, spiral-sliced into noodles

1 lime, cut into 8 wedges

1. In a large saucepan over medium heat, heat the coconut oil until melted and shimmering. Add the onion and sauté until just translucent, about 5 minutes.

2. Stir in the jalapeño, curry paste, and garlic and sauté until fragrant, about 1 minute. Add the broth and coconut milk and whisk until fully combined. Bring to a simmer.

3. Add the bell pepper, chicken, and fish sauce and simmer until the chicken is cooked through, about 5 minutes. Remove from the heat and stir in the cilantro.

4. Divide the zucchini noodles among 8 soup bowls and ladle the soup over them; the heat of the soup will make the noodles tender.

5. Serve with a lime wedge on the side.

EVERYDAY TIP:

If you aren't serving all the soup at once, the extra zucchini noodles will keep well in a covered container for a day or two.

NUTRITIONAL INFORMATION:

CALORIES: 277 | FAT: 20.3g | PROTEIN: 18.2g | CARBS: 6.6g | FIBER: 1.2g

BROWNED BUTTER MUSHROOM SOUP

This soup is so simple and yet so deliciously filling. Between the umami taste of the mushrooms and the nuttiness of the browned butter, your taste buds will be doing a happy dance.

6 tablespoons (¾ stick) salted butter

2 tablespoons chopped fresh sage leaves

1 pound cremini or button mushrooms, sliced

¾ teaspoon salt

½ teaspoon black pepper

4 cups chicken broth, store-bought or homemade (page 58)

½ cup heavy cream

Fresh thyme leaves or sprigs, for garnish (optional)

1. In a large saucepan over medium heat, cook the butter until it turns a deep amber color, 3 to 4 minutes. Watch carefully so it doesn't burn. Add the sage and cook for 1 minute more.

2. Add the mushrooms, salt, and pepper and stir to coat them in the butter. Sauté until the mushrooms are tender and golden brown, about 5 minutes.

3. Stir in the broth and bring to a simmer. Reduce the heat to medium-low and cook for 5 minutes. Transfer to a blender or food processor and puree until smooth.

4. Return the soup to the pot and stir in the cream. Serve immediately, garnished with thyme, if desired.

NUTRITIONAL INFORMATION:
CALORIES: 198 | FAT: 17.7g | PROTEIN: 4.6g | CARBS: 4.6g | FIBER: 0.6g

SLOW COOKER BROCCOLI CHEESE SOUP

This is one of those dump-and-run recipes: dump all the ingredients into your slow cooker and go read a book or play with your kids. A few hours later, soup's on! It's thick, it's creamy, and it's insanely satisfying.

YIELD: **6 servings**   PREP TIME: **5 minutes**   COOK TIME: **2 hours on high or 4 hours on low**

1 pound frozen broccoli

4 ounces cream cheese (½ cup)

¼ cup chopped onions

2 tablespoons salted butter

2 cloves garlic, peeled

3 cups chicken broth, store-bought or homemade (page 58)

1 teaspoon salt

½ teaspoon black pepper

2 cups shredded cheddar cheese (about 8 ounces)

1 packed cup fresh spinach leaves

1. Place the broccoli, cream cheese, onions, butter, and garlic in a 5-quart or larger slow cooker. Pour in the broth and sprinkle with the salt and pepper. Cover and cook on high for 2 hours or on low for 4 hours.

2. Add the shredded cheese and spinach and stir until the cheese is melted. Use an immersion blender to blend until smooth. Alternatively, you can blend the soup in batches in a blender or food processor.

3. Season to taste with additional salt and pepper. Serve immediately.

EVERYDAY TIPS:
You can use fresh broccoli here, too, but using frozen broccoli cuts down on your prep time and makes this soup extra-easy. I keep a bag in the freezer at all times for whenever the mood strikes.

Cream cheese is a great way to thicken creamy low-carb soups without using flour.

NUTRITIONAL INFORMATION:
CALORIES: 291 | FAT: 20.2g | PROTEIN: 14.3g | CARBS: 8g | FIBER: 2.3g

ITALIAN WEDDING SOUP

My kids love the not-so-healthy canned Italian wedding soup, so I decided that I needed to create a keto-friendly version. They love it and don't even bat an eye that it contains cauliflower rice instead of pasta.

YIELD: **6 servings**   PREP TIME: **30 minutes**   COOK TIME: **25 minutes**

MEATBALLS:

1 pound ground beef or ground pork

½ cup crushed pork rinds (see Tip, page 148)

½ ounce Parmesan cheese, grated (about ½ cup)

1 teaspoon Italian seasoning

¾ teaspoon salt

½ teaspoon black pepper

1 large egg

SOUP:

2 tablespoons avocado oil

¼ cup chopped onions

4 stalks celery, chopped

1 teaspoon salt

½ teaspoon black pepper

3 cloves garlic, minced

6 cups chicken broth, store-bought or homemade (page 58)

1 teaspoon dried oregano leaves

2 cups riced cauliflower (see page 276)

2 packed cups spinach leaves

Grated Parmesan cheese, for garnish

TO MAKE THE MEATBALLS:

1. In a large bowl, use your hands to mix together all the ingredients for the meatballs.

2. Form the mixture into ½-inch meatballs and place on a waxed paper–lined tray. Refrigerate until ready to add to the soup.

TO MAKE THE SOUP:

1. In a large saucepan or stockpot over medium heat, heat the oil until shimmering. Add the onions, celery, salt, and pepper and sauté until the vegetables are tender, about 7 minutes. Stir in the garlic and cook for another minute.

2. Add the broth and oregano. Bring just to a boil, then reduce the heat and simmer for 10 minutes.

3. Add the riced cauliflower and meatballs and continue to simmer until the meatballs are cooked through and float to the top, about 5 minutes.

4. Add the spinach and cook until wilted, 2 minutes more. Season to taste with additional salt and pepper. Garnish each serving with a sprinkle of grated Parmesan.

EVERYDAY TIP:
You can make the meatballs a day ahead and keep them in the fridge.

EVERYDAY SWAP:
Substitute ½ cup of almond flour for the pork rinds in the meatballs.

NUTRITIONAL INFORMATION:
CALORIES: 303 | FAT: 20.2g | PROTEIN: 29.5g | CARBS: 5.7g | FIBER: 1.9g

DILLED CUCUMBER SALAD

I make this salad all summer long when my cucumbers are growing like mad. It's light and refreshing and the whole family loves it. It's a perfect side for grilled meat.

YIELD: **6 servings** PREP TIME: **5 minutes** COOK TIME: —

2 medium cucumbers

¼ cup avocado oil mayonnaise, store-bought or homemade (page 65)

2 tablespoons chopped fresh dill

1 tablespoon fresh lemon juice

1 clove garlic, minced

½ teaspoon salt

½ teaspoon black pepper

1. Trim the ends from the cucumbers, then cut them lengthwise into quarters. Slice the quarters crosswise about ¼ inch thick.

2. In a large bowl, toss the cucumbers with the mayo, dill, lemon juice, and garlic. Add the salt and pepper just before serving.

EVERYDAY TIP:
The moment you add the salt, it begins drawing out water from the cucumbers. It's best to add the salt right before serving so you don't end up with a lot of liquid in the bottom of the bowl.

NUTRITIONAL INFORMATION:
CALORIES: 85 | FAT: 7.5g | PROTEIN: 0.7g | CARBS: 4.1g | FIBER: 0.6g

TABBOULEH

I distinctly remember the first time I tried tabbouleh when a friend brought it to a potluck. It quickly became one of my favorite summer salads. I can still enjoy it by replacing the bulgur with riced cauliflower. I honestly think this version is just as good!

YIELD: **8 servings**   PREP TIME: **15 minutes**   COOK TIME: —

4 cups riced cauliflower (see page 276)

1 lightly packed cup fresh parsley leaves, chopped

1 medium cucumber, chopped

1 medium tomato, chopped

2 green onions, white and light green parts only, chopped

2 tablespoons fresh lemon juice

2 tablespoons extra-virgin olive oil

¾ teaspoon salt

½ teaspoon ground cumin

1. Place all the ingredients in a large bowl. Toss well to combine.

2. Adjust the seasonings to taste. Serve at room temperature or chilled. Store leftovers in the refrigerator for up to 4 days.

EVERYDAY TIP:
If you prefer your cauliflower a little more tender, you can cook it for just a few minutes in the microwave. Place it in a microwave-safe bowl and cover with plastic wrap, then cook on high for about 3 minutes.

EVERYDAY SWAP:
You can replace the olive oil with avocado oil if you prefer, but a really good extra-virgin olive oil gives the tabbouleh that true Mediterranean flavor.

NUTRITIONAL INFORMATION:
CALORIES: 58 | FAT: 3.5g | PROTEIN: 2g | CARBS: 5.9g | FIBER: 2.2g

FRIED GOAT CHEESE SALAD

How can you resist warm, melty rounds of goat cheese with a crispy fried coating? They turn a plain garden salad into something spectacular.

YIELD: 4 servings **PREP TIME:** 10 minutes **COOK TIME:** 2 minutes

1 (8-ounce) log fresh goat cheese

DRY "BREADING":

1 cup crushed pork rinds (see Tip, page 148)

2 tablespoons grated Parmesan cheese

1 teaspoon garlic powder

1 teaspoon dried oregano leaves

¾ teaspoon salt

¼ teaspoon black pepper

⅛ teaspoon red pepper flakes

EGG WASH:

1 large egg

1 tablespoon heavy cream

¼ cup lard or avocado oil, for the pan

2 cups mixed salad greens, for serving

1. Using a sharp knife, cut the goat cheese crosswise into 8 even slices. Using your hands, press them into circles about ⅝ inch thick.

2. In a shallow bowl, whisk together the pork rinds, Parmesan, garlic powder, oregano, salt, pepper, and red pepper flakes. In another shallow bowl, whisk together the egg and cream until well combined.

3. Dip each slice of goat cheese into the egg mixture, then dredge in the pork rind mixture, making sure to coat each slice well.

4. In a large skillet over medium-high heat, heat the lard or oil until shimmering. Add the coated goat cheese slices and fry until golden brown, about 1 minute per side.

5. Divide the salad greens among 4 small plates. Top each salad with 2 fried goat cheese rounds and serve.

SERVING SUGGESTION:
You can pass Dijon Vinaigrette (page 67) around the table for anyone who wants a little dressing, but this salad is good just as it is, no dressing necessary.

NUTRITIONAL INFORMATION:
CALORIES: 422 | FAT: 33.3g | PROTEIN: 23.5g | CARBS: 1.7g | FIBER: 0.5g

GRILLED VEGETABLE SALAD WITH FETA AND PINE NUTS

In warm weather, you can find me grilling out almost every weekend. My husband and I love to make big batches of grilled vegetables to eat all week long.

OPTION

YIELD: **6 servings**   PREP TIME: **15 minutes**   COOK TIME: **6 to 10 minutes**

1 small eggplant, sliced ¼ inch thick

1 medium zucchini, sliced ¼ inch thick

1 small red bell pepper, sliced into ½-inch strips

2 tablespoons extra-virgin olive oil

2 cloves garlic, minced

1 teaspoon salt

½ teaspoon black pepper

6 cups salad greens

¾ cup crumbled feta cheese (about 3 ounces)

6 tablespoons pine nuts, toasted and cooled

1 recipe Dijon Vinaigrette (page 67)

1. Preheat the grill to medium.

2. Arrange the sliced vegetables on the grill and cook until tender and slightly charred, 3 to 5 minutes per side. Transfer to a bowl and toss with the olive oil, garlic, salt, and pepper.

3. Divide the salad greens among 6 plates. Top with a few slices of each of the vegetables. Sprinkle each salad with 2 tablespoons of the feta and 1 tablespoon of the pine nuts. Serve with the vinaigrette on the side.

EVERYDAY TIP:
The eggplant takes the longest to cook, so I always put it on first and make sure it's over the hottest part of the grill.

EVERYDAY SWAPS:
Leave off the pine nuts to make this recipe nut-free. This salad is also delicious with Creamy Cilantro Dressing (page 70).

NUTRITIONAL INFORMATION (not including dressing):
CALORIES: 172   FAT: 13.2g   PROTEIN: 5.3g   CARBS: 7.5g   FIBER: 2.7g

BLACK AND BLUE STEAK SALAD

Having grown up on a beef cattle farm, I've always loved a good steak with a pat of butter floating on top. It takes a light salad and turns it into a hearty meal.

YIELD: **4 servings** PREP TIME: **15 minutes, plus 2 hours to marinate steak**
COOK TIME: **8 minutes**

1 pound chuck steak, about 1 inch thick

1 recipe Steak Marinade (page 60)

Salt and pepper

2 tablespoons salted butter

2 small heads romaine lettuce, chopped

1 medium cucumber, quartered lengthwise, then sliced crosswise

1½ cups grape or cherry tomato halves

8 small pepperoncini

⅛ red onion, thinly sliced

½ cup crumbled bleu cheese (about 2 ounces)

1 recipe Dijon Vinaigrette (page 67) or Easy Ranch Dressing (page 68)

1. Place the steak in a large glass or ceramic dish and poke it all over on both sides with a fork. Pour the marinade over the top and flip the steak over to coat both sides. Marinate in the refrigerator for 2 hours.

2. Preheat the grill to medium-high. Sprinkle the steak generously with salt and pepper. Grill until the internal temperature registers 135°F to 145°F, about 4 minutes per side. Remove to a platter and top with the butter. Let rest for 5 minutes.

3. Divide the lettuce among 4 plates. Top with the cucumber, tomatoes, and pepperoncini. Thinly slice the steak against the grain and divide among the plates. Sprinkle with the onion and bleu cheese.

4. Serve with the dressing on the side.

SERVING SUGGESTION:
This salad is also delicious with Easy Ranch Dressing (page 68).

EVERYDAY TIP:
Chuck steak is an inexpensive cut with a reputation for being tough, but it's very flavorful and perfect on this salad as long as you marinate it, don't overcook it, and slice it thinly.

NUTRITIONAL INFORMATION (not including dressing):
CALORIES: 397 | FAT: 28.1g | PROTEIN: 26.8g | CARBS: 6.8g | FIBER: 1.9g

SPICY SHRIMP AND AVOCADO SALAD

I never knew what to do with those tiny cooked bay shrimp until I created this recipe. I received some in a CSA box and had to find a way to use them. We love this spicy, tangy salad as a quick and easy meal.

YIELD: **4 servings**   PREP TIME: **10 minutes**   COOK TIME: —

2 large ripe avocados

12 ounces cooked bay shrimp

2 tablespoons avocado oil mayonnaise, store-bought or homemade (page 65)

2 tablespoons fresh lime juice

1 tablespoon Sriracha or other hot sauce

Salt and pepper

Chopped fresh cilantro or parsley, for garnish

4 lime wedges, for garnish

1. Cut the avocados in half lengthwise and remove the pits. Score the flesh into chunks, being careful not to cut through the skin, and use a large spoon to scoop the flesh into a medium bowl. Reserve the skins for serving.

2. Add the shrimp, mayonnaise, lime juice, and Sriracha to the bowl. Toss to combine well. Season to taste with salt and pepper.

3. Divide the salad among the reserved avocado skins. Sprinkle with chopped cilantro or parsley and serve each salad with a lime wedge.

EVERYDAY TIP:
You can serve this over lettuce for a bigger salad, but I love how it looks when served in the avocado skins.

NUTRITIONAL INFORMATION:
CALORIES: 231 | FAT: 15.9g | PROTEIN: 13g | CARBS: 7.4g | FIBER: 4.7g

SOUTHWESTERN CHICKEN CHOPPED SALAD

Chopped salads may take a little extra work, but they are worth it. They look particularly inviting when arranged nicely on a plate or platter. And little ones who are still trying to master their fork and knife skills find chopped salads easier to scoop up.

YIELD: **4 servings** PREP TIME: **30 minutes** COOK TIME: **10 minutes**

8 slices bacon

2 small heads romaine lettuce

3 cups chopped cooked chicken

1 large red bell pepper, diced

1 medium tomato, diced

1 avocado, diced

½ medium cucumber, diced

1 cup shredded cheddar or Pepper Jack cheese (about 4 ounces)

1 recipe Easy Ranch Dressing (page 68) or Creamy Cilantro Dressing (page 70)

1. Chop the bacon into small pieces and cook over medium heat until crisp. Transfer to a paper towel–lined plate to drain.

2. Cut the stem end off each head of lettuce, then cut each head in half lengthwise. Cut each half lengthwise again. Chop the lettuce quarters into smaller-than-bite-size pieces. Wash and dry the chopped lettuce.

3. Divide the chopped lettuce among 4 dinner plates or large bowls. Divide the chicken, bell pepper, tomato, avocado, cucumber, and bacon among the plates, arranging the ingredients as you like. Sprinkle each salad with ¼ cup of the cheese.

4. Serve with the dressing on the side.

EVERYDAY TIP:
This salad is a great way to use up leftover cooked chicken and is also fabulous with turkey. So now you know what you'll be having the day after Thanksgiving!

NUTRITIONAL INFORMATION (not including dressing):
CALORIES: 339 | FAT: 20.4g | PROTEIN: 23.6g | CARBS: 9.1g | FIBER: 4.4g

BEEF, PORK & LAMB

MEXICAN SHREDDED BEEF

My family purchased a quarter cow last year, and one package was labeled "arm roast." I had no idea what to do with it, but a little investigation proved it to be a kind of chuck roast. So I slow-cooked it with some spices and tomatoes and a new family favorite was born. I think my kids would be happy to eat this every day.

YIELD: 12 servings   PREP TIME: 5 minutes   COOK TIME: 5 hours 15 minutes

1 (4- to 5-pound) chuck roast

Salt and pepper

¼ cup bacon fat or lard

1 (15-ounce) can diced tomatoes

1 cup water

2 tablespoons liquid smoke (optional)

4 cloves garlic, minced

1 teaspoon ground cumin

1 teaspoon chipotle powder, or 1 tablespoon chili powder

1. Preheat the oven to 300°F and place an oven rack in the second-lowest position. Season the roast liberally with salt and pepper.

2. In a large Dutch oven, melt the bacon fat over medium heat. Once hot, add the roast and brown well on all sides. Stir in the tomatoes, water, liquid smoke (if using), garlic, cumin, and chipotle powder.

3. Bring to a simmer, then cover and transfer the pot to the oven. Cook the roast until it is tender and can easily be pierced with a fork, about 5 hours.

4. Remove from the oven and use two forks to shred the meat. Toss the meat in the juices that have collected at the bottom of the pot to moisten it.

5. Store leftovers in the refrigerator for up to 3 days. The meat can also be wrapped tightly in foil and frozen for up to a month.

SERVING SUGGESTION:
Serve over Cilantro-Lime Cauliflower Rice (page 280) with chopped avocado. It's also great sprinkled with shredded cheddar cheese and garnished with fresh cilantro.

EVERYDAY TIP:
This recipe easily feeds a crowd, so it's a good one to make when guests are coming. But it also makes fabulous leftovers, and I can get two full meals out it for my family of five. I've even been known to eat it for breakfast!

NUTRITIONAL INFORMATION:
CALORIES: 416 | FAT: 27.8g | PROTEIN: 29.5g | CARBS: 1.9g | FIBER: 0.5g

RED WINE BRAISED SHORT RIBS

Short ribs are one of my favorite cuts of meat because they are so fatty and unctuous. Slow cooking makes them incredibly tender, too.

YIELD: 4 servings PREP TIME: 5 minutes COOK TIME: 1 hour 40 minutes

2 to 2½ pounds bone-in short ribs

Salt and pepper

2 tablespoons lard, bacon fat, or coconut oil

1 cup beef broth or chicken broth, store-bought or homemade (page 58)

½ cup red wine

¼ cup chopped red onions

2 tablespoons tomato paste

½ teaspoon dried thyme leaves

1. Preheat the oven to 300°F and season the short ribs liberally with salt and pepper.

2. In a large Dutch oven that can accommodate all of the ribs in a single layer, melt the lard over medium-high heat. Add the ribs, fat side down, and cook undisturbed for 3 to 4 minutes, until golden brown. Flip the ribs over and cook for another 3 to 4 minutes.

3. Add the broth, red wine, onions, tomato paste, and thyme to the bottom of the pot. Whisk together and bring to a simmer.

4. Cover the pot and transfer to the oven. Cook for 1½ hours, until the ribs are fork-tender. Remove the ribs and stir the sauce until well combined. Spoon the sauce over the ribs upon serving.

SERVING SUGGESTION:
Serve over Cheesy Cauliflower Grits (page 282).

EVERYDAY SWAP:
If you prefer not to use red wine, simply replace it with water.

NUTRITIONAL INFORMATION:
CALORIES: 397 | FAT: 31.3g | PROTEIN: 25.3g | CARBS: 3.5g | FIBER: 0.5g

GARLIC BUTTER STEAK TIPS

I lived in New England for eleven years, and in that region of the country it's common to see steak tips on the menu at local restaurants. It's also easy to find steak tips precut in grocery stores. In other locales, you are more likely to find whole sirloin tip roasts.

YIELD: 6 servings   PREP TIME: 20 minutes   COOK TIME: 5 minutes

1½ pounds sirloin tip roast

Salt and pepper

¼ cup (½ stick) salted butter, divided

6 cloves garlic, minced, divided

1. Cut the roast into small chunks no larger than 1 inch. If you are using precut steak tips, cut them accordingly. Season the steak tips liberally with salt and pepper.

2. In a large skillet over medium-high heat, melt 2 tablespoons of the butter until bubbling. Add half of the garlic and sauté until fragrant, about 30 seconds. Place half of the steak tips in a single layer in the pan and let cook undisturbed for 1 to 2 minutes.

3. Flip the steak tips over and cook until nicely browned on the outside but still a little pink on the inside, 2 or 3 minutes more. Transfer to a bowl and repeat with the remaining butter, garlic, and steak tips.

4. Pour any juices remaining in the pan over the tips.

SERVING SUGGESTION:
Serve over cauliflower rice (see page 278) or zucchini noodles (see page 274).

EVERYDAY TIP:
If you purchase precut steak tips, you will probably need to cut them up further to be no larger than an inch. This helps ensure quick and even cooking.

NUTRITIONAL INFORMATION:
CALORIES: 275 | FAT: 18.4g | PROTEIN: 23.1g | CARBS: 1.1g | FIBER: 0.1g

BEEF AND VEGGIE KEBABS

A simple and delicious way to coax great flavor out of inexpensive chuck steak.

YIELD: 6 skewers (1 per serving) PREP TIME: 15 minutes, plus 2 hours to marinate steak COOK TIME: 8 minutes

1½ pounds chuck steak

1 recipe Steak Marinade (page 60)

1 medium zucchini

1 medium-size red or yellow bell pepper, or a mix

¼ medium onion

Salt and pepper

1 recipe Chimichurri Sauce (page 72), for serving

SPECIAL EQUIPMENT:

6 bamboo or metal barbecue skewers

1. Cut the steak into 1½-inch chunks. Place in a bowl and pour the marinade over it. Toss to coat and place in the refrigerator to marinate for 2 hours. If you are using bamboo skewers, soak them for at least 1 hour prior to using.

2. Cut the zucchini in half lengthwise and then cut it crosswise into ½-inch slices. Chop the bell pepper and onion into 1-inch chunks. Separate the onion chunks into individual layers.

3. Preheat the grill to medium-high. Thread the meat and vegetables onto the skewers in an alternating pattern. Brush with the marinade from the bottom of the bowl and season liberally with salt and pepper.

4. Place on the preheated grill and cook for about 8 minutes (4 minutes per side), until the beef chunks are cooked to medium-rare and the vegetables have grill marks.

5. Remove from the grill and serve on or off the skewers, with the Chimichurri Sauce on the side.

EVERYDAY TIP:
Cutting the meat into chunks before you marinate it allows more of the surface area to come in contact with the marinade. Your beef will be much more tender!

NUTRITIONAL INFORMATION (not including Chimichurri Sauce):
CALORIES: 224 | FAT: 10.2g | PROTEIN: 23.1g | CARBS: 3.6g | FIBER: 0.9g

EXTRA-BEEFY SPAGHETTI BOLOGNESE

This sauce is so beefy, it could almost pass as chili. My kids love it so much I always make a double batch. It freezes really well, too.

OPTION OPTION

YIELD: 4 servings PREP TIME: 5 minutes COOK TIME: 30 minutes

1 (14½-ounce) can diced tomatoes (with juices), or 1 pound tomatoes, skinned, seeded, and coarsely chopped (with juices)

2 tablespoons salted butter or lard

2 cloves garlic, minced

1 pound ground beef

¾ teaspoon salt

½ teaspoon black pepper

½ teaspoon dried oregano leaves or Italian seasoning

Dash of red pepper flakes

2 medium zucchini, spiral-sliced into noodles

1. Puree the tomatoes in a blender or food processor.

2. In a large skillet over medium heat, melt the butter or lard. Sauté the garlic in the butter until fragrant, about 1 minute.

3. Add the beef, salt, and pepper and cook until the beef is no longer pink, breaking up any clumps with the back of a wooden spoon.

4. Stir in the pureed tomatoes, oregano, and pepper flakes. Bring to a simmer and then reduce the heat to low. Cook until much of the liquid has evaporated, about 15 minutes. Adjust seasonings to taste.

5. To serve, divide the zucchini noodles among 4 plates and microwave each for 30 seconds (for al dente noodles). Spoon the sauce over the top of each plate.

EVERYDAY TIP:
You can use fresh or canned tomatoes in this recipe. It's heavenly with summer tomatoes from your garden or farmer's market.

EVERYDAY SWAPS:
Use lard, coconut oil, or even bacon fat in place of the butter for a dairy-free and Paleo sauce.

NUTRITIONAL INFORMATION:
CALORIES: 397 | FAT: 25.5g | PROTEIN: 31.8g | CARBS: 8g | FIBER: 2.4g

LASAGNA-STUFFED PEPPERS

Traditional lasagna may be off-limits, but nothing says you can't enjoy all the yummy fillings. Just stuff it all into a bell pepper for a pasta-free lasagna experience.

YIELD: 8 servings PREP TIME: 20 minutes COOK TIME: 40 minutes

1 pound ground beef or ground pork

1¼ teaspoons salt, divided

½ teaspoon black pepper

2 cloves garlic, minced

½ teaspoon red pepper flakes

4 ounces frozen spinach, thawed and drained

1 cup whole-milk ricotta cheese

½ ounce Parmesan cheese, grated (about ½ cup)

4 large bell peppers, any color

2 tablespoons tomato paste

⅓ cup water

¼ teaspoon garlic powder

1 cup shredded mozzarella cheese (about 4 ounces)

¼ cup chopped fresh basil, for garnish

1. Preheat the oven to 400°F.

2. Heat a large skillet over medium heat. Add the ground beef and sprinkle with ¾ teaspoon of the salt and the pepper. Cook until no longer pink, about 10 minutes, breaking up any clumps with a wooden spoon. Add the garlic and red pepper flakes and cook for another minute.

3. Squeeze the spinach to remove the excess moisture. In a large bowl, combine the ricotta, spinach, and Parmesan. Add the cooked beef and stir to combine.

4. Cut each bell pepper in half lengthwise and remove the seeds and ribs, keeping the stem end as intact as possible. Set the pepper halves into a 9 by 13-inch baking dish. Spoon the beef and ricotta mixture into each half, mounding it on top.

5. In a medium bowl, whisk the tomato paste with the water until smooth. Whisk in the garlic powder and remaining ½ teaspoon of salt. Spoon the tomato sauce over the peppers. Sprinkle with the mozzarella.

6. Bake for 30 minutes, then turn the oven to broil and broil the peppers 6 inches from the heat for 1 to 3 minutes, until lightly browned. Remove from the oven and sprinkle with the chopped basil.

7. Store leftovers in the refrigerator for up to 4 days.

EVERYDAY TIP:
You can purchase no-sugar-added tomato sauce, but I just whip some up with a little tomato paste, water, and some seasonings. It's great as a pizza sauce, too.

NUTRITIONAL INFORMATION:
CALORIES: 297 | FAT: 17.7g | PROTEIN: 24.7g | CARBS: 8g | FIBER: 2.3g

EASY TACO PIE

I love creating new recipes so much that I rarely make the same thing twice. So when I tell you that I've made this pie more times than I can count, that's saying A LOT. This is one of my easy go-to family pleasers.

YIELD: 8 servings PREP TIME: 5 minutes COOK TIME: 40 minutes

1 pound ground beef

3 tablespoons Taco Seasoning (page 63)

6 large eggs

1 cup heavy cream

2 cloves garlic, minced

½ teaspoon salt

¼ teaspoon black pepper

1 cup shredded cheddar cheese (about 4 ounces)

1. Preheat the oven to 350°F and grease a 9-inch glass or ceramic pie pan.

2. Brown the ground beef in a large skillet over medium heat until no longer pink, about 7 minutes, breaking up any clumps with a wooden spoon. Add the taco seasoning and stir until combined. Spread the beef mixture in the greased pie pan.

3. In a large bowl, combine the eggs, cream, garlic, salt, and pepper. Pour slowly over the beef mixture in the pan.

4. Sprinkle with the cheese and bake for 30 minutes, or until the center is set and the cheese is browned. Remove from the oven and let sit for 5 minutes before serving.

5. Store leftovers in the refrigerator for up to 4 days.

SERVING SUGGESTION:
Serve with your favorite taco toppings, like sour cream, sliced avocado, and Pico de Gallo (page 76).

NUTRITIONAL INFORMATION:
CALORIES: 302 | FAT: 21.2g | PROTEIN: 20.2g | CARBS: 2.1g | FIBER: 0.2g

SLOW COOKER KIELBASA AND CABBAGE

Kielbasa and cabbage go together like peanut butter and jelly. I've made this dish in the slow cooker and in the oven and it's a hit both ways. The vinegar and caraway seeds make the cabbage reminiscent of sauerkraut.

YIELD: 4 servings PREP TIME: 5 minutes COOK TIME: 4 to 6 hours

2 tablespoons bacon fat or lard

½ large head cabbage, chopped

1 teaspoon caraway seeds

1 teaspoon salt

½ teaspoon black pepper

½ teaspoon garlic powder

½ teaspoon mustard powder

1 cup chicken broth, store-bought or homemade (page 58)

2 tablespoons apple cider vinegar

1 pound smoked kielbasa or other smoked sausage

1. Grease a 4-quart or larger slow cooker with the bacon fat. Arrange the chopped cabbage over the bottom. Sprinkle with the caraway seeds, salt, pepper, garlic powder, and mustard powder.

2. Pour the broth and vinegar over the cabbage. Arrange the kielbasa on top and cover the slow cooker.

3. Cook on low for 4 to 6 hours, until the cabbage is tender. Remove the sausage and cut it into chunks for serving.

VARIATION:
Oven-Baked Kielbasa and Cabbage. To make this dish in the oven, preheat the oven to 350°F. Grease a 9 by 13-inch glass or ceramic baking dish with the bacon fat and proceed as directed in Steps 1 and 2. Cover the casserole dish tightly with aluminum foil and bake for 2 hours, until the cabbage is tender.

SERVING SUGGESTION:
If you don't need this dish to be dairy-free, it is extra-delicious with some shredded Swiss cheese on top. Add the cheese just before serving.

NUTRITIONAL INFORMATION:
CALORIES: 426 | FAT: 33.9g | PROTEIN: 15.7g | CARBS: 7.4g | FIBER: 2.1g

NEW MEXICO–STYLE SMOTHERED PORK CHOPS

I was inspired to make these chops after watching an episode of *Burger Land* that featured burgers smothered in the famous New Mexico Hatch chilies. I got to wondering what else I could smother in all that lovely green chile sauce!

YIELD: 4 servings   PREP TIME: 10 minutes   COOK TIME: 20 to 25 minutes

GREEN CHILE SAUCE:

1 tablespoon avocado oil

2 medium jalapeño peppers, seeded and chopped

2 cloves garlic, minced

1 teaspoon ground cumin

2 (4-ounce) cans chopped Hatch green chilies, with juices (if you can't find these, any mild green chilies will do)

2 tablespoons water

¼ teaspoon salt

PORK CHOPS:

4 bone-in pork loin chops, about 1 inch thick

Salt and pepper

2 tablespoons avocado oil

Green Chile Sauce (from above)

1½ cups shredded Pepper Jack cheese (about 6 ounces)

Chopped fresh cilantro, for garnish (optional)

TO MAKE THE CHILE SAUCE:

1. In a medium skillet over medium heat, heat the avocado oil until shimmering. Add the jalapeños, garlic, and cumin and stir until fragrant, about 1 minute.

2. Stir in the canned chilies, water, and salt. Bring to a simmer and cook until the liquids are slightly reduced, about 4 minutes.

3. Transfer to a blender or food processor and puree until smooth.

TO MAKE THE PORK CHOPS:

1. Pat the pork chops dry and season liberally with salt and pepper.

2. Heat a large ovenproof skillet over medium-high heat. Add the oil and swirl to coat the bottom. Arrange the pork chops in the pan so that they don't overlap and sear the first side for 3 minutes.

3. Reduce the heat to medium and turn the chops. Continue to cook until the internal temperature reaches 135°F to 140°F on an instant-read thermometer, 7 to 10 minutes.

4. Place an oven rack in the second-highest position and preheat the broiler. Smother the pork chops in the green chile sauce and sprinkle with the shredded cheese. Transfer the skillet to the oven and broil until the cheese is melted and beginning to brown, 2 to 4 minutes. Serve garnished with chopped cilantro, if desired.

SERVING SUGGESTION:
Make it a full New Mexico–style meal by pairing the chops with some basic cauliflower rice (see page 278) and a few slices of avocado.

NUTRITIONAL INFORMATION:
CALORIES: 477 | FAT: 37.8g | PROTEIN: 39.1g | CARBS: 5.3g | FIBER: 2.2g

EVERYDAY TIPS:

Pan-searing pork chops is my favorite way to cook them. It's a method I learned from *Cook's Illustrated,* and it works perfectly on chops that are no more than 1 inch thick. Any thicker and it's best to finish them off in the oven to ensure they cook through properly without burning the outside.

I will be the first to admit that this is a hefty meal, with a lot of fat and a lot of protein. Personally, I eat half a chop for dinner and eat the rest the next day for breakfast!

PORK MEDALLIONS WITH BROWNED BUTTER AND CRISPY SAGE

Tenderloin is one of the leanest cuts of pork, but when it's cooked properly, it's juicy and flavorful. It's also something of a blank slate, allowing you to add the flavors that suit your palate. This combination of browned butter and sage certainly suits my palate!

YIELD: 4 servings   PREP TIME: 10 minutes   COOK TIME: 15 to 20 minutes

1 (1- to 1½-pound) pork tenderloin

Salt and pepper

2 tablespoons avocado oil or light olive oil, divided

¼ cup (½ stick) salted butter, cut into 4 pieces

10 fresh sage leaves, coarsely chopped

1. Cut the tenderloin into 1-inch-thick slices. Pound each slice gently with a kitchen mallet to a ¼-inch thickness. Sprinkle with salt and pepper.

2. In a large skillet over medium heat, heat 1 tablespoon of the oil until shimmering. Add half of the pork medallions to the pan and cook until well browned, 2 to 3 minutes per side. Remove to a paper towel–lined plate and repeat with the remaining oil and pork medallions.

3. When all the pork medallions are cooked, add the butter to the skillet. Let it melt and cook until it begins to darken. Add the chopped sage leaves and continue to cook until the butter is a deep amber color, 3 to 4 minutes.

4. Place the pork medallions on a serving platter and pour the butter and sage mixture over the top.

SERVING SUGGESTION:
Serve over zucchini noodles (see page 274) or cauliflower rice (see page 278).

EVERYDAY TIP:
This is one of those dishes that pleases almost every palate. It's easy to double or even triple the recipe if you need to serve guests.

NUTRITIONAL INFORMATION:
CALORIES: 242 | FAT: 14.5g | PROTEIN: 24.6g | CARBS: 1.2g | FIBER: 0.5g

DRY RUB FALL-OFF-THE-BONE RIBS

I don't know why most restaurants feel the need to slather ribs in heavy, sugary sauces. Really good ribs don't need that treatment. Braising them in the oven and then quickly grilling or broiling them makes ribs so tender that they fall apart at the slightest touch.

YIELD: 8 servings PREP TIME: 5 minutes COOK TIME: 1 hour 40 minutes

1 (3- to 4-pound) rack pork spareribs

2 tablespoons Basic Spice Rub (page 62)

1 cup water

1. Preheat the oven to 425°F. Rub the spice rub all over both sides of the ribs.

2. Lay the ribs in a large roasting pan (cut the rack in half if necessary to make it fit). Add the water and cover the pan tightly with aluminum foil.

3. Bake for 1½ hours, until the meat is very tender. Check the water level once or twice and add more water if it is evaporating too quickly. The water should be about ½ inch deep at all times. Finish the ribs on the grill by following Step 4, or finish them under the broiler by following Step 5.

4. To grill the ribs, preheat the grill to medium. Lay the ribs fat side down on the grill and grill for 5 minutes, watching carefully for flare-ups. Turn the ribs over and grill for another 3 minutes.

5. To broil the ribs, preheat the broiler and place the ribs about 6 inches from the heat, fat side up. Broil for 6 to 8 minutes, until nicely browned, watching carefully so that they do not burn.

6. Store leftovers in the refrigerator for up to 3 days.

EVERYDAY TIP:
Although you can use this same method for baby-back ribs, I always purchase spareribs. They are fattier, and all that fat means that they will be more tender after cooking. They're often less expensive as well.

NUTRITIONAL INFORMATION:
CALORIES: 445 | FAT: 31.9g | PROTEIN: 24.8g | CARBS: 1.4g | FIBER: 0.6g

BBQ PULLED PORK

Some keto pulled pork, some coleslaw, and some good friends are all it takes to make me happy. Seriously, I am that easy to please!

YIELD: 8 to 10 servings PREP TIME: 10 minutes COOK TIME: 3 hours, 10 minutes

2 tablespoons lard or bacon fat

1 (3- to 4-pound) bone-in pork shoulder roast

2 tablespoons Basic Spice Rub (page 62)

1 cup water

1 cup Low-Carb BBQ Sauce (page 73)

Salt and pepper

1. Preheat the oven to 300°F. Heat the lard in a large Dutch oven over medium heat.

2. Rub the pork roast all over with the spice rub. Place the roast in the Dutch oven and brown on all sides. Add the water to the pot and bring to a boil. Cover and transfer the pot to the oven.

3. Cook for 3 hours, until the pork is tender and can easily be pierced with a fork. Remove from the oven and use 2 forks to shred the meat off the bone; discard the bone.

4. Pour the BBQ sauce over the meat and toss to coat. Season with salt and pepper to taste and toss again to combine.

5. Store leftovers in the refrigerator for up to 3 days or freeze for up to a month.

SERVING SUGGESTIONS:
This pulled pork makes a delicious filling for lettuce wraps. I like to serve it with sliced avocado, tomatoes, and a squeeze of lime. It's also wonderful served over cauliflower rice (see page 278) or coleslaw.

NUTRITIONAL INFORMATION (based on 8 servings):
CALORIES: 402 | FAT: 25.3g | PROTEIN: 34.7g | CARBS: 3.9g | FIBER: 1.2g | ERYTHRITOL: 4.5g

CHEESY SHEPHERD'S PIE

Shepherd's pie is the ultimate comfort food. Hearty and flavorful, it warms you up on a chilly winter night.

YIELD: 10 servings PREP TIME: 15 minutes COOK TIME: 55 minutes

FILLING:

2 pounds ground lamb

¼ cup chopped onions

1 teaspoon salt

½ teaspoon black pepper

2 cloves garlic, minced

2 tablespoons coconut flour

½ cup dry red wine

2 tablespoons chopped fresh rosemary

TOPPING:

1 pound cauliflower florets

2 cloves garlic

¼ cup sour cream

2 tablespoons salted butter

½ teaspoon salt

¼ teaspoon black pepper

1 cup shredded cheddar cheese (about 4 ounces)

TO MAKE THE FILLING:

1. Brown the lamb in a large skillet over medium heat until cooked through, 10 to 12 minutes, breaking up any clumps with a wooden spoon. Using a slotted spoon, remove the lamb to a large casserole dish.

2. Add the onions, salt, and pepper to the skillet and cook until the onions are translucent, about 5 minutes. Add the garlic and cook until fragrant, 1 minute more.

3. Whisk the coconut flour into the pan juices until well combined. Add the red wine and simmer until reduced by about half. Stir in the rosemary, then pour the mixture over the lamb.

TO MAKE THE TOPPING:

1. Set a steamer basket in a large stockpot and pour an inch of water into the bottom of the pot. Add the cauliflower and garlic cloves and steam until very tender, 6 to 8 minutes.

2. Drain the cauliflower and garlic well, then transfer to a blender or food processor. Add the sour cream, butter, salt, and pepper and blend until smooth.

TO ASSEMBLE:

1. Preheat the oven to 400°F.

2. Spread the cauliflower mixture over the lamb filling and sprinkle the top with the cheddar cheese. Bake for 25 minutes, or until the cheese is melted and the filling is bubbling.

3. Turn the broiler on high and broil 4 to 6 inches from the heat for 2 to 4 minutes to brown the cheese. Remove from the oven and let sit for a few minutes before serving.

4. Store leftovers in the refrigerator for up to 3 days.

NUTRITIONAL INFORMATION:
CALORIES: 382 | FAT: 25.1g | PROTEIN: 27.7g | CARBS: 5g | FIBER: 1.8g

EVERYDAY SWAP:

If you're not a lamb fan, you can always use ground beef in its place. Technically, that would be a "cottage" pie.

EVERYDAY TIPS:

This is a recipe that feeds a crowd, but it's easy to make a half batch if you think you might be overwhelmed by the leftovers. They do make a tasty breakfast, though. Just sayin'!

ROSEMARY LAMB SKEWERS

Lamb is such flavorful meat, it really needs very little besides some chopped herbs, salt, and pepper. Skewering it with rosemary sprigs makes for a beautiful presentation.

YIELD: 4 servings PREP TIME: 10 minutes, plus 2 hours to marinate
COOK TIME: 6 to 8 minutes

4 long, woody rosemary sprigs (about 10 inches each) (see Tips)

¼ cup avocado oil

1 tablespoon apple cider vinegar

4 cloves garlic, minced

1 teaspoon salt

1 teaspoon black pepper

½ teaspoon dried ground marjoram

1 pound boneless leg of lamb (see Tips), cut into 1½-inch chunks

1. Strip the leaves from the rosemary sprigs, leaving an inch of leaves attached at the top. Chop 3 tablespoons of the rosemary leaves. Reserve the sprigs for use as skewers.

2. In a large bowl, combine the oil, vinegar, garlic, salt, pepper, marjoram, and chopped rosemary. Add the lamb and toss well to coat. Refrigerate for 2 hours.

3. Preheat the grill to medium and prepare it for indirect heat. For a gas grill, turn off one element. For a charcoal grill, push all the hot coals to one side. Lay a strip of aluminum foil over the cool side of the grill.

4. Cut the woody end of each rosemary sprig on the diagonal to sharpen it, then thread the lamb onto the sprigs.

5. Lay the lamb skewers over the hot side of the grill, with the leafy ends lying on the foil so they don't burn. Grill for 3 to 4 minutes, then flip them over and grill for another 3 to 4 minutes for medium-rare, or until done to your liking.

SERVING SUGGESTION:
Serve on the skewers over basic cauliflower rice (see page 278) or mashed cauliflower.

EVERYDAY TIPS:
The rosemary sprigs need to be quite woody and thick to serve as skewers. If you can't find any like this, bamboo skewers will be fine. The aluminum foil on the grill helps keep the pretty leafy ends of the rosemary sprigs from burning.

A leg of lamb works best here because it has a good fat content. If you are using a leaner cut or stew meat, marinate it longer to make it more tender.

NUTRITIONAL INFORMATION:
CALORIES: 276 | FAT: 22.1g | PROTEIN: 21.2g | CARBS: 1.4g | FIBER: 0.3g

CHICKEN & EGGS

CRISPY BAKED BUFFALO CHICKEN

My son loves Buffalo wings and orders them almost every time we go out to eat. This is one of his favorite home-cooked meals. It's also one of the most popular recipes on my blog, so it would seem that other people feel the same way!

YIELD: **6 servings** PREP TIME: **5 minutes** COOK TIME: **1 hour 10 minutes**

2½ pounds chicken drumsticks (about 12 drumsticks) or bone-in, skin-on chicken thighs (about 6 thighs), or a combination

1½ tablespoons baking powder

¼ teaspoon salt

¼ teaspoon black pepper

¼ cup Buffalo sauce, room temperature, plus more to taste

1 tablespoon salted butter, melted

1. Preheat the oven to 250°F and set a wire baking rack over a large rimmed baking sheet. Spray the rack with coconut oil spray or brush it with oil to prevent sticking.

2. Pat the chicken pieces very dry and place them in a large sealable plastic bag. Add the baking powder, salt, and pepper and seal the bag. Shake vigorously to coat the chicken.

3. Lay the chicken pieces in a single layer on the prepared baking rack and place the pan in the lower third of the oven. Bake for 30 minutes.

4. Increase the oven temperature to 425°F and move the pan to the upper third of the oven. Bake for another 30 to 40 minutes, until the chicken is well browned and crisp.

5. In a small bowl, whisk together the Buffalo sauce and melted butter. Brush the sauce over the drumsticks or toss them in a bowl to coat. If you prefer your sauce baked on, you can return the chicken to the oven for another 5 to 10 minutes.

6. Add more Buffalo sauce if desired.

EVERYDAY TIPS:
Because of the sauce, these don't stay crispy for long after they're baked, so serve them immediately. They do warm up nicely but never get as crisp as they are straight from the oven.

Because the baking powder contains sodium, you don't want to add a lot of extra salt to these. If you are sensitive to salt, hold off on adding any in Step 2 and see how they taste to you.

SERVING SUGGESTION:
I like to serve these with veggies and Easy Ranch Dressing (page 68) or bleu cheese dressing, just like Buffalo wings.

NUTRITIONAL INFORMATION:
CALORIES: 323 | FAT: 21.7g | PROTEIN: 33.3g | CARBS: 0.4g | FIBER: 0g

SHEET PAN CHICKEN AND VEGGIES

This is the dinner recipe that has people walking into your house and asking what smells so good! I was worried that the Brussels sprouts would become mushy and flavorless, but instead they soaked up all the juices from the chicken and became very flavorful. We all fought over the last of them!

OPTION OPTION ★

YIELD: **6 servings** PREP TIME: **10 minutes** COOK TIME: **35 to 40 minutes**

2 tablespoons salted butter or coconut oil, melted

2 cloves garlic, minced

1½ teaspoons salt, divided

1 teaspoon black pepper, divided

¾ teaspoon ground cumin

½ teaspoon ground coriander

½ teaspoon paprika

⅛ teaspoon cayenne pepper

6 bone-in, skin-on chicken thighs

1 medium head cauliflower, cut into 1-inch florets

½ pound Brussels sprouts, quartered

4 slices thick-cut bacon, cut into 1-inch pieces

2 tablespoons avocado oil

1. Preheat the oven to 450°F.

2. In a small bowl, stir together the melted butter, garlic, ¾ teaspoon of the salt, ½ teaspoon of the pepper, cumin, coriander, paprika, and cayenne. Brush the mixture over the tops of the chicken thighs.

3. In a large bowl, combine the cauliflower, Brussels sprouts, and bacon. Drizzle with the avocado oil and sprinkle with the remaining ¾ teaspoon of salt and ½ teaspoon of pepper. Toss to coat well.

4. Spread out the cauliflower and Brussels sprouts in a rimmed baking sheet. Place the chicken thighs on top. Bake for 35 to 40 minutes, until the center of the chicken registers 165°F on an instant-read thermometer.

5. Turn on the broiler and set the pan on the second-highest rack of the oven. Broil for 2 to 4 minutes to brown the chicken.

EVERYDAY TIP:
You can make this recipe with any chicken parts, including breasts, whole legs, or drumsticks. Your cooking time will vary, so have that thermometer close at hand. Boneless, skinless chicken might dry out a little more easily, so skip the broiling step if you choose to go that route.

EVERYDAY SWAP:
For a dairy-free and Paleo version, use coconut oil rather than butter.

NUTRITIONAL INFORMATION:
CALORIES: 437 | FAT: 29.4g | PROTEIN: 35.2g | CARBS: 8.8g | FIBER: 3.5g

PAN-SEARED CHICKEN THIGHS WITH CREAMY ROSEMARY MUSHROOMS

Mushrooms sautéed in butter and garlic...could anything be better? Add some crispy chicken thighs and you've got magic in a pan. I would not be above licking my plate with this meal.

YIELD: **4 servings**   PREP TIME: **10 minutes**   COOK TIME: **25 to 30 minutes**

4 bone-in, skin-on chicken thighs

Salt and pepper

2 tablespoons avocado oil

CREAMY MUSHROOMS:

2 tablespoons salted butter

8 ounces cremini or button mushrooms, sliced

2 tablespoons chopped fresh rosemary

2 cloves garlic, minced

½ teaspoon salt

½ teaspoon black pepper

¼ cup heavy cream

1. Preheat the oven to 375°F. Pat the chicken dry and season liberally with salt and pepper.

2. In a large skillet over medium heat, heat the oil until shimmering. Add the chicken, skin side down. Cook undisturbed for 5 to 7 minutes, until the skin is golden and crisp. Flip over and cook for another 4 minutes.

3. Transfer the chicken to a baking dish and place in the oven. Bake for 15 minutes or until the internal temperature reaches 165°F on an instant-read thermometer.

4. While the chicken is baking, prepare the mushrooms: Melt the butter in the hot skillet. Add the mushrooms and sauté until golden brown, about 5 minutes. Add the rosemary, garlic, salt, and pepper and cook for 1 more minute. Stir in the cream and simmer until thickened.

5. Add the chicken and any accumulated juices back to the pan. Spoon the mushrooms and sauce over the thighs as you serve them.

EVERYDAY TIP:
To really get that skin to crisp up, it's imperative not to disturb the chicken during the first 5 minutes of cooking. Don't try to peek at them; they're doing just fine!

NUTRITIONAL INFORMATION:
CALORIES: 405 | FAT: 34.8g | PROTEIN: 20.7g | CARBS: 4.9g | FIBER: 1.2g

CHICKEN CORDON BLEU ROLL-UPS

I need to shake the hand of the person who first decided to stuff chicken breasts with ham and Swiss cheese. Because yum!

OPTION

YIELD: **4 servings** PREP TIME: **15 minutes** COOK TIME: **30 minutes**

1 tablespoon salted butter

2 large boneless, skinless chicken breast halves (about ½ pound each)

Salt and pepper

8 slices deli ham

4 ounces Emmentaler or Swiss cheese, thinly sliced

1 tablespoon avocado oil mayonnaise, store-bought or homemade (page 65)

1 tablespoon Dijon mustard

¼ cup finely chopped nuts or crushed pork rinds (see Tip, page 148)

Chopped fresh parsley, for garnish (optional)

1. Preheat the oven to 350°F. Place the butter in a glass or ceramic baking dish and place the dish in the oven to melt the butter.

2. Lay the chicken breasts on a work surface. Holding one hand on top of the chicken, carefully slice each breast horizontally into two thin slices. Season with salt and pepper.

3. Cover each slice of chicken with two slices of ham and two slices of cheese. Starting from the small end, roll up each piece of chicken tightly and secure with a toothpick.

4. Remove the baking dish from the oven and swirl to cover the bottom with the melted butter. Put the chicken roll-ups in the dish.

5. In a small bowl, stir together the mayonnaise and mustard. Spread the mixture over the chicken and sprinkle with the chopped nuts or crushed pork rinds. Bake for 30 minutes, until the chicken is cooked through and the cheese is melted. Garnish with chopped parsley before serving, if desired.

EVERYDAY TIP:
Don't forget to remove the toothpicks before serving.

EVERYDAY SWAP:
Be sure to use crushed pork rinds instead of nuts if you need this dish to be nut-free.

NUTRITIONAL INFORMATION:
CALORIES: 281 | FAT: 18g | PROTEIN: 23.4g | CARBS: 3.9g | FIBER: 1.1g

EASY CAPRESE CHICKEN

This recipe turns a classic salad into a winner winner chicken dinner. It's quick and easy and captures the fresh flavors of summer tomatoes and basil.

YIELD: **4 servings** PREP TIME: **10 minutes** COOK TIME: **35 minutes**

4 boneless, skinless chicken thighs

Salt and pepper

2 tablespoons avocado oil or coconut oil

4 ounces fresh mozzarella, cut into 4 slices

1 medium tomato, cut into 4 slices

¼ cup chopped fresh basil

1. Preheat the oven to 375°F. Season the chicken thighs with salt and pepper.

2. In a large skillet, heat the oil over medium heat until shimmering. Add the chicken and cook until golden brown, about 3 minutes per side.

3. Arrange the chicken in a single layer in a glass or ceramic baking dish. Top each thigh with one slice of mozzarella and one slice of tomato.

4. Bake for 25 to 28 minutes, until the cheese is melted and bubbling and the chicken is cooked through. Turn the broiler on for 2 to 3 minutes to brown the cheese.

5. Remove from the oven and sprinkle with the basil. Serve immediately.

EVERYDAY SWAP:
For a higher fat content, you can use bone-in, skin-on chicken thighs. They might take a little longer to cook through, so be ready to check the temperature with an instant-read thermometer. Chicken should always be cooked to an internal temperature of 165°F.

NUTRITIONAL INFORMATION:
CALORIES: 343 | FAT: 20.4g | PROTEIN: 35.8g | CARBS: 1.4g | FIBER: 0.5g

CHICKEN AND ASPARAGUS STIR-FRY

I love the fresh flavors of stir-fries, especially when they aren't drowned in sugary sauces. They are so easy to make at the end of a busy day, too.

YIELD: 4 servings PREP TIME: 5 minutes (not including time to make teriyaki sauce) **COOK TIME: 15 to 20 minutes**

1 pound boneless, skinless chicken breasts

Salt

1 bunch asparagus (about 12 ounces)

4 tablespoons coconut oil or avocado oil, divided

½ recipe Teriyaki Sauce (page 74)

1. Cut the chicken into 1-inch chunks and sprinkle liberally with salt. Trim the ends from the asparagus and cut the spears into 1- to 2-inch pieces.

2. Heat 2 tablespoons of the oil in a large skillet or wok over medium-high heat until shimmering. Add the chicken and stir-fry until lightly browned and cooked through, 7 to 10 minutes. Transfer to a bowl.

3. Heat the remaining 2 tablespoons of oil in the skillet, then add the asparagus. Sauté until bright green and just tender, 5 to 7 minutes.

4. Return the chicken to the pan and drizzle with the teriyaki sauce. Toss to coat well and cook for 1 to 2 more minutes to warm through.

SERVING SUGGESTION:
Serve over basic cauliflower rice (see page 278).

EVERYDAY TIP:
Cutting the chicken and veggies into bite-size pieces allows for quick and even cooking.

EVERYDAY SWAP:
Feel free to substitute your favorite vegetables for the asparagus. Choose foods that cook quickly, like zucchini, peppers, and sugar snap peas. Bok choy would be delicious, too.

NUTRITIONAL INFORMATION:
CALORIES: 285 | FAT: 16g | PROTEIN: 27.4g | CARBS: 5.2g | FIBER: 1.8g

BACON, SPINACH, AND FETA FRITTATA

A frittata was one of the first meals I made for my husband back when we started dating. I remember being immensely pleased with my kitchen skills. Don't tell him that frittatas are ridiculously easy to make, okay? It's our little secret.

YIELD: **One 10-inch frittata (6 servings)** PREP TIME: **10 minutes**
COOK TIME: **30 minutes**

6 slices bacon, diced

1 clove garlic, minced

6 ounces fresh spinach, roughly chopped

¼ cup chopped roasted red peppers (jarred)

¾ cup crumbled feta cheese (about 3 ounces)

7 large eggs

¼ cup heavy cream

½ teaspoon salt

½ teaspoon black pepper

1. In a 10-inch ovenproof skillet over medium heat, cook the diced bacon until crisp. Transfer the bacon to a paper towel–lined plate and remove all but 2 tablespoons of the bacon fat from the pan.

2. Preheat the oven to 350°F.

3. Add the garlic to the skillet and sauté until fragrant, about 30 seconds. Stir in the spinach and cook until just wilted, 1 to 2 minutes.

4. Remove the skillet from the heat. Spread the spinach evenly across the bottom of the pan. Sprinkle with the roasted peppers, feta, and bacon.

5. In a large bowl, whisk together the eggs, cream, salt, and pepper until well combined. Pour over the spinach mixture in the pan. Return the skillet to low heat and cook until the edges are set and beginning to brown.

6. Transfer the skillet to the oven and bake for 10 to 15 minutes, until the frittata is puffed and cooked through in the center. Remove and serve warm or let cool to room temperature.

EVERYDAY TIP:
The trick to a good frittata is slow cooking. Don't try to hurry it along by turning up the heat or it will become dry and tough.

NUTRITIONAL INFORMATION:
CALORIES: 218 | FAT: 15.5g | PROTEIN: 13.8g | CARBS: 3g | FIBER: 0.6g

BRIE AND MUSHROOM QUICHE

Real men do eat quiche. At least my husband does, and I'm pretty sure he's a real man.

YIELD: **8 servings**   PREP TIME: **10 minutes** (not including time to make crust)
COOK TIME: **45 minutes**

¼ cup (½ stick) salted butter

8 ounces cremini or button mushrooms, sliced

2 cloves garlic, minced

1 teaspoon salt, divided

1 par-baked Savory Pie Crust (page 80)

5 large eggs

½ cup heavy cream

½ teaspoon black pepper

4 ounces Brie cheese, thinly sliced

1. Preheat the oven to 325°F.

2. In a large sauté pan, heat the butter over medium heat until melted and hot. Add the mushrooms and toss to coat in the butter. Add the garlic and ½ teaspoon of the salt and sauté until the mushrooms are golden brown, about 5 minutes. Spoon the mushrooms into the par-baked crust.

3. In a medium bowl, whisk together the eggs, cream, remaining ½ teaspoon of salt, and pepper. Pour this mixture over the mushrooms and arrange the slices of Brie over the top.

4. Bake for 30 to 40 minutes, until the quiche is just set in the center. Let cool for 10 minutes before serving.

EVERYDAY TIP:
If the edges of the crust are getting a little too brown during baking, cover them with strips of aluminum foil, leaving the filling open to the heat of the oven.

EVERYDAY SWAP:
If you don't like Brie, any cheese will go well here.

NUTRITIONAL INFORMATION:
CALORIES: 372 | FAT: 32.9g | PROTEIN: 12.6g | CARBS: 6.8g | FIBER: 2.5g

GOAT CHEESE SOUFFLÉS

These individual soufflés make an elegant brunch, lunch, or dinner. They're also a lot easier to make than you might think. I enjoy the leftovers warmed up the next day for breakfast, too.

YIELD: 4 soufflés **PREP TIME:** 20 minutes **COOK TIME:** 30 minutes

2 tablespoons salted butter

¼ cup (25g) blanched almond flour

1 tablespoon unflavored whey protein powder

½ teaspoon salt, divided

¼ teaspoon black pepper

¼ teaspoon garlic powder

½ cup heavy cream

3 ounces fresh goat cheese, room temperature

½ ounce Parmesan cheese, grated (about ½ cup)

2 tablespoons chopped fresh chives

4 large eggs, separated, room temperature

¼ teaspoon cream of tartar

8 pieces fresh chives (2 to 3 inches long), for garnish (optional)

1. Preheat the oven to 350°F and grease four 8-ounce ramekins. Set the ramekins on a rimmed baking sheet.

2. Melt the butter in a medium saucepan over medium heat. Whisk in the almond flour, protein powder, ¼ teaspoon of the salt, pepper, and garlic powder until well combined. Slowly whisk in the cream until fully incorporated.

3. Remove the pan from the heat and whisk in the goat cheese, Parmesan, and chopped chives until melted and smooth. Whisk in the egg yolks one at a time.

4. In a large bowl, beat the egg whites with the cream of tartar and the remaining ¼ teaspoon of salt until they hold stiff peaks. Carefully fold about one-third of the egg whites into the cream and cheese mixture to lighten it. Then fold the cream and cheese mixture back into the egg whites until no streaks remain.

5. Divide the mixture among the prepared ramekins and bake for 20 to 25 minutes, until the soufflés are puffed and the tops are golden brown. Top with chive pieces, if using, and serve immediately.

EVERYDAY TIP:
Get ready to rush these to the table! Like any soufflé, they only stay puffed for a few minutes and begin to deflate rapidly. But they look impressive and taste even better.

NUTRITIONAL INFORMATION:
CALORIES: 259 | FAT: 20.1g | PROTEIN: 14.8g | CARBS: 2.5g | FIBER: 0.8g

FISH & SEAFOOD

CEDAR-PLANKED SALMON WITH PESTO

Cedar planking is the ultimate grilled salmon experience. The fish comes off the grill so lusciously tender, it barely needs anything besides salt and pepper. But my family loves it with a little freshly made pesto from our summer basil.

**YIELD: 3 servings   PREP TIME: 5 minutes, plus 1 hour to soak plank
COOK TIME: 12 minutes**

1 (1-pound) salmon fillet, preferably skin-on

Salt and pepper

½ teaspoon garlic powder

¼ cup plus 2 tablespoons pesto, store-bought or homemade (page 71)

Lemon wedges, for serving (optional)

SPECIAL EQUIPMENT:

1 cedar grilling plank, about 12 inches long

1. Set the cedar grilling plank in a large baking dish filled with water and weight it down with cans or something heavy so it is completely submerged. Let it soak for at least 1 hour.

2. Preheat the grill to medium-high and prepare it for indirect heat. For a gas grill, turn off one burner. For a charcoal grill, push all of the coals to one side.

3. Remove the plank from the water and pat it dry with a tea towel. Lay the salmon skin side down on the plank and season liberally with salt and pepper. Sprinkle with the garlic powder.

4. Set the plank over direct heat for 3 to 4 minutes, until the plank begins to smoke and char a bit

5. Move the plank to indirect heat and continue to cook for another 7 to 12 minutes, until the fish is opaque and cooked through at the thickest part. The cooking time will depend on the thickness of the fillet.

6. Remove the plank from the grill and spread the pesto over the salmon. Let rest for a few minutes before serving. Serve with lemon wedges, if desired.

EVERYDAY TIP:
It's important to soak the plank for at least 1 hour; otherwise it could catch fire during grilling.

Sometimes you can reuse the cedar plank, if it isn't too badly charred. It depends somewhat on the heat and flaring of your grill. Remember to soak it again before the next use.

NUTRITIONAL INFORMATION:
CALORIES: 330 │ FAT: 20.2g │ PROTEIN: 24.5g │ CARBS: 1.7g │ FIBER: 0.4g

FISH SALTIMBOCCA

This recipe will make a fish lover out of anyone! It is easily one of my favorite ways to serve whitefish.

YIELD: 4 servings   **PREP TIME:** 5 minutes (not including time to make sauce)
COOK TIME: 15 minutes

4 (4-ounce) firm whitefish fillets, such as halibut (see Tip)

Salt and pepper

4 large slices prosciutto

4 sage leaves

2 tablespoons salted butter

1 recipe Roasted Tomato Cream Sauce (page 77)

1. Pat the fish dry with paper towels and season generously with salt and pepper. Wrap each fillet in a slice of prosciutto and lay a sage leaf across the top. Secure the sage and prosciutto with toothpicks.

2. In a large skillet, melt the butter over medium heat. When the butter is hot and beginning to brown, add the fish, sage side down, and cook for 4 minutes, until the prosciutto is crisp. Flip the fish and cook for another 4 to 6 minutes, until cooked through.

3. Turn off the heat and transfer the fish to a plate. Add the sauce to the still-hot pan to warm through, stirring it into the pan juices.

4. Divide the sauce evenly between four plates and place a wrapped fish fillet on top. Serve immediately.

EVERYDAY TIP:
Try to find fish that is at least ½ inch thick so that it doesn't cook too quickly. You want time for the prosciutto to crisp up nicely.

NUTRITIONAL INFORMATION:
CALORIES: 271 | FAT: 15.9g | PROTEIN: 26.1g | CARBS: 4.3g | FIBER: 1.1g

SOLE FLORENTINE

Creamy shallot sauce over tender spinach-stuffed fish. Be careful, you might find yourself tipping the last of the sauce straight into your mouth.

YIELD: **4 servings**   PREP TIME: **10 minutes**   COOK TIME: **25 minutes**

2 tablespoons salted butter, divided

1 medium shallot, minced

1 cup heavy cream

½ teaspoon dried thyme leaves

¾ teaspoon salt

½ teaspoon black pepper

8 ounces frozen spinach, thawed and squeezed dry

2 ounces cream cheese (¼ cup), softened

½ ounce Parmesan cheese, grated (about ½ cup)

4 (4- to 6-ounce) sole fillets

1. Preheat the oven to 425°F. Place 1 tablespoon of the butter in a glass or ceramic baking dish and place in the oven to melt.

2. Melt the remaining tablespoon of butter in a medium skillet over medium heat. Add the shallot and cook until softened, about 2 minutes. Add the cream and thyme and cook until the sauce has thickened, 3 to 4 minutes. Stir in the salt and pepper.

3. In a medium bowl, stir together the spinach, cream cheese, and Parmesan. Add half of the shallot cream sauce and mix well.

4. Lay the sole fillets on a work surface and season them with a few pinches of salt and pepper. Divide the spinach filling among them, mounding it in the center of each fillet. Fold the ends of the fish over the filling, overlapping them in the center.

5. Remove the pan from the oven and swirl to coat the bottom with the melted butter. Place the fish seam side down in the baking dish and pour the remaining sauce over the fish.

6. Bake for 15 to 20 minutes, until the sauce is bubbling and the fish flakes easily with a fork.

EVERYDAY TIP:
It's important to squeeze as much moisture as possible out of the thawed spinach so it doesn't water down the sauce during baking.

NUTRITIONAL INFORMATION:
CALORIES: 434 | FAT: 33.3g | PROTEIN: 22.8g | CARBS: 5.5g | FIBER: 1.5g

CRISPY FISH NUGGETS

This is my healthy and ever-so-much-tastier answer to commercial fish sticks. My kids love them. Take that, fast-food chains!

OPTION · OPTION

YIELD: 4 servings **PREP TIME:** 20 minutes **COOK TIME:** 10 minutes

2 tablespoons avocado oil

1½ cups crushed pork rinds (see Tip, page 148)

½ ounce Parmesan cheese, grated (about ½ cup)

1 teaspoon chili powder

1 teaspoon salt

½ teaspoon black pepper

½ teaspoon garlic powder

1 large egg

1 tablespoon water

1 pound firm whitefish fillets, such as mahi mahi, cut into 2-inch pieces

1. Preheat the oven to 425°F. Place the oil in a large rimmed baking sheet and place in the oven while it preheats.

2. In a medium shallow bowl, whisk together the pork rinds, Parmesan, chili powder, salt, pepper, and garlic powder. In another bowl, whisk the egg with the water until well combined.

3. Dip the chunks of fish into the egg mixture and shake off the excess, then dredge them in the pork rind mixture, making sure to coat both sides.

4. Remove the pan from the oven and swirl to coat the bottom with the oil.

5. Place the fish nuggets in the pan and bake for 5 minutes. Carefully flip the nuggets and bake for another 5 minutes or until the fish flakes easily with a fork.

SERVING SUGGESTION:
Serve with lemon wedges and Roasted Tomato Cream Sauce (page 77) for dipping. These nuggets are also great as a crispy addition to a salad.

EVERYDAY SWAP:
To make this recipe dairy-free and Paleo, simply omit the grated Parmesan.

NUTRITIONAL INFORMATION:
CALORIES: 277 | FAT: 16.5g | PROTEIN: 35.5g | CARBS: 1.2g | FIBER: 0.3g

OLD BAY CRAB CAKES

OPTION   OPTION

Because crabmeat is so fragile, most crab cakes take copious amounts of breadcrumbs. But I've found that you can get away without any filler if you refrigerate the cakes first and are very careful when flipping them.

YIELD: 4 crab cakes (2 servings as a meal) PREP TIME: 10 minutes, plus 30 minutes to chill COOK TIME: 8 minutes

8 ounces lump crabmeat (canned is fine)

1 large egg

2 tablespoons chopped fresh parsley

1 tablespoon avocado oil mayonnaise, store-bought or homemade (page 65)

1 teaspoon Old Bay seasoning

1 teaspoon dry mustard

½ teaspoon salt

½ teaspoon black pepper

2 tablespoons salted butter

1. In a large bowl, combine the crabmeat, egg, parsley, mayonnaise, Old Bay seasoning, dry mustard, salt, and pepper. Mix well, breaking up larger chunks of crab with a fork, until the mixture is cohesive.

2. Shape the mixture by hand into 4 even patties no thicker than 1 inch. Refrigerate for 30 minutes.

3. In a large skillet, heat the butter over medium heat until melted and hot. Add the crab cakes and cook undisturbed for 3 to 4 minutes, until the underside is golden brown. Carefully flip them over and cook for another 3 to 4 minutes, until golden brown on the second side.

4. Serve immediately.

SERVING SUGGESTION:
Serve each crab cake with a dollop of Spicy Cajun Mayonnaise (page 66) on top.

EVERYDAY TIP:
Serve these crab cakes immediately; they don't do very well when reheated.

EVERYDAY SWAP:
To make these crab cakes dairy-free and Paleo, substitute avocado oil or coconut oil for the butter.

NUTRITIONAL INFORMATION (not including Spicy Cajun Mayo):
CALORIES: 264 | FAT: 17.4g | PROTEIN: 22.7g | CARBS: 1.5g | FIBER: 0.5g

SPICY SHRIMP AND CUCUMBER NOODLES

This light and fresh meal comes together in a matter of moments. It's perfect for warm summer days when you don't want anything heavy.

OPTION   OPTION

YIELD: **4 servings**   PREP TIME: **5 minutes**   COOK TIME: **5 minutes**

SHRIMP:

1 pound medium shrimp, peeled and deveined (tails on or off)

1 to 1½ teaspoons Asian chili garlic sauce

½ teaspoon ground cumin

½ teaspoon salt

¼ teaspoon garlic powder

2 tablespoons salted butter

CUCUMBER NOODLES:

2 medium cucumbers

1½ tablespoons toasted sesame oil

Salt and pepper

Sesame seeds, for garnish

1. In a medium bowl, toss the shrimp with the chili garlic sauce, cumin, salt, and garlic powder until each shrimp is coated.

2. Heat the butter in a large skillet over medium-high heat until melted and frothy. Swirl to coat the pan with the butter. Add the shrimp and sauté until cooked through and bright pink, about 3 minutes. Transfer to a plate to cool.

3. Use a spiral vegetable slicer to cut the cucumbers into long noodles. In a medium bowl, toss the cucumber noodles with the sesame oil. Season to taste with salt and pepper.

4. Divide the cucumber noodles among 4 plates or bowls. Top with the shrimp and sprinkle with sesame seeds.

EVERYDAY TIPS:
Don't salt the cucumber noodles until you are ready to serve this dish. They release a lot of moisture when combined with salt.

Be aware that Asian chili garlic sauce is not the same thing as sweet chili garlic sauce, which has tons of added sugar. Huy Fong, the maker of Sriracha, also makes a chili garlic sauce in small jars that is really spicy and has no sugar. It's quite powerful, so a little goes a long way.

EVERYDAY SWAP:
Use coconut oil in place of the butter for a dairy-free and Paleo version.

NUTRITIONAL INFORMATION:
CALORIES: 199 | FAT: 12g | PROTEIN: 16.5g | CARBS: 4.3g | FIBER: 1g

BROCCOLI DRUNKEN NOODLES WITH SHRIMP

Drunken noodles used to be one of my favorite Thai dishes. I had a lot of fun re-creating it with broccoli stem noodles.

YIELD: **4 servings**   PREP TIME: **15 minutes**   COOK TIME: **10 minutes**

3 large broccoli stalks

3 tablespoons coconut oil

1 clove garlic, minced

1 pound medium shrimp, deveined and peeled (tails on or off)

2 large eggs

¼ cup chopped tomatoes

2 tablespoons fish sauce

2 tablespoons coconut aminos

1 Thai chile, seeded and chopped, or ¼ jalapeño pepper, seeded and chopped

2 teaspoons grated lime zest

¼ cup chopped fresh basil

Lime wedges, for serving

1. Wash the broccoli stalks and trim the ends. Cut the stalks into thin noodles with a spiral vegetable slicer.

2. In a large skillet or wok, heat the coconut oil over medium-high heat. Once hot, add the garlic and cook until fragrant, about 30 seconds. Add the shrimp and stir-fry until it is almost cooked through, 2 to 3 minutes. Stir in the eggs until they are just starting to set.

3. Add the tomatoes, fish sauce, coconut aminos, chile, and lime zest and stir to combine. Stir in the broccoli stem noodles until they are hot and coated with sauce, about 2 more minutes.

4. Turn off the heat and stir in the basil. Serve immediately with lime wedges.

EVERYDAY SWAP:
This recipe can also be made with chicken. Use 1 pound of thinly sliced boneless chicken thighs, and make sure the chicken is cooked through before adding the eggs.

NUTRITIONAL INFORMATION:
CALORIES: 249 | FAT: 13.8g | PROTEIN: 22.3g | CARBS: 8.5g | FIBER: 2g

SPICY TUNA STUFFED AVOCADOS

Just because you can't have sushi doesn't mean you can't enjoy sushi *flavors.* This recipe takes one of my favorite sushi flavors and turns it into a light meal that I can enjoy without guilt.

YIELD: **4 avocado halves (1 per serving)** PREP TIME: **10 minutes**
COOK TIME: —

½ pound sushi-grade ahi tuna, finely diced

1 tablespoon avocado oil mayonnaise, store-bought or homemade (page 65)

1 tablespoon coconut aminos

1 to 2 teaspoons Sriracha or other hot sauce

1 teaspoon toasted sesame oil

2 medium avocados

Salt

Black and white sesame seeds, for garnish

1. In a medium bowl, stir together the tuna, mayonnaise, coconut aminos, Sriracha, and sesame oil until well combined.

2. Cut the avocados in half and remove the pits. Sprinkle the cut sides with salt. Mound the tuna mixture into each avocado half and sprinkle with sesame seeds.

3. Serve immediately.

EVERYDAY TIPS:
You can make the spicy tuna filling a few hours ahead and stuff the avocados when you are ready to serve them. Because this dish contains raw fish, it should be eaten the same day it's made.

Please note that consuming raw or undercooked meats, poultry, seafood, shellfish, or eggs may increase your risk of food-borne illness, especially if you have certain medical conditions.

NUTRITIONAL INFORMATION:
CALORIES: 245 | FAT: 16.3g | PROTEIN: 15.3g | CARBS: 8.1g | FIBER: 5.1g

SIDE DISHES

HOW TO COOK ZUCCHINI NOODLES

Zucchini noodles, or "zoodles," are easy to make as long as you have a spiral vegetable slicer. You hardly need a recipe for that! Simply follow the instructions that came with your spiral slicer. What's trickier, however, is figuring out how to cook them without turning them into a soggy mess.

1 medium zucchini (about 7 ounces) will give you 2 servings of cooked zoodles.

Here are my best tips for delicious al dente zoodles.

MICROWAVE:

This method works well if you want to serve the zoodles under a sauce, like spaghetti. I like to do this serving by serving so the zoodles are hot for each person.

1. Place the desired amount of zucchini noodles in a microwave-safe bowl or on a plate and heat on high for 30 to 60 seconds. They should be warmed through but not too soft.

2. Season with salt and pepper only after cooking.

STOVETOP:

1. Heat a little oil or butter in a skillet set over medium-high heat. Add the zucchini noodles and toss lightly in the oil.

2. Cook, tossing frequently, until the zoodles are al dente, 3 to 7 minutes. How long they take will depend on how much you are trying to cook at once and how thick the zoodles are. For 2 to 4 servings, use a large skillet. For more servings, you may need to work in batches.

3. Season with salt and pepper only after cooking.

ADDING TO SOUP:

Add the zucchini noodles only in the last minute of cooking. I also find that pouring the hot broth over the zoodles in individual serving bowls works well.

STORING:

You can make the zucchini noodles up to 3 days ahead. Simply store them in a plastic or glass container in the refrigerator. Unfortunately, they don't freeze well.

HOW TO RICE CAULIFLOWER

As with zucchini noodles, cauliflower "rice" is a mainstay of the ketogenic diet. It is infinitely useful for re-creating many high-carb dishes in a healthier, low-carb fashion. I find myself eating it at least once or twice a week. It's become such a popular health-food item that many stores are selling it riced and ready to go, both fresh and frozen. If you do purchase it at a store, be sure to check the ingredients. A few brands offer flavored varieties that have a higher carb count.

There are plenty of options to make your own riced cauliflower at home. It's easy to do, and you can freeze it for later use. You don't even need any sort of fancy equipment.

One medium head of cauliflower will produce 12 to 16 ounces of riced cauliflower, or 4 to 5 cups.

FOOD PROCESSOR:

1. Cut a medium head of cauliflower into florets and discard the stem.

2. If your food processor has a grating blade, set that up and feed the florets through the tube a few at a time.

3. Alternatively, you can put all of the florets in the processor with the S-blade and pulse until the cauliflower resembles grains of rice. I find that this method leaves me with some larger chunks that I have to process a second time.

HIGH-POWERED BLENDER:

A reader told me about this one, and now it's my go-to method. You do need a really high-powered blender for this.

1. Cut a medium head of cauliflower into florets no larger than 1 inch. Discard the stem.

2. Place half the florets in the blender and add enough water to cover. Secure the lid and pulse 5 or 6 times, until the cauliflower resembles grains of rice.

3. Drain the riced cauliflower in a fine-mesh sieve.

4. Repeat with the remaining cauliflower florets.

BOX GRATER:

If you don't own a food processor or a high-powered blender, you can still make your own cauliflower rice. It's a little more labor-intensive, but think of it as good exercise!

1. Cut a medium head of cauliflower into large florets (easier to hold on to while grating). Discard the stem.

2. Use the large holes on the box grater to grate the cauliflower into fine grains.

TO FREEZE:

Simply portion the cauliflower rice into resealable bags or containers and freeze. If you use the blender method, allow the cauliflower rice to air-dry in a single layer for a few hours first.

The rice can be frozen for up to 3 months. Let it thaw slightly on the counter before cooking.

HOW TO COOK BASIC CAULIFLOWER RICE

You have a number of options when it comes to cooking cauliflower rice. Pan-frying in a skillet is my favorite method.

MICROWAVE:

Place the cauliflower rice in a microwave-safe bowl and cover with plastic wrap (no need to add any liquid). Microwave on high for 5 to 7 minutes, depending on how soft you like it. Five minutes is great for cauli-rice that still has a little crunch to it, whereas 7 minutes will produce soft "grains." Season to taste.

SAUCEPAN:

Put the cauliflower rice and a few tablespoons of water in a saucepan. Cover and bring just to a simmer over medium heat, then reduce the heat to low and cook until tender, 5 to 10 minutes. Season to taste.

SKILLET:

Preheat a skillet over medium heat. Put a tablespoon or two of oil or butter in the skillet. When the oil is melted and hot, add the cauliflower rice and toss to coat, then sauté until tender, 5 to 7 minutes. Season to taste.

CILANTRO-LIME CAULIFLOWER RICE

If I am forced to eat fast food on the go, I keep my eye out for a place like Chipotle. I know I am getting fresh food with an emphasis on sustainability, and there are plenty of low-carb options. Chipotle's cilantro-lime rice isn't low-carb, of course, but it turns out that those same flavors make great cauliflower rice, too.

OPTION   OPTION

YIELD: 4 servings   PREP TIME: 5 minutes   COOK TIME: 5 to 7 minutes

2 tablespoons salted butter

4 cups riced cauliflower (see page 276)

3 tablespoons chopped fresh cilantro

2 tablespoons fresh lime juice

Salt and pepper

1. In a large skillet over medium heat, melt the butter until it begins to froth.

2. Add the riced cauliflower and toss to coat in the butter. Cook, stirring frequently, until the rice is crisp-tender and beginning to brown, 5 to 7 minutes.

3. Remove from the heat and add the cilantro, lime juice, and salt and pepper to taste.

SERVING SUGGESTIONS:
Oh so many delicious possibilities! This rice is perfect topped with my Mexican Shredded Beef (page 206) or Garlic Butter Steak Tips (page 210). It's also good with BBQ Pulled Pork (page 228).

EVERYDAY SWAP:
Use coconut oil or avocado oil in place of the butter for a dairy-free and Paleo version.

NUTRITIONAL INFORMATION:
CALORIES: 79 | FAT: 5.6g | PROTEIN: 2.2g | CARBS: 6.1g | FIBER: 2.2g

CHEESY CAULIFLOWER GRITS

Confession time: I don't actually like conventional grits. Maybe they are too heavy, or maybe I've just never had good ones, but I am not a fan. However, I love this lightened-up cauliflower version. It's the perfect accompaniment to Red Wine Braised Short Ribs (page 208).

YIELD: 6 servings   PREP TIME: 10 minutes   COOK TIME: 20 minutes

2 tablespoons salted butter

4 cups riced cauliflower (see page 276)

¾ teaspoon salt

¼ cup heavy cream

1½ cups shredded cheddar cheese (about 6 ounces), divided

Chopped fresh parsley, for garnish (optional)

1. In a large saucepan over medium heat, melt the butter. Add the riced cauliflower and salt and toss to coat well. Cook for 5 minutes, stirring frequently, until crisp-tender.

2. Reduce the heat to low, stir in the cream, and cover. Cook for about 10 minutes, until the cauliflower rice is tender but not mushy.

3. Use an immersion blender to blend the mixture to a slightly creamier consistency, while still keeping some texture. Stir in 1 cup of the shredded cheese until melted.

4. Sprinkle with the remaining cheese and the parsley, if using, just before serving.

EVERYDAY TIP:
Prepackaged cauliflower rice works well in this recipe. If you are cooking it from frozen, be aware that the cooking time may be longer.

NUTRITIONAL INFORMATION:
CALORIES: 166 | FAT: 12.7g | PROTEIN: 6.5g | CARBS: 5g | FIBER: 1.8g

CHEESY SPINACH CAULIFLOWER WAFFLES

Cooking foods in a waffle iron somehow makes them more appealing. These waffles are like cauliflower fritters, but they're more fun to eat!

YIELD: 8 mini or 4 large waffles (2 mini or 1 large per serving)
PREP TIME: 15 minutes   COOK TIME: about 25 minutes

3 cups riced cauliflower (see page 276)

8 ounces frozen spinach, thawed

1 cup shredded mozzarella cheese (about 4 ounces)

½ ounce Parmesan cheese, grated (about ½ cup)

2 large eggs

2 cloves garlic, minced

¾ teaspoon salt

½ teaspoon black pepper

1. Set a tea towel in a sieve and place it in the sink or over a bowl. Place the riced cauliflower in a microwave-safe bowl and cover with plastic wrap. Microwave on high for 10 minutes.

2. Carefully remove the plastic wrap and drain the cauliflower in the towel-lined sieve until cool enough to handle.

3. Preheat a waffle maker to medium-high and brush with oil.

4. Add the spinach to the towel-lined sieve and gather the ends together. Squeeze out as much liquid as possible, then transfer the mixture to a large bowl.

5. Stir in the mozzarella, Parmesan, eggs, garlic, salt, and pepper until well combined.

6. For mini waffles, spoon about ¼ cup of the mixture into each section of the waffle maker. For large waffles, spoon ½ cup of the mixture into each section of the waffle maker.

7. Close the lid and cook until the waffle is nicely browned on both sides. Remove and repeat with the remaining batter.

SERVING SUGGESTIONS:
These waffles are a wonderful side with a meat or chicken dish like Dry Rub Fall-Off-the-Bone Ribs (page 226) or Chicken Cordon Bleu Roll-Ups (page 242). They are also delicious for breakfast with a fried egg on top. They are perfect for soaking up runny egg yolks.

EVERYDAY TIPS:
If you don't own a waffle iron, you can shape these into individual patties and fry them in a skillet as fritters. Keep them on the small side to help them hold together.

Waffle irons vary quite a bit from brand to brand. Some are very deep, whereas others are quite shallow. The cooking time will vary depending on these factors.

NUTRITIONAL INFORMATION:
CALORIES: 170 | FAT: 9.1g | PROTEIN: 14g | CARBS: 7.8g | FIBER: 3.1g

EASY ROASTED BROCCOLI

Roasted broccoli has become one of my favorite low-carb side dishes; I make it at least once a week. I like mine extra-crispy, and I love the little tiny pieces that get really browned. I find myself sneaking those bits as I serve up this dish to my family.

I fancy myself as something of a roasted broccoli expert, so be sure to check out my tips below for making the best roasted broccoli at home.

YIELD: 6 servings **PREP TIME:** 5 minutes **COOK TIME:** 20 to 30 minutes

1 pound broccoli

2 tablespoons avocado oil or light olive oil

Salt and pepper

1. Preheat the oven to 400°F.

2. Cut the broccoli into florets. If some of the florets are very large, cut those in half or even into quarters. Slice the first few inches of the stem crosswise into ½-inch rounds.

3. Spread the broccoli florets and stems out on a large rimmed baking sheet. Drizzle with the oil and sprinkle with salt and pepper. Toss with a spatula to combine.

4. Roast for 15 to 20 minutes, until the broccoli is lightly browned and crispy. For extra-crispy broccoli, turn off the oven and leave the broccoli inside for another 5 to 10 minutes. Add more salt and pepper to taste.

EVERYDAY TIPS:

I've found that using a liquid oil like avocado or olive oil makes for the crispiest broccoli. Butter and coconut oil seem to make it a little soggy.

Be sure to dry your broccoli well after washing. Too much moisture on the surface makes it soft and soggy.

Roast the broccoli directly on the pan, not on foil or parchment paper.

VARIATION:

Garlic Parmesan Roasted Broccoli. Follow the directions above, but in Step 3, sprinkle 2 cloves of minced garlic on the broccoli along with the oil, salt, and pepper. After removing the broccoli from the oven, sprinkle it with ¼ cup of grated Parmesan cheese. *Note:* For a dairy-free or Paleo version, replace the Parmesan with 2 to 3 tablespoons of nutritional yeast.

NUTRITIONAL INFORMATION (plain version):

CALORIES: 47 | FAT: 4.7g | PROTEIN: 2.2g | CARBS: 5.1g | FIBER: 2g

NUTRITIONAL INFORMATION (Garlic Parmesan version):

CALORIES: 53 | FAT: 5g | PROTEIN: 2.6g | CARBS: 5.5g | FIBER: 2g

TUSCAN ROASTED VEGETABLES

Back when we lived in the Boston area, my kids loved going to Bertucci's. While they ate pizza, I ate wings and this delicious Tuscan vegetable side dish. I always came away satisfied. And what a way to use summer's bounty!

OPTION   OPTION

YIELD: 8 servings   **PREP TIME:** 15 minutes   **COOK TIME:** 20 to 25 minutes

1 small eggplant, cut into 1-inch pieces

1 small zucchini, cut into 1-inch pieces

1 large red bell pepper, cut into 1-inch pieces

2 medium tomatoes, cut into 1-inch pieces

8 ounces cremini or button mushrooms, quartered

6 ounces marinated artichoke hearts, drained and quartered

¼ cup avocado oil

6 cloves garlic, minced

2 teaspoons chopped fresh rosemary

1½ teaspoons salt

½ teaspoon black pepper

½ ounce Parmesan cheese, grated (about ½ cup)

1. Preheat the oven to 400°F.

2. In a large bowl, combine the eggplant, zucchini, bell pepper, tomatoes, mushrooms, and artichoke hearts. Drizzle with the avocado oil, then add the garlic, rosemary, salt, and pepper. Toss well to combine.

3. Spread the vegetables in a single layer on a large rimmed baking sheet. Roast for 20 to 25 minutes, until the vegetables are tender and beginning to brown and caramelize.

4. Remove from the oven and sprinkle with grated Parmesan cheese. Add more salt and pepper to taste.

EVERYDAY TIPS:
Try to cut the vegetables as uniformly as possible so that they all roast evenly. I find that they roast and brown better when I don't line the baking sheet with foil or parchment paper.

EVERYDAY SWAP:
For a dairy-free and Paleo version, leave out the Parmesan cheese.

NUTRITIONAL INFORMATION:
CALORIES: 122 | FAT: 8.2g | PROTEIN: 3.9g | CARBS: 8.9g | FIBER: 3.2g

ROASTED CABBAGE WEDGES WITH BLEU CHEESE AND BACON

I modeled this recipe after the famous iceberg lettuce wedge salad. The nutty flavor of roasted cabbage goes so well with bacon and bleu cheese.

YIELD: **4 servings**   PREP TIME: **5 minutes**   COOK TIME: **30 to 35 minutes**

½ large head green cabbage (with core intact)

4 slices bacon, cooked crisp and crumbled, drippings reserved

Salt and pepper

¼ cup crumbled bleu cheese (about 1 ounce)

1. Preheat the oven to 400°F.

2. Cut the cabbage into 4 even wedges, making sure each wedge has some of the core, and brush both sides of each wedge with the reserved bacon drippings. Sprinkle with salt and pepper.

3. Roast for 20 minutes, then flip each wedge and roast for another 10 to 15 minutes, until tender and lightly browned.

4. Sprinkle each wedge with bacon and bleu cheese.

EVERYDAY TIP:
I find that by leaving the core intact when I cut into the cabbage, my wedges stay together better during cooking.

NUTRITIONAL INFORMATION:
CALORIES: 160 | FAT: 11.6g | PROTEIN: 6.2g | CARBS: 7.1g | FIBER: 2.9g

SAUTÉED GREEN BEANS WITH CRISPY PROSCIUTTO

My favorite way to cook green beans is to flash-fry them in a hot pan with butter or oil. Topped with crispy prosciutto and shallots, they make a stunning side dish.

OPTION   OPTION

YIELD: **6 servings** PREP TIME: **5 minutes** COOK TIME: **8 minutes**

3 tablespoons salted butter, divided

2 ounces prosciutto, chopped

2 small shallots, thinly sliced

1 pound green beans, trimmed

Salt and pepper

1. In a large skillet over medium heat, melt 1 tablespoon of the butter. When the froth begins to subside, add the prosciutto and shallots. Cook until the prosciutto is crispy, about 3 minutes. Remove the prosciutto and shallots from the pan.

2. Add the remaining 2 tablespoons of butter and let it melt. Add the green beans and sauté until tender and just a little browned, 4 to 5 minutes.

3. Add the prosciutto and shallots back to the pan and toss to combine. Season to taste with salt and pepper.

EVERYDAY SWAP:
You can easily make this recipe Paleo and dairy-free by replacing the butter with coconut oil or avocado oil. Avocado oil is more neutral in flavor, which will allow the prosciutto and shallots to shine through.

NUTRITIONAL INFORMATION:
CALORIES: 98 | FAT: 6.6g | PROTEIN: 4.2g | CARBS: 6.5g | FIBER: 2.3g

DEEP-FRIED BRUSSELS SPROUTS

There's a restaurant near my house that I love to go to for one single thing: the fried Brussels sprouts. The rest of the food is meh, but the sprouts are to die for. It turns out that it's not hard to make them at home.

OPTION   OPTION

YIELD: **4 servings**   PREP TIME: **10 minutes**   COOK TIME: **5 minutes**

2 quarts light olive oil or other heat-stable oil, for frying

1 pound Brussels sprouts, trimmed and cut into quarters

Coarse salt and black pepper

½ ounce Parmesan cheese, grated (about ½ cup)

¼ teaspoon red pepper flakes

1. In a large, deep saucepot or Dutch oven with a lid, heat the oil to 375°F. Add the Brussels sprouts and immediately cover with the lid to prevent splattering. Fry, stirring occasionally, until the sprouts are golden brown, 4 to 5 minutes.

2. Transfer the sprouts to a paper towel–lined plate to drain and season immediately with salt and pepper. Let sit for 3 to 4 minutes.

3. Transfer the sprouts to a large bowl and toss with the grated Parmesan and red pepper flakes. Serve hot.

SERVING SUGGESTION:
These are delicious dipped in Spicy Cajun Mayonnaise (page 66).

EVERYDAY TIPS:
Brussels sprouts are full of moisture, which is why they sizzle and spit like crazy when they hit the hot oil. Have that lid handy to cover the pot when they first go in. They will calm down after 30 seconds or so.

The frying oil can be saved and reused, to save on expense. I strain mine through a fine-mesh sieve and then store it in its original container in my cool basement. It will keep for about a month and can be used once or twice more.

EVERYDAY SWAP:
To make these sprouts Paleo, or if you want the same flavor without dairy, try sprinkling the fried Brussels with 4 to 5 tablespoons of nutritional yeast instead of Parmesan cheese.

NUTRITIONAL INFORMATION:
CALORIES: 182 | FAT: 14.3g | PROTEIN: 5.1g | CARBS: 10.5g | FIBER: 4.4g

It is difficult to ascertain how much oil the sprouts absorb when deep-fried. Studies indicate that foods with a high moisture content actually absorb very little oil, particularly when not coated in any sort of breading.

SHEET PAN EGGPLANT PARMESAN

A cross between eggplant Parmesan and mini eggplant pizzas.

YIELD: **8 servings** PREP TIME: **15 minutes, plus 30 minutes to drain eggplant**
COOK TIME: **25 to 30 minutes**

1 medium eggplant (about 1¼ pounds), sliced into ¼-inch-thick rounds

Salt

1 tablespoon avocado oil

DRY "BREADING":

1½ cups crushed pork rinds (see Tip, page 148)

1 teaspoon Italian seasoning

½ teaspoon garlic powder

½ teaspoon salt

½ teaspoon black pepper

EGG WASH:

1 large egg

1 tablespoon water

1 recipe Roasted Tomato Cream Sauce (page 77)

1½ cups shredded mozzarella cheese (about 6 ounces)

1. Spread the eggplant slices in a single layer on a large tea towel and sprinkle both sides with salt. Let the eggplant sit for 30 minutes, then blot dry with another tea towel.

2. Preheat the oven to 350°F. Brush a rimmed baking sheet with the avocado oil.

3. In a shallow bowl, whisk together the pork rinds, Italian seasoning, garlic powder, salt, and pepper. In another shallow bowl, whisk the egg and water together.

4. Dip each eggplant slice in the egg wash and then dredge it in the pork rind mixture, making sure to coat it well. Lay the coated slices on the prepared baking sheet.

5. Bake the eggplant for 10 minutes, then flip each slice carefully and bake for another 10 minutes.

6. Remove from the oven and spoon about 1 tablespoon of sauce over each slice. Sprinkle with the shredded cheese and return to the oven until the cheese is melted and bubbly, another 5 to 10 minutes.

EVERYDAY TIP:
In some recipes you can get away without salting the eggplant, but for a good eggplant Parmesan, getting out some of the excess moisture before baking is well worth the effort.

NUTRITIONAL INFORMATION:
CALORIES: 201 | FAT: 14.7g | PROTEIN: 13.1g | CARBS: 7.2g | FIBER: 2.7g

GARLIC PARMESAN SPAGHETTI SQUASH

It's amazing how Mother Nature came up with her own healthy answer to pasta. Spaghetti squash is right there, waiting for you to add delicious sauces and toppings.

OPTION

1 medium spaghetti squash

¼ cup (½ stick) salted butter

4 cloves garlic, minced

¼ cup chopped parsley, loosely packed

1 ounce Parmesan cheese, grated (about 1 cup), divided

Salt and pepper

6 slices bacon, cooked crisp and crumbled

YIELD: **6 servings**   PREP TIME: **5 minutes**   COOK TIME: **65 to 80 minutes**

1. Preheat the oven to 350°F and line a large rimmed baking sheet with foil or parchment paper.

2. Cut the spaghetti squash in half crosswise and use a spoon to scrape out the seeds. Remove the upper rack from the oven to allow room for the spaghetti squash. Place the halves on the prepared baking sheet, cut side down, and bake for 60 to 75 minutes, until the squash is tender enough to be easily squeezed. Remove and set aside.

3. In a large skillet, melt the butter over medium heat. When hot, add the garlic and sauté for 1 minute.

4. Scoop the flesh of the spaghetti squash out of the skin and add the flesh to the pan. Toss to coat in the butter and garlic. Stir in the parsley and three-quarters of the grated Parmesan. Season with salt and pepper.

5. Sprinkle with the crumbled bacon and the remaining Parmesan just before serving.

EVERYDAY TIP:
Spaghetti squash can be hard to cut in half. Make sure you use a very large, very sharp chef's knife or a cleaver for hard winter squash like this. Sometimes I put the whole cutting board right on the floor so I can get above it and put more weight on the knife.

EVERYDAY SWAP:
Leave out the bacon for a lovely vegetarian dish.

NUTRITIONAL INFORMATION:
CALORIES: 162 | FAT: 11.6g | PROTEIN: 5.6g | CARBS: 7.8g | FIBER: 1.6g

CREAMY SPINACH AND MUSHROOM GRATIN

Let's face it, the French know how to make vegetables taste good: lots of butter, lots of cream, and top it all off with plenty of cheese. This is such a rich side dish, it could almost be a meal unto itself!

YIELD: **8 servings**   PREP TIME: **10 minutes**   COOK TIME: **45 minutes**

6 tablespoons (¾ stick) salted butter, divided

2 cloves garlic, minced

10 ounces button mushrooms, sliced

1 teaspoon salt

½ teaspoon black pepper

24 ounces fresh baby spinach

1 cup heavy cream

¼ teaspoon ground nutmeg

½ ounce Parmesan cheese, grated (about ½ cup)

¾ cup shredded Gruyère cheese (about 3 ounces)

1. Preheat the oven to 425°F.

2. Melt 4 tablespoons of the butter in a large skillet over medium heat. Add the garlic and cook for 1 minute. Add the mushrooms and sprinkle with the salt and pepper. Sauté until the mushrooms are golden brown, 5 to 7 minutes.

3. Add the spinach and continue to cook until the spinach has wilted. Transfer the mixture to a 1½- to 2-quart oval baker or a 9 by 13-inch baking dish.

4. In the same skillet, melt the remaining 2 tablespoons of butter over medium heat. Add the cream and nutmeg and cook until bubbles appear around the edges. Stir in the Parmesan and continue to cook until the mixture has thickened, 3 to 4 minutes.

5. Pour the cream mixture over the spinach and mushrooms. Sprinkle with the Gruyère cheese. Bake for 18 to 22 minutes, until the cheese is bubbly and lightly browned.

EVERYDAY TIP:
This recipe makes a lot, so it's a great side dish to serve at holiday meals. But any leftovers will keep for a few days, and the gratin is delicious when warmed up.

NUTRITIONAL INFORMATION:
CALORIES: 303 | FAT: 25.8g | PROTEIN: 11.1g | CARBS: 6g | FIBER: 2.2g

SESAME GINGER BOK CHOY

Bok choy is one of my new favorite vegetables. The stems are always deliciously crisp and add plenty of crunch to a stir-fry.

YIELD: 4 servings   PREP TIME: 5 minutes   COOK TIME: 5 minutes

2 tablespoons coconut aminos

½ teaspoon garlic powder

½ teaspoon ginger powder

1 tablespoon avocado oil

4 heads baby bok choy, coarsely chopped

1 tablespoon toasted sesame oil

¾ teaspoon salt

Sesame seeds, for garnish

1. In a small bowl, whisk together the coconut aminos and garlic and ginger powders.

2. Heat the avocado oil in a large skillet or wok over medium-high heat until shimmering. Add the bok choy and sauté until the stalks are just tender and the leaves are just wilted, about 4 minutes.

3. Add the coconut aminos mixture and toss to coat. Cook for 1 more minute, then drizzle with the toasted sesame oil and sprinkle with the salt.

4. Sprinkle with sesame seeds before serving.

EVERYDAY TIPS:

Toasted sesame oil has a deep, rich sesame flavor. Because it's already cooked and deepened in flavor, it's best used as a finishing oil rather than a cooking oil. It's great in salad dressings and drizzled over vegetables.

Soy sauce can always be substituted for coconut aminos, but keep in mind that it's not considered Paleo-friendly.

NUTRITIONAL INFORMATION:
CALORIES: 88 | FAT: 8.5g | PROTEIN: 2.2g | CARBS: 5g | FIBER: 1.6g

CAULIFLOWER SPINACH CURRY

I love the sharp, pungent flavors of curry. I don't make it often enough, but I've vowed to change that, starting with this delicious vegetarian dish.

YIELD: **6 servings**   PREP TIME: **10 minutes**   COOK TIME: **about 30 minutes**

2 tablespoons coconut oil

¼ cup chopped onions

½ jalapeño pepper, seeded and minced (optional)

2 tablespoons curry powder

1 medium head cauliflower, cut into florets

¾ cup chopped tomatoes (preferably fresh)

½ cup water

6 ounces fresh spinach, chopped

¾ cup full-fat coconut milk

Chopped fresh cilantro, for garnish (optional)

1. In a large skillet, heat the coconut oil over medium heat until melted and shimmering. Add the onions and sauté until translucent, about 4 minutes. Add the jalapeño (if using) and curry powder and continue to cook for another 30 seconds.

2. Add the cauliflower, tomatoes, and water and stir to combine. Bring to a simmer, then cover the pan and reduce the heat to low. Cook for 15 to 20 minutes, until the cauliflower is fork-tender.

3. Add the spinach and let it wilt, then stir in the coconut milk. Cook for 2 more minutes, until warmed through. Serve garnished with chopped cilantro, if desired.

EVERYDAY TIPS:

I recently learned that in Indian cooking, it's important to get the spices right at the beginning of the recipe. You can't really add flavor after the curry has come together (and I've tried, believe me!). So add a little more at the beginning than you think you need. If the end result is too spicy for you, you can always thin it out with a little more coconut milk. Greek yogurt works well, too.

NUTRITIONAL INFORMATION:

CALORIES: 140 | FAT: 10.9g | PROTEIN: 3.8g | CARBS: 9.4g | FIBER: 4.1g

CHAPTER 14

DESSERTS &
SWEET TREATS

RASPBERRY LEMONADE GUMMIES

These gummies are fun and easy to make, and kids love them. They're also a great way to get a little gelatin into your diet.

YIELD: **2 cups (6 servings)** PREP TIME: **5 minutes, plus 2 hours to chill**
COOK TIME: **10 minutes**

1 cup raspberries (fresh or frozen)

½ cup water

½ cup fresh lemon juice

¼ cup powdered erythritol sweetener

¼ cup grass-fed gelatin

SPECIAL EQUIPMENT (optional):

Silicone mold(s)

1. In a medium saucepan over medium heat, bring the raspberries and water to a boil. Mash the berries with a wooden spoon.

2. Strain the berries through a fine-mesh sieve into a 2-cup or larger glass measuring cup, pressing on the solids to release as much juice as possible. Discard the solids.

3. Add the lemon juice and enough water to bring the mixture to 2 cups of liquid. Return the mixture to the pan. Whisk in the sweetener and gelatin and bring to a simmer, stirring until the gelatin dissolves.

4. Spoon into silicone molds and refrigerate until firm, about 2 hours. You can also line a 9-inch square pan with parchment paper and pour the mixture into the pan to chill.

5. To unmold, simply push the gummies out from the bottom of the silicone mold. Or lift out the parchment and cut into squares.

6. Store in the refrigerator for up to a week.

EVERYDAY TIPS:
Silicone molds are not a requirement for this recipe, but they are fun and inexpensive. Kids love eating heart- and flower-shaped gummies. How many pieces you get will depend on the size of your mold(s) or how big you cut your squares.

NUTRITIONAL INFORMATION:
CALORIES: 33 | FAT: 0g | PROTEIN: 4.4g | CARBS: 3.7g | FIBER: 0.7g | ERYTHRITOL: 10g

EASY PEANUT BUTTER CUPS

Peanut butter is my kryptonite, and I'm not afraid to admit it. One of the first sweet treats I successfully made low-carb was peanut butter cups, but carefully painting chocolate over the bottom and sides of the molds is fiddly work. You don't need that, and I don't need that. This easy version gets the deliciousness into your mouth that much faster.

YIELD: 12 cups (1 per serving)   **PREP TIME:** 10 minutes, plus 75 minutes to chill   **COOK TIME:** —

½ cup creamy peanut butter (unsweetened and salted)

¼ cup (½ stick) unsalted butter

3 ounces cacao butter, chopped

⅓ cup powdered erythritol sweetener

½ teaspoon vanilla extract

4 ounces sugar-free dark chocolate chips or chunks, store-bought or homemade (page 322), chopped

1. Line a standard 12-cup muffin pan with parchment paper cupcake liners or silicone liners.

2. Melt the peanut butter, butter, and cacao butter in a medium saucepan over low heat, stirring until smooth. Stir in the sweetener and vanilla extract until well combined and no lumps remain.

3. Divide the mixture among the prepared muffin cups, filling each one-quarter full. Refrigerate until firm, about 1 hour.

4. Set a heatproof bowl over a pan of barely simmering water. Put the chocolate in the bowl and stir until melted and smooth. Drizzle about 1 teaspoon of the melted chocolate over each peanut butter cup and spread it to the edges. Return the cups to the refrigerator until set, another 10 to 15 minutes.

5. Store in the refrigerator for up to a week (if they last that long!).

EVERYDAY TIP:
Cacao butter is critical for getting the right consistency for the peanut butter layer, so the cups aren't overly soft as you pick them up. It's readily available online and at some specialty grocery stores.

EVERYDAY SWAP:
If you don't tolerate peanuts, you can easily make these cups with another nut butter. You can also use sunflower seed butter for a nut-free version.

NUTRITIONAL INFORMATION:
CALORIES: 200 | FAT: 19g | PROTEIN: 2.9g | CARBS: 6.2g | FIBER: 3.6g | ERYTHRITOL: 12g

WHITE CHOCOLATE RASPBERRY CUPS

These fat bombs create their own layered effect as the raspberry powder sinks to the bottom of the cup. My kids adore them, and I love knowing they are getting a great source of fat.

YIELD: 10 cups (1 per serving) **PREP TIME:** 5 minutes, plus 1 hour to chill
COOK TIME: 10 minutes

½ cup freeze-dried raspberries

½ cup coconut oil

2 ounces cacao butter, chopped

¼ cup powdered erythritol sweetener

1. Line a standard 12-cup muffin pan with 10 parchment paper cupcake liners or silicone liners.

2. In a coffee grinder or food processor, grind the freeze-dried berries until they resemble a powder.

3. In a small saucepan over low heat, melt the coconut oil and cacao butter until smooth. Remove the pan from the heat.

4. Stir in the raspberry powder and sweetener until the sweetener is mixed in. Much of the raspberry powder will sink to the bottom. Divide the mixture among the prepared muffin cups, filling each one-quarter full, making sure to scoop some of the solids from the bottom of the pan into each cup.

5. Chill until set, at least 1 hour. Store in the refrigerator; they will keep for several weeks.

EVERYDAY TIP:
Freeze-dried raspberries and other berries are available in many stores, often in the aisle with the other fruit snacks. They don't usually have any added sugars, but check the labels.

NUTRITIONAL INFORMATION:
CALORIES: 153 | FAT: 16.6g | PROTEIN: 0.2g | CARBS: 1.2g | FIBER: 0.4g | ERYTHRITOL: 6g

SALTED CHOCOLATE MACADAMIA NUT FAT BOMBS

Macadamia nuts are like Mother Nature's fat bombs, so very buttery and rich. But there's no reason you can't improve on Mother Nature by adding a little chocolate and sea salt!

YIELD: **10 cups (1 per serving)**   PREP TIME: 15 minutes, plus 75 minutes to chill
COOK TIME: 5 minutes

¾ cup roasted, unsalted macadamia nuts

2 teaspoons avocado oil or macadamia nut oil

1 ounce unsweetened chocolate, chopped

2 tablespoons coconut oil

¼ cup powdered erythritol sweetener

2 tablespoons cocoa powder

½ teaspoon vanilla extract

⅛ teaspoon fine sea salt

Flaked sea salt, for garnish

1. Line a standard 12-cup muffin pan with 10 parchment paper cupcake liners or silicone liners. Set aside 10 of the macadamia nut halves for garnish.

2. Grind the remaining nuts in a food processor or blender until they resemble coarse crumbs. Add the avocado oil and continue to process until the mixture becomes a smooth butter.

3. In a heatproof bowl set over a pan of barely simmering water, combine the macadamia nut butter, chocolate, and coconut oil. Stir until melted and smooth.

4. Whisk in the sweetener, cocoa powder, vanilla extract, and fine sea salt. Divide the mixture evenly between the prepared cups, filling each about one-third full. Refrigerate for 15 minutes, then gently press a macadamia nut half into the top of each cup. Sprinkle lightly with flaked sea salt.

5. Refrigerate until firm, about 1 hour. Store in the refrigerator for up to 2 weeks.

EVERYDAY SWAP:
If you want these fat bombs to be a little firmer and able to stay out of the fridge for a few hours, replace the coconut oil with ½ ounce of cacao butter. They will travel much better.

NUTRITIONAL INFORMATION:
CALORIES: 122 | FAT: 12.6g | PROTEIN: 1.4g | CARBS: 2.9g | FIBER: 1.7g | ERYTHRITOL: 6g

CHOCOLATE GANACHE

This rich, smooth chocolate glaze is divine poured over any sort of cake or brownies. It also makes amazing sugar-free truffles (page 318)!

YIELD: About 1½ cups (12 servings)   PREP TIME: 5 minutes   COOK TIME: 10 minutes

1 cup heavy cream

¼ cup (½ stick) unsalted butter

4 ounces unsweetened chocolate, finely chopped

½ cup Swerve confectioners'-style sweetener or equivalent powdered erythritol sweetener

1 teaspoon vanilla extract

1. In a medium saucepan over medium heat, bring the cream and butter just to a simmer, then remove the pan from the heat.

2. Add the chocolate and let it sit for 5 minutes to melt, then add the sweetener and vanilla extract and whisk until smooth.

3. If using the ganache as a glaze or frosting, let it sit for a few minutes until slightly thickened, then pour or spread it over the cake or brownies. It does not reheat well, so be sure to use it while still warm. Once refrigerated, the ganache thickens up perfectly for making truffles.

SERVING SUGGESTION:
Pour over Coconut Oil Brownies (page 330) for a truly decadent treat! I suggest using a half batch of the ganache to top the brownies because it's rich.

EVERYDAY TIPS:
It's important to use both unsweetened chocolate and powdered erythritol sweetener for this recipe, as the fiber content helps thicken the ganache properly. Swerve is the best choice, but other powdered erythritol sweeteners will work. I don't recommend using any sort of sucralose or stevia, which would make the ganache very bitter.

Try not to take the cream and butter mixture to a full boil, which could seize the chocolate. If you do bring the mixture to a boil, allow it to cool for a few minutes until the froth has subsided.

This recipe makes enough ganache to frost the top and sides of a two-layer 9-inch cake. If you want just a thin coating of chocolate, simply make a half batch.

NUTRITIONAL INFORMATION:
CALORIES: 165 | FAT: 15.2g | PROTEIN: 1.8g | CARBS: 3.3g | FIBER: 1.6g | ERYTHRITOL: 10g

CHOCOLATE TRUFFLES

The classic holiday confection gets a ketogenic makeover.

YIELD: 30 truffles (2 per serving) PREP TIME: 5 minutes, plus 3 hours to chill (not including time to make ganache) COOK TIME: —

1 recipe Chocolate Ganache (page 316)

3 to 4 tablespoons cocoa powder

1. Chill the ganache in the refrigerator for 2 to 3 hours, until firm enough to handle.

2. Spread the cocoa powder in a shallow bowl.

3. Scoop about 1 tablespoon of the chilled ganache into your hands and roll it into a ball, squeezing it together if it cracks or crumbles. The heat of your hands will bring it back together.

4. Roll the ball in the cocoa powder to coat it thoroughly. Repeat with the remaining ganache.

5. Store the truffles in the refrigerator for up to a week.

EVERYDAY TIP:
While these should be stored in the refrigerator, I find that they are best eaten at room temperature, so take them out 30 minutes before serving.

NUTRITIONAL INFORMATION:
CALORIES: 132 | FAT: 12.2g | PROTEIN: 1.4g | CARBS: 2.6g | FIBER: 1.3g | ERYTHRITOL: 8g

CHOCOLATE SAUCE

Looking for a rich, fudgy sauce to drizzle over your low-carb ice cream? Look no further than this easy chocolate sauce.

OPTION

YIELD: About 1 cup (8 servings) **PREP TIME:** 5 minutes **COOK TIME:** 10 minutes

1 cup heavy cream

2 ounces unsweetened chocolate, finely chopped

⅓ cup Swerve confectioners'-style sweetener or other powdered erythritol sweetener

½ teaspoon vanilla extract

1. In a medium saucepan over medium heat, bring the cream just to a simmer.

2. Remove the pan from the heat and add the chocolate. Let sit for 5 minutes, until the chocolate is melted.

3. Add the sweetener and vanilla extract and whisk until smooth. Let sit for 5 to 10 minutes to thicken.

4. Store in the refrigerator for up to a week. Reheat very gently in a saucepan over low heat or microwave on low until melted.

EVERYDAY TIP:
As with the ganache (page 316), the best ingredients for this sauce are unsweetened chocolate and Swerve confectioners'-style sweetener. They give it the right consistency and help it thicken as it cools.

EVERYDAY SWAP:
For a dairy-free version, use full-fat coconut milk in place of the cream. The sauce will be a little thinner but will still be delicious.

NUTRITIONAL INFORMATION:
CALORIES: 155 | FAT: 14g | PROTEIN: 1.6g | CARBS: 3.1g | FIBER: 1.2g | ERYTHRITOL: 9.9g

HOMEMADE SUGAR-FREE DARK CHOCOLATE CHUNKS AND CHIPS

Good-quality sugar-free chocolate chips can be expensive, so I came up with a homemade solution. You can pour the chocolate mixture into a little mold to make hexagon-shaped chips, as pictured opposite (see the Tips below), or simply make them into bars and chop them up into small chunks when needed, as shown below.

YIELD: About 1¾ cups (14 servings) PREP TIME: 5 minutes, plus 1 hour to chill COOK TIME: 10 minutes

3 ounces cacao butter (see Tips)

2 ounces unsweetened chocolate, chopped

½ cup powdered erythritol sweetener, sifted

⅔ cup cocoa powder

½ teaspoon vanilla extract

SPECIAL EQUIPMENT (optional):

Mold for making chocolate bars or hexagon-shaped chips (see Tips)

1. In a heatproof bowl set over a pan of barely simmering water, melt the cacao butter and chocolate. Stir in the sifted sweetener and cocoa powder until smooth.

2. Remove from the heat and stir in the vanilla extract.

3. Pour into a chocolate mold or spread in an 8-inch square pan lined with parchment paper. Refrigerate until firm, then chop into small chunks. (*Note:* If you use the kitchen hack described below, simply pop the "chips" out of the mold.)

4. The chocolate can be stored in the pantry for several weeks. It can also be frozen in a sealable bag for up to 3 months.

EVERYDAY TIPS:

It's important to use cacao butter here. Butter and coconut oil make the chips too soft, and they would melt away when baked into recipes.

A reader told me about a kitchen hack for making evenly sized chocolate chips using a honeycomb-patterned silicone trivet (basically a potholder or hot pad) as the mold. Simply pour the chocolate into the trivet and place in the fridge to firm up. You will have perfect little hexagon-shaped "chips."

NUTRITIONAL INFORMATION:

CALORIES: 83 | FAT: 8.4g | PROTEIN: 1.3g | CARBS: 3.5g | FIBER: 1.8g | ERYTHRITOL: 8.6g

DUCK FAT CHOCOLATE CHIP COOKIES

I created this recipe when I was looking for a really good dairy-free cookie for my lactose-intolerant sister. I tried coconut oil, of course, but I didn't love the consistency. I tried lard and bacon fat, and then I gave duck fat a try. It was the clear winner in both consistency and flavor. You wouldn't know that these cookies are made without butter if I didn't tell you so.

YIELD: 24 cookies (2 per serving) **PREP TIME:** 10 minutes
COOK TIME: 12 to 14 minutes

2 cups (200g) blanched almond flour

1 teaspoon baking powder

½ teaspoon salt

½ cup duck fat, room temperature

½ cup granulated erythritol sweetener

½ teaspoon vanilla extract

1 large egg, room temperature

3 ounces sugar-free chocolate chips or chunks, store-bought or homemade (page 322)

1. Preheat the oven to 325°F and line 2 baking sheets with parchment paper or silicone baking mats.

2. In a medium bowl, whisk together the almond flour, baking powder, and salt.

3. In a large bowl, beat the duck fat, sweetener, and vanilla extract with an electric mixer until well combined. Beat in the egg, then beat in the almond flour mixture until the dough comes together. Stir in the chocolate chips.

4. Form the dough into 1½-inch balls and place them 2 inches apart on the prepared baking sheets. Press each ball with the heel of your hand to ½-inch thickness. Bake for 12 to 14 minutes, until beginning to brown. The centers will still be soft to the touch.

5. Remove from the oven and let cool completely on the pan. The cookies will firm up as they cool. Store on the counter for up to 3 days or in the refrigerator for up to a week.

EVERYDAY SWAP:
If you would rather use butter in place of the duck fat, simply use ½ cup (1 stick) of unsalted butter. The cookies are delicious that way, of course. But if you can get your hands on duck fat at some point, I highly recommend giving it a try!

NUTRITIONAL INFORMATION:
CALORIES: 214 | FAT: 19.5g | PROTEIN: 4.8g | CARBS: 6.7g | FIBER: 3g | ERYTHRITOL: 11.5g

NO-BAKE HAYSTACK COOKIES

Remember when you were a kid and you made no-bake cookies at school? You proudly brought them home to your parents, absolutely delighted with your cooking skills. Well, relive those memories with these easy keto no-bake cookies.

YIELD: 12 cookies (1 per serving) PREP TIME: 10 minutes, plus 30 minutes to chill COOK TIME: 5 minutes

⅓ cup creamy almond butter (unsweetened and salted) or other nut butter of choice

2 ounces unsweetened chocolate, chopped

2 tablespoons coconut oil

⅔ cup Swerve confectioners'-style sweetener or equivalent powdered erythritol sweetener

¼ cup cocoa powder

½ teaspoon vanilla extract

¾ cup unsweetened coconut flakes

¾ cup chopped pecans or other nuts

1. Line a large baking sheet with parchment paper or waxed paper.

2. In a large saucepan over low heat, combine the almond butter, chocolate, and coconut oil. Stir until melted and smooth. Remove the pan from the heat.

3. Whisk in the sweetener, cocoa powder, and vanilla extract until smooth. Add the coconut flakes and chopped pecans and stir until well combined.

4. Drop the mixture by large rounded spoonfuls onto the prepared baking sheet and refrigerate until set, about 30 minutes. Keep refrigerated until ready to serve; they will keep for up to a week.

EVERYDAY TIPS:
Whichever nut butter you choose to use here, make sure to mix in any of the separated oils really well before measuring out the nut butter. Too much of those oils can significantly affect the consistency of these cookies.

Swerve works best here for consistency.

NUTRITIONAL INFORMATION:
CALORIES: 172 | FAT: 15.6g | PROTEIN: 3.4g | CARBS: 5.7g | FIBER: 3.3g | ERYTHRITOL: 13.3g

BUTTER PECAN COOKIES

I had visions of these cookies being like pecan shortbread, so I was disappointed when they came out of the oven flat and crisp. I thought they were ruined . . . and then I tasted one. They were so buttery, and so delicious, I decided not to change a thing.

YIELD: **20 cookies (2 per serving)** PREP TIME: **15 minutes**
COOK TIME: **15 to 17 minutes**

½ cup (1 stick) unsalted butter, softened

½ cup granulated erythritol sweetener

1¾ cups (175g) blanched almond flour

2 tablespoons (14g) coconut flour

½ teaspoon vanilla extract

½ teaspoon salt

½ cup chopped, toasted pecans

1. Preheat the oven to 325°F and line 2 baking sheets with parchment paper or silicone baking mats.

2. In a large bowl, beat the butter and sweetener with an electric mixer until lightened and fluffy, about 2 minutes. Add the almond flour, coconut flour, vanilla extract, and salt and beat until well combined. Stir in the pecans.

3. Roll the dough into 1-inch balls and place the balls a few inches apart on the prepared baking sheets. Flatten slightly with your palm.

4. Bake for 5 minutes, then remove from the oven and use a flat-bottomed glass to flatten the cookies again to about ¼ inch thick. Return to the oven and bake for another 10 to 12 minutes, until the edges are golden brown.

5. Let cool completely on the baking sheet. Store on the counter for up to 4 days or in the refrigerator for up to a week. The cookies can also be frozen for up to a month.

EVERYDAY TIP:
Cookies made without flour and sugar don't really spread during baking the way conventional cookies do. I like to help them along a bit by pressing them down partway through baking.

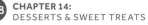
NUTRITIONAL INFORMATION:
CALORIES: 240 | FAT: 22.3g | PROTEIN: 5g | CARBS: 5.3g | FIBER: 3.1g | ERYTHRITOL: 12g

COCONUT OIL BROWNIES

Whether you are a cakey brownie fan or a fudgy brownie fan, this recipe is for you. I like to take them out of the oven before they are completely done for serious fudginess.

YIELD: 16 brownies (1 per serving) PREP TIME: 15 minutes
COOK TIME: 18 to 23 minutes

⅔ cup granulated erythritol sweetener (see Tips)

¼ cup cocoa powder

2 tablespoons (14g) coconut flour

1 teaspoon baking powder

½ teaspoon salt

½ cup coconut oil

4 ounces unsweetened chocolate, chopped

5 large eggs

½ teaspoon vanilla extract

¼ cup brewed coffee or water, cold

1. Preheat the oven to 325°F and lightly grease a 9-inch square baking pan.

2. In a medium bowl, whisk together the sweetener, cocoa powder, coconut flour, baking powder, and salt.

3. In a large saucepan over low heat, gently melt the coconut oil and chocolate, stirring until smooth. Take the pan off the heat, then add the eggs and vanilla extract and whisk until well combined.

4. Whisk in the dry ingredients and then the coffee or water until the batter is smooth. Pour into the greased baking pan and bake for 18 to 23 minutes, until the edges are set and the center no longer jiggles.

5. Remove from the oven and let cool in the pan. Store leftover brownies in the refrigerator for up to 5 days.

SERVING SUGGESTION:
If you want to be all hard-core decadent, I highly recommend frosting these brownies with a half batch of Chocolate Ganache (page 316).

EVERYDAY TIPS:
During baking, the sides of these brownies will rise higher than the center. Fear not; this is normal, and the sides will sink as the brownies cool.

These brownies have a deep bittersweet chocolate flavor. If you prefer sweeter brownies, you can add a full cup of sweetener.

The less time you bake these brownies, the fudgier they will be. You can take them out of the oven when the center still seems a little wet, and they will continue to firm up and cook through. For cakier brownies, bake on the longer end of the time range and until the center no longer looks wet. I always aim for fudgy brownies, which are what you see pictured here.

EVERYDAY SWAP:
This recipe works perfectly well with unsalted butter, too!

NUTRITIONAL INFORMATION:
CALORIES: 137 | FAT: 12.2g | PROTEIN: 3.4g | CARBS: 3.5g | FIBER: 2g | ERYTHRITOL: 9.4g

NO-BAKE BROWNIE CHEESECAKE BARS

This is a fun little twist on one of the most popular recipes on my blog: brownie cheesecake. Now in no-bake bar form!

OPTION

YIELD: 16 bars (1 per serving)   PREP TIME: 15 minutes, plus 3 hours to chill
COOK TIME: —

BROWNIE BASE:

½ cup creamy almond butter

½ cup coconut oil, softened

1½ cups (150g) blanched almond flour

½ cup cocoa powder

6 tablespoons powdered erythritol sweetener

1 teaspoon vanilla extract

¼ teaspoon salt

1 to 2 tablespoons water

CHEESECAKE FILLING:

2 (8-ounce) packages cream cheese, softened

½ cup powdered erythritol sweetener

½ teaspoon vanilla extract

¼ cup heavy cream, room temperature

TO MAKE THE BROWNIE BASE:

1. Line an 8-inch square baking pan with parchment paper, leaving a 1-inch overhang for easy removal. Lightly grease the paper.

2. In a large bowl, stir together the almond butter and coconut oil. Add the almond flour, cocoa powder, sweetener, vanilla extract, and salt and mix well. Add the water 1 tablespoon at a time until the mixture resembles a stiff dough.

3. Press the base evenly into the prepared baking pan. Top with another layer of parchment or waxed paper and use a flat-bottomed glass or measuring cup to press it firmly into the pan. Chill the base while you prepare the filling.

TO MAKE THE CHEESECAKE FILLING:

1. In a large bowl, beat the cream cheese with the sweetener and vanilla extract with an electric mixer until smooth. Beat in the cream until well combined.

2. Spread the filling over the brownie base. Chill for at least 3 hours to set. Lift it out of the pan using the overhanging parchment and cut into bars.

3. Store leftovers in the refrigerator; they will keep nicely for up to 4 days. The bars can also be frozen individually, wrapped tightly.

SERVING SUGGESTION:
You can cut these bars as big or small as you like. The recipe makes 16 good-sized servings, but I cut them into 25 bars when I took them to a party recently. They look elegant with a few fresh berries on top.

EVERYDAY SWAPS:
You can make these bars nut-free by using sunflower seed butter in place of the almond butter and sunflower seed flour (page 84) in place of the almond flour.

NUTRITIONAL INFORMATION:
CALORIES: 288 | FAT: 26.1g | PROTEIN: 6.2g | CARBS: 6.6g | FIBER: 2.9g | ERYTHRITOL: 13.1g

NEW YORK–STYLE CHEESECAKE

Who needs a crust when you have a beautiful tall, creamy New York cheesecake in front of you?

YIELD: One 9-inch cake (12 servings) PREP TIME: 15 minutes, plus 4 hours to chill
COOK TIME: 70 to 90 minutes

3 (8-ounce) packages cream cheese, softened

5 tablespoons unsalted butter, softened

1 cup powdered erythritol sweetener

3 large eggs, room temperature

¾ cup sour cream, room temperature

2 teaspoons grated lemon zest

1½ teaspoons vanilla extract

1. Preheat the oven to 300°F and generously grease a 9-inch springform pan. Cut a circle of parchment paper to fit the bottom of the pan and grease the paper. Wrap 2 pieces of aluminum foil around the outside of the pan to cover the bottom and most of the way up the sides.

2. In a large bowl, beat the cream cheese and butter until smooth, then beat in the sweetener until well combined. Add the eggs one at a time, beating after each addition. Clean the beaters and scrape down the sides of the bowl as needed.

3. Add the sour cream, lemon zest, and vanilla extract and beat until the batter is smooth and well combined. Pour into the prepared springform pan and smooth the top.

4. Set the springform pan inside a roasting pan large enough to prevent the sides from touching. Place the roasting pan in the oven and carefully pour boiling water into the roasting pan until the water reaches halfway up the sides of the springform pan.

5. Bake for 70 to 90 minutes, until the cheesecake is mostly set but still jiggles just a little in the center when shaken. Remove from the oven, then carefully remove the springform pan from the water bath. Let cool to room temperature.

6. Run a sharp knife around the edges of the cake to loosen, then release the sides of the pan. Refrigerate for at least 4 hours before serving.

NUTRITIONAL INFORMATION:
CALORIES: 287 | FAT: 24.7g | PROTEIN: 5.3g | CARBS: 2.9g | FIBER: 0g | ERYTHRITOL: 20g

SERVING SUGGESTION:

Serve with Wild Blueberry Syrup (page 78), raspberry syrup (see the tip on page 78), or Chocolate Sauce (page 320) Or simply top the cheesecake with some fresh berries.

EVERYDAY TIP:

It is critical to have all your ingredients at room temperature before proceeding with this recipe. Adding cold eggs or cold sour cream to the cream cheese mixture will make it clump up.

EVERYDAY SWAPS:

You can substitute any sweetener you like in this recipe. Make sure to figure out how much of your sweetener equals 1 cup of sugar in sweetness (see the sweetener chart on page 36 for guidance).

For a lovely citrusy flavor, try swapping lemon extract for the vanilla extract.

SUPER-SIMPLE VANILLA ICE CREAM

I couldn't possibly write a ketogenic cookbook without a recipe for vanilla ice cream! This one is quite easy and requires no heating or cooking, so you can mix up the ingredients and toss them into your ice cream maker any time the mood strikes.

YIELD: 3 cups (6 servings) **PREP TIME: 5 minutes, plus 2½ hours to churn and freeze**
COOK TIME: —

2½ cups heavy cream, chilled

⅓ cup powdered erythritol sweetener (or more if you prefer it sweeter)

2 tablespoons vodka

¾ teaspoon vanilla extract

Pinch of salt

¼ teaspoon xanthan gum

SPECIAL EQUIPMENT:

Ice cream maker

1. In a large bowl, whisk together the cream, sweetener, vodka, vanilla extract, and salt until well combined. Taste for sweetness and add more sweetener if desired.

2. Sprinkle the surface with the xanthan gum and whisk vigorously to combine.

3. Pour the mixture into an ice cream maker and churn according to the manufacturer's directions.

4. Transfer to an airtight container and chill until firm but not rock-hard, about 2 hours. Leftover ice cream will freeze a little harder but softens nicely after 10 to 15 minutes on the counter.

EVERYDAY TIPS:
Since alcohol doesn't freeze, using a little vodka in homemade ice cream helps keep it from getting too icy and hard in the freezer. Xanthan gum helps, too.

Many ice cream makers require the canister to be frozen for at least 12 hours prior to churning. I've forgotten to do this many a time. Fortunately, the ice cream base can be kept in the fridge overnight if you do forget.

Did you know that foods taste less sweet when they are cold than when they are at room temperature or warm? Keep this in mind as you add sweetener to the ice cream base. If it tastes "just right" before it's churned, you may want to sweeten it a little more.

EVERYDAY SWAP:
Because this recipe does not rely on erythritol for consistency, you can use any sweetener you prefer.

NUTRITIONAL INFORMATION:
CALORIES: 346 | FAT: 34.8g | PROTEIN: 2g | CARBS: 2.8g | FIBER: 0g | ERYTHRITOL: 13.3g

NO-CHURN STRAWBERRY SOUR CREAM ICE CREAM

Fear not, my friends! This ice cream is neither sour nor tangy, but instead has a deliciously sweet strawberry flavor. The sour cream simply gives this no-churn treat some structure so that it can be made without an ice cream maker. My son declares it to be the best ice cream I've ever made.

12 ounces strawberries (fresh or frozen and thawed)

½ cup powdered erythritol sweetener, divided

1½ cups full-fat sour cream

1 teaspoon vanilla extract

1½ cups heavy cream

YIELD: About 5 cups (10 servings)   **PREP TIME:** 20 minutes, plus 6 hours to freeze   **COOK TIME:** —

1. Place the strawberries and ¼ cup of the sweetener in a blender or food processor. Blend until almost pureed but some chunks remain.

2. In a large bowl, whisk together the sour cream, vanilla extract, and strawberry mixture until thoroughly combined.

3. In another large bowl, whip the cream with the remaining ¼ cup of sweetener until it holds stiff peaks. Gently fold the whipped cream into the strawberry mixture until just a few streaks remain.

4. Transfer to an airtight container and freeze until firm, at least 6 hours.

EVERYDAY SWAP:
You could really use any sweetener here that you prefer, since ice cream doesn't rely on bulk sweeteners for texture. Stevia extract would be fine; just be sure to use the amount that equals about ½ cup of sugar in sweetness (see the sweetener chart on page 36).

NUTRITIONAL INFORMATION:
CALORIES: 202 | FAT: 18.6g | PROTEIN: 1.7g | CARBS: 4.4g | FIBER: 0.6g | ERYTHRITOL: 9g

BROWNED BUTTER ICE CREAM

There is something magical about browned butter—how it becomes nutty and slightly caramel-like in flavor. It's wonderful in both sweet and savory dishes. This is a classic custard-based ice cream made with egg yolks. It's a little more work but has an incredibly smooth and creamy consistency.

YIELD: About 1 quart (8 servings) **PREP TIME:** 20 minutes, plus 4½ hours to churn and chill **COOK TIME:** 20 minutes

½ cup (1 stick) salted butter, cut into 4 pieces

2 cups heavy cream

½ cup unsweetened almond milk

½ cup granulated erythritol sweetener

5 large egg yolks

1 teaspoon vanilla extract

¼ teaspoon xanthan gum (optional)

SPECIAL EQUIPMENT:

Ice cream maker

1. Set a large bowl over an ice bath and set aside.

2. Melt the butter in a medium skillet over medium heat. Cook, swirling occasionally, until the butter is a rich amber color and has a nutty fragrance, 4 to 5 minutes. Transfer to a large bowl and set aside until cool.

3. Combine the cream, almond milk, and sweetener in a medium saucepan over medium heat. Stir until the sweetener dissolves and the mixture reaches 170°F on an instant-read thermometer.

4. Add the egg yolks to the cooled browned butter and whisk to combine well. Slowly add about 1 cup of the hot cream mixture to the yolks and butter, whisking continuously. Then slowly whisk the yolk/butter/cream mixture back into the remaining cream mixture in the pan.

5. Continue to cook, whisking continuously, until the mixture thickens enough to coat the back of a wooden spoon and reaches 175°F.

6. Pour the mixture into the bowl set over the ice bath and allow to cool for 10 minutes. Cover the bowl tightly with plastic wrap and chill for at least 3 hours and up to overnight.

7. Stir in the vanilla extract, then sprinkle the surface with the xanthan gum, if using, and whisk vigorously to combine. Pour into an ice cream maker and churn according to the manufacturer's directions.

8. Once the ice cream is churned, transfer to an airtight container and freeze until firm but not rock-hard, another hour or two. If frozen longer, it will be harder to scoop, but it softens nicely after 10 to 15 minutes on the counter.

NUTRITIONAL INFORMATION:
CALORIES: 347 | FAT: 34.4g | PROTEIN: 3.1g | CARBS: 2.2g | FIBER: 0g | ERYTHRITOL: 15g

BANANA PUDDING POPS

Be a kid again! Enjoy a cold treat on a hot day. These pudding pops are so low in carbs, you could eat two if you so desired.

OPTION

YIELD: **8 pops (1 per serving)** PREP TIME: **3 minutes, plus 5 hours to freeze**
COOK TIME: **10 minutes**

¾ cup heavy cream

¾ cup unsweetened almond milk or coconut milk

3 large egg yolks

¼ cup plus 2 tablespoons powdered erythritol sweetener

Pinch of salt

2 tablespoons unsalted butter, cut into 2 pieces

1½ teaspoons banana extract

SPECIAL EQUIPMENT:

8 (3-ounce) ice pop molds

1. In a medium saucepan over medium heat, combine the cream and milk. Bring just to a simmer. Meanwhile, in a medium bowl, whisk the egg yolks with the sweetener and salt until well combined.

2. Slowly whisk about half of the hot cream mixture into the yolk mixture, whisking continuously. Then slowly whisk the yolk-cream mixture back into the saucepan and cook until thickened, 4 to 5 more minutes, whisking continuously.

3. Remove from the heat and whisk in the butter and banana extract until the butter is melted.

4. Divide the mixture among 8 medium ice pop molds. Freeze for 1 hour, then press a wooden stick about two-thirds of the way into the center of each pop. Return to the freezer until completely firm, at least another 4 hours.

5. To unmold the pops, run the ice pop mold under hot water and gently tug and twist the wooden sticks until the pops release.

EVERYDAY TIPS:
Wooden sticks work far better than plastic ones. The wood surface is not entirely smooth, so the frozen mixture has something to grab onto. I find that the plastic ones tend to pull right out and then the ice pop is stuck inside the mold.

Any size of ice pop mold can be used to make these pops, but keep in mind that the nutritional info is based on a 3-ounce pop.

EVERYDAY SWAP:
Use coconut milk rather than almond milk to make these pops nut-free.

NUTRITIONAL INFORMATION:
CALORIES: 127 | FAT: 12.4g | PROTEIN: 1.6g | CARBS: 1g | FIBER: 0g | ERYTHRITOL: 11.3g

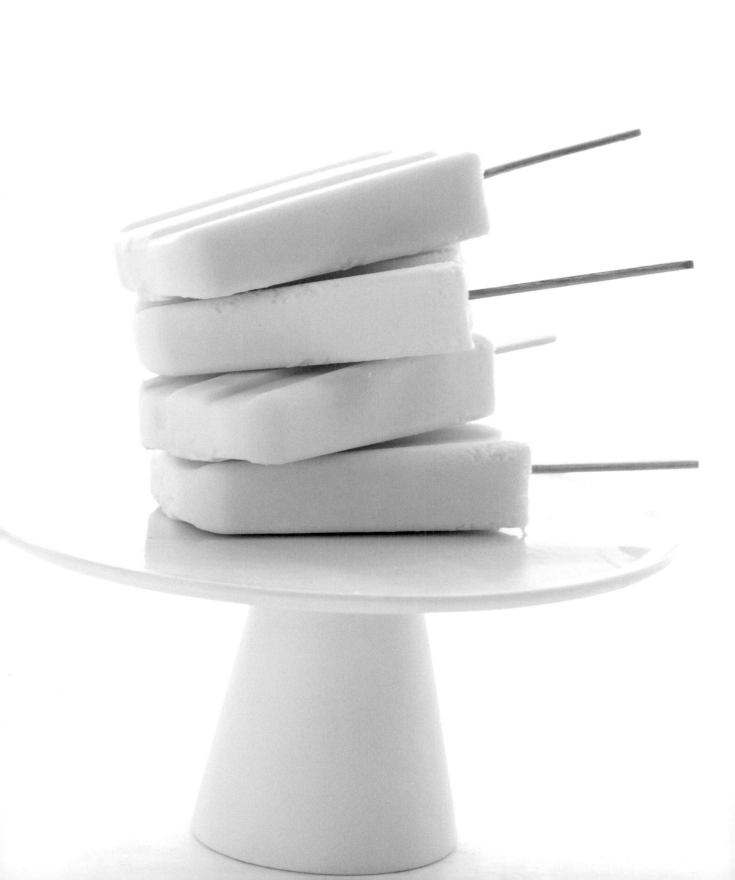

ALMOST-INSTANT BLENDER CHOCOLATE MOUSSE

After seeing a friend post a high-carb, sugar-laden blender mousse recipe, I had to try my hand at a keto version. It took several attempts to get it right. At first it was too thick, and then it was too thin. And then it was *juuuuuuust riiiiight.*

OPTION

YIELD: 4 servings **PREP TIME:** 10 minutes, plus 1 hour to chill
COOK TIME: 5 minutes

2 ounces unsweetened chocolate, coarsely chopped

¼ cup Swerve confectioners'-style sweetener or equivalent powdered erythritol sweetener

2 tablespoons cocoa powder

½ teaspoon instant espresso powder (optional)

¼ teaspoon xanthan gum

½ cup heavy cream

½ cup unsweetened almond milk or cashew milk

¼ cup (½ stick) unsalted butter

2 large eggs

1. In a blender, combine the chocolate, sweetener, cocoa powder, espresso powder (if using), and xanthan gum. Pulse a few times to combine.

2. In a small saucepan over medium heat, combine the cream, milk, and butter. Bring to a full boil, then immediately pour the scalded cream mixture into the blender and blend until smooth.

3. Quickly add the eggs to the blender and blend again until smooth. Pour the mousse into 4 dessert cups and chill for at least 1 hour to set.

EVERYDAY TIPS:
It's really important to have the cream-milk mixture hot hot hot when you add it to the blender. And it's important that it's still hot when you add the eggs and blend them in, as this is what helps set the mousse. The eggs in this recipe are technically raw, although they do get heated when added to the hot chocolate mixture. If you are concerned about consuming raw eggs, feel free to use pasteurized eggs, such as Safest Choice brand.

Be sure to use unsweetened chocolate, as the fiber content is higher, and that sets the mousse properly. Look for a good-quality chocolate, like Ghirardelli or Scharffen Berger. Baker's chocolate is more prone to seizing.

Swerve confectioners'-style sweetener is the best choice of sweetener for this recipe; other sweeteners may change the consistency of the mousse.

EVERYDAY SWAPS:
I have successfully made a dairy-free version of this mousse by using coconut cream for the heavy cream and coconut oil for the butter. My sister, who is lactose intolerant, is a huge fan.

NUTRITIONAL INFORMATION:
CALORIES: 342 | FAT: 31g | PROTEIN: 6.4g | CARBS: 6.7g | FIBER: 3.4g | ERYTHRITOL: 15g

EASY RASPBERRY MOUSSE

When I want a quick keto dessert, I know I can always toss some berries and cream cheese in the blender and end up with something delicious.

YIELD: 6 servings PREP TIME: 15 minutes, plus 1 hour to chill COOK TIME: —

¾ cup raspberries, fresh or frozen and thawed

2 tablespoons water

1 (8-ounce) package cream cheese, softened

¼ cup plus 2 tablespoons powdered erythritol sweetener, divided

1 cup heavy cream

½ teaspoon vanilla extract

1. Combine the raspberries and water in a blender and blend until smooth. Add the cream cheese and ¼ cup of the sweetener and blend again until well combined.

2. In a large bowl, beat the cream with the remaining 2 tablespoons of sweetener and the vanilla extract until stiff peaks form.

3. Fold the raspberry–cream cheese mixture into the whipped cream until no streaks remain. Divide the mousse among 6 dessert cups and chill until set, about 1 hour.

SERVING SUGGESTION:
Eat the mousse as is or top it with a little whipped cream and some fresh berries.

EVERYDAY SWAPS:
If you are dairy-free, don't despair. You can make recipes like this, but you need to find a good cream cheese replacement. Many of them are soy-based and quite high in carbs, but Kite Hill brand makes a really good almond milk–based cream cheese. It has only 2 grams of carbs per ounce, just like real cream cheese, and it's pretty tasty. You can then substitute coconut whipped cream for the dairy whipped cream, and you're in business!

NUTRITIONAL INFORMATION:
CALORIES: 280 | FAT: 25g | PROTEIN: 3.3g | CARBS: 4.4g | FIBER: 0.5g | ERYTHRITOL: 15g

TIRAMISU MOUSSE CUPS

These cups have all the flavor of the classic Italian dessert with none of the carbs and sugars.

YIELD: 4 mousse cups (1 per serving)   **PREP TIME:** 20 minutes, plus 1 hour to chill   **COOK TIME:** 5 minutes

CHOCOLATE CUPS:

2 ounces sugar-free dark chocolate, chopped, store-bought or homemade (page 322)

2 teaspoons unsalted butter or coconut oil

TIRAMISU MOUSSE:

4 ounces mascarpone cheese (½ cup), softened

2 ounces cream cheese (¼ cup), softened

3 tablespoons powdered erythritol sweetener

½ teaspoon vanilla extract

½ cup heavy cream, chilled

1 teaspoon instant espresso powder

2 teaspoons cocoa powder, for garnish

TO MAKE THE CHOCOLATE CUPS:

1. In a heatproof bowl set over a pan of barely simmering water, stir together the chocolate and butter until melted and smooth. Remove from the heat.

2. Set 4 parchment paper or silicone liners into a standard muffin pan. Spoon about 1 tablespoon of the melted chocolate into each liner and use the back of the spoon to coat the bottom and sides thoroughly. Refrigerate until set, about 10 minutes.

3. Divide any remaining chocolate between the cups and recoat the sides to cover any thin parts. Refrigerate again until completely set, about 20 minutes.

TO MAKE THE TIRAMISU MOUSSE:

1. In a large bowl, beat the mascarpone, cream cheese, sweetener, and vanilla extract until well combined and smooth.

2. In another large bowl, combine the cream and espresso powder. Beat until it holds stiff peaks. Gently fold the whipped cream into the mascarpone mixture until well combined.

TO ASSEMBLE:

1. Remove the chocolate cups from the refrigerator and carefully peel off the parchment paper or silicone liners.

2. Pipe or spoon the mousse into the chilled chocolate cups. Return the filled cups to the refrigerator and chill at for least 30 minutes.

3. Sprinkle with cocoa powder before serving.

NUTRITIONAL INFORMATION:
CALORIES: 351 | FAT: 35g | PROTEIN: 4.4g | CARBS: 7.7g | FIBER: 3.2g | ERYTHRITOL: 20g

EVERYDAY TIPS:
Only silicone or parchment paper liners will work for the chocolate cups. Regular paper cupcake liners will stick to the chocolate too much and won't peel away properly.

The chocolate cups can be made up to 2 days in advance, and the mousse can be made 1 day in advance.

EVERYDAY SWAP:
The mousse does not rely on bulk sweeteners for consistency, so feel free to use whichever sweetener you prefer (see the sweetener chart on page 36).

CRUSTLESS LEMON MERINGUE PIES

Everyone knows that the best part of a lemon meringue pie is the lemon filling and the meringue topping! Who needs a crust?

YIELD: Four 4-inch pies (1 per serving) PREP TIME: 20 minutes, plus 3 hours to chill
COOK TIME: 25 to 30 minutes

LEMON FILLING:

1 cup water

2 teaspoons grated lemon zest

¼ teaspoon salt

4 large egg yolks

⅓ cup fresh lemon juice

1½ teaspoons grass-fed gelatin

⅓ cup powdered erythritol sweetener

3 tablespoons unsalted butter, cut into 3 pieces

¼ teaspoon xanthan gum

MERINGUE TOPPING:

3 large egg whites, room temperature

¼ teaspoon cream of tartar

Pinch of salt

3 tablespoons powdered erythritol sweetener

2 tablespoons granulated erythritol sweetener

¼ teaspoon vanilla extract

TO MAKE THE LEMON FILLING:

1. In a medium saucepan over medium heat, combine the water, lemon zest, and salt. Bring to just a boil.

2. In a medium bowl, whisk the egg yolks until smooth. Slowly add about ½ cup of the water mixture to the egg yolks, whisking continuously. Then gradually whisk the egg yolks back into the pan of water and reduce the heat to low. Cook for 1 minute more, whisking continuously. Remove from the heat.

3. In a small bowl, stir together the lemon juice and gelatin. Let sit for 2 minutes until gelled. Whisk this mixture into the hot water–egg yolk mixture. Whisk in the sweetener and butter until dissolved and smooth. Sprinkle the surface with the xanthan gum and whisk vigorously to combine.

4. Divide the filling among four 4-inch ramekins or baking cups. Let the filling cool on the counter while you prepare the topping.

TO MAKE THE MERINGUE TOPPING:

1. Preheat the oven to 300°F.

2. In a large bowl, with an electric mixer, beat the egg whites with the cream of tartar and salt until frothy. With the beaters still going, slowly add the sweeteners and vanilla extract and continue to beat until stiff peaks form.

3. Dollop the meringue over the filling and spread it to the edges of the ramekins. Swirl the top decoratively with the back of a spoon.

4. Bake for 20 to 25 minutes, until the topping is golden and just firm to the touch. Remove the ramekins from the oven and let cool for 20 minutes, then refrigerate for at least 3 hours, until set.

NUTRITIONAL INFORMATION:
CALORIES: 159 | FAT: 12.4g | PROTEIN: 6.3g | CARBS: 2.4g | FIBER: 0.2g | ERYTHRITOL: 37.5g

EVERYDAY SWAP:
In the meringue, you can use all powdered or all granulated sweetener if you like. However, I find that a combination of the two gives the meringue the best consistency. You can't use anything other than erythritol; I have never successfully gotten meringue to stay light and fluffy with stevia or xylitol.

CANNOLI TART

In Boston's Italian district, known as the North End, there is a famous pastry shop called Mike's Pastry. I had my first taste of cannoli there and fell in love. This tart captures all the same flavors in one neat little low-carb package.

YIELD: One 10-inch tart (12 servings) **PREP TIME:** 10 minutes, plus time to chill
COOK TIME: 70 to 85 minutes

CRUST:

1½ cups (150g) blanched almond flour

¼ cup granulated erythritol sweetener

¼ teaspoon salt

¼ cup (½ stick) unsalted butter, melted

FILLING:

1½ cups whole-milk ricotta cheese, room temperature

5 ounces cream cheese (½ cup plus 2 tablespoons), softened

2 large eggs, room temperature

¼ cup granulated erythritol sweetener

¼ cup powdered erythritol sweetener

¾ teaspoon vanilla extract

⅓ cup sugar-free dark chocolate chips, store-bought or homemade (page 322)

CHOCOLATE DRIZZLE (OPTIONAL):

1 ounce sugar-free dark chocolate, chopped

½ tablespoon unsalted butter

TO MAKE THE CRUST:

1. Preheat the oven to 325°F.

2. In a medium bowl, whisk together the flour, granulated sweetener, and salt. Stir in the melted butter until the dough resembles coarse crumbs.

3. Turn the dough out into a 10-inch glass or ceramic tart pan. Press it firmly into the bottom and up the sides of the pan. Use a flat-bottomed glass or measuring cup to even out the bottom of the crust. Prick the bottom all over with a fork.

4. Par-bake the crust for 10 minutes, then remove from the oven and let cool while you prepare the filling.

TO MAKE THE FILLING:

1. In a food processor, combine the ricotta, cream cheese, eggs, sweeteners, and vanilla extract. Process on high until the mixture is smooth. Stir in the chocolate chips.

2. Pour the batter into the par-baked crust. Set the tart pan inside a large roasting pan and fill the roasting pan with water until the water reaches halfway up the sides of the tart pan.

3. Carefully place the roasting pan in the oven and bake for 60 to 75 minutes, until the filling is just set in the center. Cover the edge of the crust with strips of aluminum foil if it is browning too quickly during baking.

4. Remove the tart from the water bath and let cool in the pan for 20 minutes. Refrigerate until firm, at least 1 hour and up to overnight, before serving.

NUTRITIONAL INFORMATION:
CALORIES: 257 | FAT: 21.4g | PROTEIN: 8.6g | CARBS: 7.6g | FIBER: 3.2g | ERYTHRITOL: 16.8g

TO MAKE THE CHOCOLATE DRIZZLE:

Place the chopped chocolate and butter in a heatproof bowl set over a pan of barely simmering water. Stir until melted and smooth.

TO SERVE:

1. Drizzle the chocolate mixture over the chilled tart and slice the tart into 12 pieces.

2. Store leftovers in the refrigerator for up to 5 days.

EVERYDAY TIP:

It is essential to use a glass or ceramic tart pan for this recipe, as it is baked in a water bath. Metal tart pans typically have removable bottoms, and water would seep into your crust. Soggy cannoli tart is not exactly what we are going for here! If you don't have a tart pan, you can use a 9-inch glass or ceramic pie pan.

CHOCOLATE CREPE CAKE

This is a stunner of a dessert. Once you have the crepes ready, it takes just a few short minutes to put this cake together.

YIELD: One 8-inch cake (10 servings) PREP TIME: 15 minutes (not including time to cook crepes) COOK TIME: —

2 cups heavy cream, chilled

¼ cup powdered erythritol sweetener

1 teaspoon vanilla extract

1 recipe Chocolate Crepes (page 110)

1 cup mixed fresh berries, for garnish

1. In a large bowl, using an electric mixer, beat the cream, sweetener, and vanilla extract until stiff peaks form.

2. Place one crepe on a serving platter and spread a thin layer of whipped cream all the way to the edges. Top with another crepe. Repeat until all of the crepes and whipped cream have been used. Finish with a layer of whipped cream.

3. Chill for 2 hours to set the cake. Top the cake with berries just before serving. Store leftovers in the refrigerator for up to 4 days.

EVERYDAY TIP:
To cut this cake into neat slices, your best bet is to use a large sharp knife that has been warmed up. I often hold my knife over the open flame of a gas burner for 10 seconds or so, but you can also run it under hot water.

EVERYDAY SWAP:
You can use any powdered or liquid sweetener here, but I find that Swerve confectioners'-style sweetener gives the whipped cream more body and stability.

NUTRITIONAL INFORMATION:
CALORIES: 278 | FAT: 25.1g | PROTEIN: 5.6g | CARBS: 5.4g | FIBER: 1.7g | ERYTHRITOL: 14g

GINGERBREAD CAKE ROLL

Cake rolls are a little finicky to make, but boy, is the end result gorgeous! This gingerbread cake roll is going to become your favorite holiday dessert. Your guests will be amazed that it's low-carb.

YIELD: One 12-inch cake roll (12 servings) **PREP TIME:** 40 minutes, plus 1 hour to chill **COOK TIME:** 10 to 12 minutes

CAKE:

1 cup (100g) blanched almond flour

¼ cup powdered erythritol sweetener

2 tablespoons cocoa powder

1 tablespoon grass-fed gelatin

1 teaspoon ginger powder

1 teaspoon ground cinnamon

¼ teaspoon ground cloves

4 large eggs, room temperature, separated

4 tablespoons granulated erythritol sweetener, divided

1 teaspoon vanilla extract

¼ teaspoon salt

¼ teaspoon cream of tartar

VANILLA CREAM FILLING:

2 ounces cream cheese (¼ cup), softened

1½ cups heavy cream, divided

¼ cup powdered erythritol sweetener

½ teaspoon vanilla extract

Additional powdered erythritol sweetener, for dusting

TO MAKE THE CAKE:

1. Preheat the oven to 350°F and line a 12 by 17-inch rimmed baking sheet with parchment paper. Grease the parchment paper and the sides of the pan very well.

2. In a medium bowl, whisk together the almond flour, powdered sweetener, cocoa powder, gelatin, ginger, cinnamon, and cloves.

3. In another medium bowl, beat the egg yolks with 2 tablespoons of the granulated sweetener until thickened and lighter yellow in color. Beat in the vanilla extract.

4. In a large clean bowl, using clean beaters, beat the egg whites with the salt and cream of tartar until frothy. Beat in the remaining 2 tablespoons of granulated sweetener until stiff peaks form.

5. Gently fold the egg yolk mixture into the whites. Then gently fold in the almond flour mixture, taking care not to deflate the whites, until no streaks remain.

6. Spread the batter evenly into the prepared baking sheet. Bake for 10 to 12 minutes, until the top springs back when touched.

7. Remove from the oven and let cool in the pan for a few minutes, then run a knife around the edges to loosen the cake. Cover with another large piece of parchment paper and then a kitchen towel. Place another large baking sheet over the top and flip the whole thing over.

8. Gently peel the parchment from what is now the top of the cake. While the cake is still warm, gently roll it up inside the kitchen towel, starting from one of the shorter ends. Don't roll it too tightly or it will crack. Let it cool while you prepare the filling.

NUTRITIONAL INFORMATION:
CALORIES: 206 | FAT: 18.1g | PROTEIN: 5.6g | CARBS: 4g | FIBER: 1.5g | ERYTHRITOL: 15g

TO MAKE THE VANILLA CREAM FILLING:

1. In a small bowl, beat the cream cheese with ¼ cup of the cream until smooth.

2. In a large bowl, beat the remaining 1¼ cups of cream with the powdered sweetener and vanilla extract until it holds soft peaks. Add the cream cheese mixture and continue to beat until stiff peaks form. Do not overbeat. Remove ½ cup of the filling and set it aside for decorating.

TO ASSEMBLE:

1. Gently and carefully unroll the cake. Do not try to lay it completely flat; let it curl up on the ends. Spread the filling to within ½ inch of each edge of the cake. Gently roll it back up without the kitchen towel. Place the cake seam side down on a serving platter.

2. Sprinkle the cake with powdered sweetener, if desired. Pipe the remaining vanilla cream mixture in stars or other shapes down the center of the top of the cake.

3. Refrigerate the assembled cake for 1 hour before slicing. Store leftovers in the refrigerator for up to 5 days.

EVERYDAY TIP:
Gelatin really is useful here. Cake rolls, especially gluten-free ones, are prone to cracking, and I've found that the gelatin gives it a bit more flexibility.

MOLTEN CHOCOLATE CAKES FOR TWO

Nothing, and I mean nothing, beats a melty molten chocolate lava cake.

YIELD: **2 cakes (2 servings)**   PREP TIME: **10 minutes**   COOK TIME: **18 minutes**

Cocoa powder, for dusting

¼ cup (½ stick) unsalted butter

1 ounce unsweetened chocolate, chopped

3 tablespoons granulated erythritol sweetener

1 large egg

1 large egg yolk

¼ teaspoon vanilla extract

3 tablespoons (19g) blanched almond flour

⅛ teaspoon salt

1. Preheat the oven to 375°F and generously grease two 4-ounce ramekins. Lightly dust the ramekins with cocoa powder.

2. In a small saucepan over low heat, melt the butter, chocolate, and sweetener, stirring until smooth. Remove from the heat, add the egg, egg yolk, and vanilla extract, and whisk until smooth. Stir in the almond flour and salt. Divide the batter evenly between the 2 prepared ramekins.

3. Bake for about 15 minutes, until the sides are set but the middle jiggles slightly when shaken. The cakes will still look slightly wet on top. Remove and let cool in the ramekins for 5 minutes.

4. Run a sharp knife around the edge of each cake. Place a plate upside down over each ramekin and invert. Holding the plate and ramekin firmly, give each cake a good shake until it comes free of the ramekin. Serve immediately.

SERVING SUGGESTION:
Serve alone or top with a scoop of Super-Simple Vanilla Ice Cream (page 336).

EVERYDAY TIP:
These delicious little cakes don't always like to come free of the ramekins, so both greasing and dusting the ramekins with cocoa powder is important.

NUTRITIONAL INFORMATION:
CALORIES: 368 | FAT: 33.7g | PROTEIN: 6.3g | CARBS: 6.5g | FIBER: 3.5g | ERYTHRITOL: 22.5g

ZUCCHINI SPICE SHEET CAKE

I love sheet cakes for a number of reasons. They are easy to make and can feed a crowd if you need them to. But the major selling point for me is that they have a high frosting-to-cake ratio.

YIELD: One 12 by 17-inch cake (20 servings) **PREP TIME:** 15 minutes, plus 1 hour to drain zucchini **COOK TIME:** 25 to 30 minutes

CAKE:

2½ cups finely shredded zucchini

Salt

3 cups (300g) blanched almond flour

½ cup granulated erythritol sweetener

1 tablespoon baking powder

2 teaspoons ground cinnamon

½ teaspoon ginger powder

¼ teaspoon salt

⅛ teaspoon ground cloves

3 large eggs

½ cup melted coconut oil or unsalted butter

⅓ cup water

FROSTING:

1 (8-ounce) package cream cheese, softened

¼ cup plus 2 tablespoons powdered erythritol sweetener

1 teaspoon vanilla extract

⅔ cup heavy cream, room temperature

½ cup chopped toasted pecans or walnuts, for garnish

TO MAKE THE CAKE:

1. Place the zucchini in a sieve set in the sink or over a bowl. Sprinkle lightly with salt and toss to combine. Let drain for 1 hour, then wrap the zucchini in a tea towel and squeeze out as much moisture as possible.

2. Preheat the oven to 325°F and generously grease a 12 by 17-inch rimmed baking sheet.

3. In a large bowl, whisk together the almond flour, granulated sweetener, baking powder, cinnamon, ginger, salt, and cloves.

4. Stir in the drained zucchini, eggs, coconut oil, and water until well combined. Spread the batter in the greased baking sheet.

5. Bake for 25 to 30 minutes, until the top of the cake is golden brown and just firm to the touch. Let cool completely in the pan.

TO MAKE THE FROSTING:

1. In a large bowl, beat the cream cheese, powdered sweetener, and vanilla extract until well combined.

2. Beat in the cream until the frosting is smooth.

TO ASSEMBLE:

1. Spread the frosting over the cooled cake. Sprinkle with the chopped nuts.

2. Store leftovers in the refrigerator for up to a week.

EVERYDAY TIP:
When measuring the shredded zucchini, don't pack it into the measuring cup or you will change the amount by a lot.

NUTRITIONAL INFORMATION:
CALORIES: 226 | FAT: 20.8g | PROTEIN: 5.5g | CARBS: 5.2g | FIBER: 2.1g | ERYTHRITOL: 10.5g

EVERYDAY KETOGENIC RESOURCES

EASY KETO SNACKS AND OTHER USEFUL PRODUCTS

I don't purchase or recommend many prepackaged products because fresh and homemade is always best. But I have found a few goodies that live up to my healthy standards, without any added fillers, preservatives, or other questionable ingredients. We can all use a few convenience items in the chaos of everyday life. Here are a few of my all-time favorites.

4505 Meats Chicharrones (4505meats.com/chicharrones)—Stick with the Classic Chile & Salt variety; the other flavors contain maltodextrin.

Ayoba Yo Biltong (www.ayoba-yo.com)—These South African dried meat snacks are truly delicious, and unlike many jerkies, they have no added sugar.

Cello Whisps (cellowhisps.com)—I love these crunchy little cheese snacks!

Epic Pork Rinds and Pork Cracklings (epicbar.com/pork-skins-overview)—I am not a huge fan of their bars, but I love the pork rinds.

Good Dee's Cookie Mixes (gooddees.com)—I don't normally do boxed mixes, as I prefer to bake from scratch, but these are great in a pinch!

Keto Kookies (ketokookie.com)—I love these with a smear of peanut butter after a tough workout. They come in sealed packages of two, so they also make great travel snacks.

Keto Krate (www.ketokrate.com)—If you're looking for a fun way to try new keto products and snacks, this subscription box makes it easy. Monthly boxes show up at your door with a variety of samples.

Lakanto Maple Syrup (www.lakanto.com/products/maple-syrup/)—This is the only sugar-free maple syrup I've tried that actually comes close to tasting like real maple syrup! And I am Canadian, so I know my maple syrup.

Lily's Chocolate Bars (lilyssweets.com)—My favorite brand of no-sugar-added chocolate, with so many great flavors. I am partial to the Salted Almond & Milk Chocolate.

Moon Cheese (www.mooncheese.com)—Similar to Cello Whisps, but with some unique flavors. I love the Pepper Jack.

Organic Prairie Mighty Bars (www.organicprairie.com/category/premium-snacks)—My favorite meat sticks. These are great when you need energy on the go.

Primal Kitchen (www.primalkitchen.com)—Primal Kitchen makes a number of products that I love. The protein bars are a little higher in carbs, but the Collagen Fuel is delicious and fits my keto diet. The full range of Paleo avocado oil mayos and salad dressings are also wonderful.

RECOMMENDED READING

BOOKS

Bernstein, Dr. Richard. *Dr. Bernstein's Diabetes Solution: The Complete Guide to Achieving Normal Blood Sugars.* Boston: Little, Brown, 1997.

Davis, Ellen. *Fight Cancer with a Ketogenic Diet, Third Edition: Using a Low-Carb, Fat-Burning Diet as Metabolic Therapy.* Gutsy Badger Publishing, 2017.

Davis, Dr. William. *Wheat Belly: Lose the Wheat, Lose the Weight, and Find Your Path Back to Health.* New York: Rodale, 2011.

Fung, Dr. Jason. *The Obesity Code: Unlocking the Secrets of Weight Loss.* Vancouver: Greystone Books, 2016.

Moore, Jimmy, and Eric Westman, MD. *Keto Clarity: Your Definitive Guide to the Benefits of a Low-Carb, High-Fat Diet.* Las Vegas: Victory Belt Publishing, 2013.

Perlmutter, Dr. David. *Grain Brain: The Surprising Truth about Wheat, Carbs, and Sugar—Your Brain's Silent Killers.* New York: Little, Brown, 2013.

Phinney, Dr. Stephen, and Dr. Jeff Volek. *The Art and Science of Low Carbohydrate Performance.* Beyond Obesity, 2012.

Rosedale, Dr. Ron, and Carol Colman. *The Rosedale Diet: Turn Off Your Hunger Switch.* New York: Harper Collins, 2005.

Teicholz, Nina. *The Big Fat Surprise: Why Butter, Meat, and Cheese Belong in a Healthy Diet.* New York: Simon & Schuster, 2014.

WEBSITES AND BLOGS

All Day I Dream About Food (alldayidreamaboutfood.com)—More great keto recipes from yours truly

Authority Nutrition (authoritynutrition.com)—Well-researched articles with citations to real studies and science

Diet Doctor (www.dietdoctor.com)—Articles, recipes, menu plans and other tools

Eating Academy (eatingacademy.com)—The blog of Dr. Peter Attia

Epilepsy Foundation (www.epilepsy.com/learn/treating-seizures-and-epilepsy/dietary-therapies/ketogenic-diet)

I Breathe, I'm Hungry (www.ibreatheimhungry.com)

Keto Adapted (mariamindbodyhealth.com)

Keto Diet Blog (ketodietapp.com/Blog)

Ketogasm (ketogasm.com)

The Nourished Caveman (thenourishedcaveman.com)

Peace, Love and Low Carb (peaceloveandlowcarb.com)

A Sweet Life Diabetes Magazine (asweetlife.org)—Takes a tough look at all things diabetes

Tasteaholics (www.tasteaholics.com)

Wheat Belly Blog (www.wheatbellyblog.com)—The blog of Dr. William Davis

KETO PLANNING RESOURCES

Diet Doctor (www.dietdoctor.com/low-carb/keto/diet-plan)

I Breathe, I'm Hungry (www.ibreatheimhungry.com/menu-plans-new)

Keto Diet App (ketodietapp.com)

Keto Size Me (ketosizeme.com/keto-diet-plan-for-beginners/)

Ketogenic Diet Resources (www.ketogenic-diet-resource.com)

WITH GRATITUDE

To my devoted readers: you've been asking for a cookbook forever, so here it is. Now quit bugging me! No, really, I am forever grateful for your support, your encouragement, and your friendship. I wouldn't be here without you. A special shout-out to the diabetes community and TypeOneGrit for making my almond flour waffles famous.

Tim, I don't ever want to do this without you. Thanks for putting up with my crazy experiments, my impulsiveness, my messes, and my chaos. Words are insufficient to express how much that means to me.

Austin, Celia, and Maggie, you are the lights of my life and my most avid and honest recipe testers. You don't love everything I make, and you don't have to. Mum, Oma, and Amanda, forgive me for being so hard to reach when I am working. I believe I owe you a phone call. I love you all.

To my blogging friends: Jennifer Farley, Erin Sellin, Lauren McPhillips Kelly, Alyssa Brantley, Brianne Izzo, Brenda Bennet, and others: so glad I have you to turn to. Who else knows the frustrations of this crazy business? And to Kyndra Holley and Mellissa Sevigny: A rising tide lifts all boats. Thanks for living those words; I've got your back, too.

Jess Apple, Andress Blackwell, and Cassidy Stockton, your faith in me is tremendous. You are my three favorite people to do business with!

To my PDX Girl Posse: Emily, Mindee, and Kachina, you've made my life so much brighter over the past two years. I am ever so grateful that I met you. I will be sure to let you know when I am in need of an entourage.

To the Victory Belt Team: Erich, Lance, Holly, Pam, and Susan, thanks for fielding all my questions and concerns and walking a total newb through the process of cookbook publishing. I am quite certain that there isn't a more supportive, enthusiastic, and encouraging publishing house on the planet. Every writer should be so lucky.

Jimmy Moore, many thanks for connecting me with Victory Belt. You are a keto rock star, and the information you provided in your own books is invaluable to me. I lost count of how many times I referenced you.

Bill and Hayley, many thanks for the beautiful cover photos.

Finally, to my wonderful father, John Currie. I miss you every day.

DIETARY RESTRICTION INDEX

O recipe can be modified

RECIPE	PAGE	🧴	🥛	🌾	🥜	🥚	⭐	👪
Slow Cooker Chicken Broth	58	✓	✓	✓		✓	✓	✓
Steak Marinade	60	✓	✓	✓		✓	✓	
Spice Rubs and Seasonings	62	✓	✓	✓	✓	✓	✓	
Blender Hollandaise Sauce	64		✓		✓		✓	
Avocado Oil Mayonnaise	65	✓	✓		✓	✓	✓	✓
Spicy Cajun Mayonnaise	66	✓	✓		✓	✓	✓	
Dijon Vinaigrette	67	✓	✓	✓	✓		✓	✓
Easy Ranch Dressing	68	✓			✓		✓	✓
Chipotle Bacon Ranch Dressing	69	✓			✓		✓	
Creamy Cilantro Dressing	70	✓			✓		✓	
Pesto	71			✓			✓	✓
Chimichurri Sauce	72	✓	✓	✓	✓	✓	✓	
Low-Carb BBQ Sauce	73	✓	✓	✓	✓		✓	✓
Teriyaki Sauce	74	✓	✓	✓	✓		✓	
Pico de Gallo	76	✓	✓	✓	✓	✓	✓	
Roasted Tomato Cream Sauce	77	O	✓	✓	✓	✓	✓	
Wild Blueberry Syrup	78	✓	✓	✓	✓		✓	✓
Easy Press-In Pie Crust—Two Ways	80			✓	✓		✓	
Magic Mozzarella Dough	82				✓			✓
Sunflower Seed Flour	84	✓	✓	✓	✓	✓	✓	✓
Baked Denver Omelet	88		✓				✓	✓
Caprese Omelet Roll	90		✓		✓		✓	✓
Smoked Salmon Scrambled Eggs	92		✓				✓	
Sausage and Egg Cups	94	O	✓			O		✓
Chorizo Gravy	96		✓	✓			✓	
Homemade Breakfast Sausage	98	✓	✓	✓			✓	✓
Salmon Cauliflower Hash	100	O	✓	✓		O	✓	
Savory Breakfast Cookies	102		✓					✓
Raspberry Ricotta Breakfast Cake	104				✓			
Coconut Flour Pancakes	106	O	✓		✓		✓	✓
Cream Cheese Waffles	108		✓		✓		✓	✓
Chocolate Crepes	110				✓			✓
Strawberry Smoothies	112			✓	✓		✓	✓
Flourless Sunflower Bread	116	✓	✓		✓		✓	
Skillet Cornbread	118	O			✓		✓	✓
Focaccia	120	O			✓	O		✓
Hamburger Buns	122		✓		✓		✓	✓
Lemon Poppyseed Quick Bread	124	O			✓			✓
Prosciutto and Arugula Flatbread	126				✓			✓
Pesto Twists	128				✓			✓
Cinnamon Rolls	130				✓			✓
Chocolate Pecan Pie Muffins	132				✓		✓	✓
Maple Bacon Pancake Muffins	134	✓					✓	✓
Apple Cider Donut Bites	136				✓			✓
Cheddar Zucchini Drop Scones	138				✓		✓	✓
Basic Almond Flour Crackers	142	O			✓	O	✓	✓
Everything Bagel Crackers	144	O			✓	O	✓	✓
Cinnamon Graham Crackers	146				✓			✓
Nacho Chips	148		✓					✓
Cheesy Broccoli Tots	150		✓		✓			✓
Fried Artichokes with Spicy Cajun Mayo	152	✓	✓		✓	✓	✓	
Grilled Zucchini Rolls with Goat Cheese and Pesto	154			✓	✓			
Baked Ricotta with Mushrooms and Thyme	156		✓	✓	✓		✓	

O recipe can be modified

RECIPE	PAGE	⬚	⬚	⬚	⬚	⬚	★	⬚
Brie and Caramelized Onion Stuffed Mushrooms	158		✓	✓	✓			
Bacon and Sun-Dried Tomato Truffles	160		✓	✓			✓	
Bacon-Wrapped Halloumi Fries	162		✓	✓			✓	✓
Spanakopita Hand Pies	164				✓			✓
Smoked Salmon Pinwheels	166		✓	✓			✓	
BBQ Slow Cooker Meatballs	168	✓	✓					✓
Old Bay Chicken Wings	170		✓	✓			✓	✓
Rich and Creamy Hot Chocolate	172	O	O	✓	O	O	✓	✓
Green Tea Frappe	174	O		✓	✓		✓	
Sweet Tea Lemonade	176	✓	✓	✓	✓		✓	
Creamy Golden Gazpacho	180	O	✓	✓	✓	O	✓	✓
Spinach Artichoke Soup	182		✓	✓			✓	✓
Thai Chicken Zoodle Soup	184	✓	✓	✓		✓	✓	
Browned Butter Mushroom Soup	186		✓	✓			✓	
Slow Cooker Broccoli Cheese Soup	188		✓	✓			✓	✓
Italian Wedding Soup	190		✓					✓
Dilled Cucumber Salad	192	✓	✓		✓	✓	✓	✓
Tabbouleh	193	✓	✓	✓	✓	✓	✓	
Fried Goat Cheese Salad	194		✓					
Grilled Vegetable Salad with Feta and Pine Nuts	196		O	✓	✓		✓	
Black and Blue Steak Salad	198		✓	✓				✓
Spicy Shrimp and Avocado Salad	200	✓	✓			✓	✓	
Southwestern Chicken Chopped Salad	202							✓
Mexican Shredded Beef	206	✓	✓	✓		✓	✓	✓
Red Wine Braised Short Ribs	208	✓	✓	✓		✓	✓	✓
Garlic Butter Steak Tips	210		✓	✓			✓	✓
Beef and Veggie Kebabs	212	✓	✓	✓		✓	✓	✓
Extra-Beefy Spaghetti Bolognese	214	O	✓	✓		O	✓	✓
Lasagna-Stuffed Peppers	216		✓	✓			✓	✓
Easy Taco Pie	218						✓	✓
Slow Cooker Kielbasa and Cabbage	220	✓	✓	✓		✓	✓	✓
New Mexico–Style Smothered Pork Chops	222		✓	✓			✓	✓
Pork Medallions with Browned Butter and Crispy Sage	224		✓	✓			✓	✓
Dry Rub Fall-Off-the-Bone Ribs	226	✓	✓	✓		✓	✓	✓
BBQ Pulled Pork	228	✓	✓	✓			✓	✓
Cheesy Shepherd's Pie	230		✓	✓			✓	✓
Rosemary Lamb Skewers	232	✓	✓	✓		✓	✓	✓
Crispy Baked Buffalo Chicken	236		✓	✓			✓	✓
Sheet Pan Chicken and Veggies	238	O	✓	✓		O	✓	✓
Pan-Seared Chicken Thighs	240		✓	✓			✓	
Chicken Cordon Bleu Roll-Ups	242		O					✓
Easy Caprese Chicken	244		✓	✓			✓	✓
Chicken and Asparagus Stir-Fry	246	✓	✓	✓			✓	
Bacon, Spinach, and Feta Frittata	248		✓				✓	
Brie and Mushroom Quiche	250				✓		✓	
Goat Cheese Soufflés	252				✓			
Cedar-Planked Salmon with Pesto	256			✓			✓	✓
Fish Saltimbocca	258		✓	✓			✓	✓
Sole Florentine	260		✓	✓			✓	
Crispy Fish Nuggets	262	O	✓			O		✓
Old Bay Crab Cakes	264	O	✓			O	✓	
Spicy Shrimp and Cucumber Noodles	266	O	✓	✓		O	✓	
Broccoli Drunken Noodles with Shrimp	268	✓	✓			✓	✓	
Spicy Tuna Stuffed Avocados	270	✓	✓			✓	✓	
Cilantro-Lime Cauliflower Rice	280	O	✓	✓	✓	O	✓	✓
Cheesy Cauliflower Grits	282		✓	✓	✓		✓	
Cheesy Spinach Cauliflower Waffles	284		✓		✓			✓

O recipe can be modified

RECIPE	PAGE							
Easy Roasted Broccoli	286	✓	✓	✓	✓	✓	✓	✓
Tuscan Roasted Vegetables	288	O	✓	✓	✓	O	✓	
Roasted Cabbage Wedges with Bleu Cheese and Bacon	290		✓	✓			✓	
Sautéed Green Beans with Crispy Prosciutto	292	O	✓	✓		O	✓	
Deep-Fried Brussels Sprouts	294	O	✓	✓	✓	O		
Sheet Pan Eggplant Parmesan	296		✓					✓
Garlic Parmesan Spaghetti Squash	298		✓	✓	O		✓	
Creamy Spinach and Mushroom Gratin	300		✓	✓	✓			
Sesame Ginger Bok Choy	302	✓	✓	✓	✓	✓	✓	
Cauliflower Spinach Curry	304	✓	✓	✓	✓	✓	✓	
Raspberry Lemonade Gummies	308	✓	✓	✓			✓	✓
Easy Peanut Butter Cups	310		✓	✓	✓		✓	✓
White Chocolate Raspberry Cups	312	✓	✓	✓	✓		✓	✓
Salted Chocolate Macadamia Nut Fat Bombs	314	✓		✓	✓		✓	
Chocolate Ganache	316		✓	✓	✓		✓	✓
Chocolate Truffles	318		✓	✓	✓		✓	✓
Chocolate Sauce	320	O	✓	✓	✓		✓	✓
Homemade Sugar-Free Dark Chocolate Chunks & Chips	322	✓	✓	✓	✓		✓	✓
Duck Fat Chocolate Chip Cookies	324	✓					✓	✓
No-Bake Haystack Cookies	326	✓		✓	✓		✓	✓
Butter Pecan Cookies	328			✓	✓		✓	✓
Coconut Oil Brownies	330	✓	✓	✓	✓		✓	✓
No-Bake Brownie Cheesecake Bars	332		O	✓	✓		✓	
New York–Style Cheesecake	334		✓		✓			
Super-Simple Vanilla Ice Cream	336		✓	✓	✓		✓	✓
No-Churn Strawberry Sour Cream Ice Cream	338		✓	✓	✓		✓	✓
Browned Butter Ice Cream	340		✓		✓			✓
Banana Pudding Pops	342		O		✓		✓	✓
Almost-Instant Blender Chocolate Mousse	344	O			✓		✓	✓
Easy Raspberry Mousse	346		✓	✓	✓		✓	
Tiramisu Mousse Cups	348		✓	✓	✓			
Crustless Lemon Meringue Pies	350		✓					✓
Cannoli Tart	352				✓			
Chocolate Crepe Cake	354				✓			✓
Gingerbread Cake Roll	356							✓
Molten Chocolate Cakes for Two	358				✓		✓	✓
Zucchini Spice Sheet Cake	360				✓			✓

RECIPE INDEX

BASICS

 58
Slow Cooker
Chicken Broth

 60
Steak Marinade

 62
Basic Spice Rub

 62
Cajun Seasoning

 63
Taco Seasoning

Blender Hollandaise
Sauce 64

 65
Avocado Oil
Mayonnaise

 66
Spicy Cajun
Mayonnaise

 67
Dijon Vinaigrette

 68
Easy Ranch Dressing

 69
Chipotle Bacon
Ranch Dressing

 70
Creamy Cilantro
Dressing

 71
Pesto

 72
Chimichurri Sauce

 73
Low-Carb
BBQ Sauce

 74
Teriyaki Sauce

76
Pico de Gallo

 77
Roasted Tomato
Cream Sauce

 78
Wild Blueberry Syrup

 80
Easy Press-In Pie
Crust—Two Ways

 82
Magic Mozzarella
Dough

 84
Sunflower Seed
Flour

BREAKFAST

88
Baked Denver Omelet

90
Caprese Omelet Roll

92
Smoked Salmon Scrambled Eggs

94
Sausage and Egg Cups

96
Chorizo Gravy

98
Homemade Breakfast Sausage

100
Salmon Cauliflower Hash

102
Savory Breakfast Cookies

104
Raspberry Ricotta Breakfast Cake

106
Coconut Flour Pancakes

108
Cream Cheese Waffles

110
Chocolate Crepes

112
Strawberry Smoothies

BREADS, MUFFINS & SCONES

116
Flourless Sunflower Bread

118
Skillet Cornbread

120
Focaccia

122
Hamburger Buns

124
Lemon Poppyseed Quick Bread

126
Prosciutto and Arugula Flatbread

128
Pesto Twists

130
Cinnamon Rolls

132
Chocolate Pecan Pie Muffins

134
Maple Bacon Pancake Muffins

136
Apple Cider Donut Bites

138
Cheddar Zucchini Drop Scones

APPETIZERS, SNACKS & BEVERAGES

142
Basic Almond Flour Crackers

144
Everything Bagel Crackers

146
Cinnamon Graham Crackers

148
Nacho Chips

150
Cheesy Broccoli Tots

152
Fried Artichokes with Spicy Cajun Mayo

154
Grilled Zucchini Rolls with Goat Cheese and Pesto

156
Baked Ricotta with Mushrooms and Thyme

158
Brie and Caramelized Onion Stuffed Mushrooms

160
Bacon and Sun-Dried Tomato Truffles

162
Bacon-Wrapped Halloumi Fries

164
Spanakopita Hand Pies

166
Smoked Salmon Pinwheels

168
BBQ Slow Cooker Meatballs

170
Old Bay Chicken Wings

172
Rich and Creamy Hot Chocolate

174
Green Tea Frappe

176
Sweet Tea Lemonade

SOUPS & SALADS

180

Creamy Golden
Gazpacho

182

Spinach Artichoke
Soup

184

Thai Chicken
Zoodle Soup

186

Browned Butter
Mushroom Soup

188

Slow Cooker Broccoli
Cheese Soup

190

Italian Wedding Soup

192

Dilled Cucumber
Salad

193

Tabbouleh

194

Fried Goat Cheese
Salad

196

Grilled Vegetable
Salad with Feta
and Pine Nuts

198

Black and Blue
Steak Salad

200

Spicy Shrimp and
Avocado Salad

202

Southwestern
Chicken Chopped
Salad

BEEF, PORK & LAMB

206
Mexican
Shredded Beef

208
Red Wine Braised
Short Ribs

210
Garlic Butter
Steak Tips

212
Beef and Veggie
Kebabs

214
Extra-Beefy
Spaghetti Bolognese

216
Lasagna-Stuffed
Peppers

218
Easy Taco Pie

220
Slow Cooker
Kielbasa and
Cabbage

222
New Mexico–Style
Smothered
Pork Chops

224
Pork Medallions
with Browned Butter
and Crispy Sage

226
Dry Rub
Fall-Off-the-Bone
Ribs

228
BBQ Pulled Pork

230
Cheesy
Shepherd's Pie

232
Rosemary
Lamb Skewers

CHICKEN & EGGS

236
Crispy Baked
Buffalo Chicken

238
Sheet Pan Chicken
and Veggies

240
Pan-Seared
Chicken Thighs with
Creamy Rosemary
Mushrooms

242
Chicken Cordon Bleu
Roll-Ups

244
Easy Caprese
Chicken

246
Chicken and
Asparagus Stir-Fry

248
Bacon, Spinach, and
Feta Frittata

250
Brie and Mushroom
Quiche

252
Goat Cheese
Soufflés

FISH & SEAFOOD

256
Cedar-Planked Salmon with Pesto

258
Fish Saltimbocca

260
Sole Florentine

262
Crispy Fish Nuggets

264
Old Bay Crab Cakes

266
Spicy Shrimp and Cucumber Noodles

268
Broccoli Drunken Noodles with Shrimp

270
Spicy Tuna Stuffed Avocados

SIDE DISHES

274
How to Cook Zucchini Noodles

276
How to Rice Cauliflower

278
How to Cook Basic Cauliflower Rice

280
Cilantro-Lime Cauliflower Rice

282
Cheesy Cauliflower Grits

284
Cheesy Spinach Cauliflower Waffles

286
Easy Roasted Broccoli

288
Tuscan Roasted Vegetables

290
Roasted Cabbage Wedges with Bleu Cheese and Bacon

292
Sautéed Green Beans with Crispy Prosciutto

294
Deep-Fried Brussels Sprouts

296
Sheet Pan Eggplant Parmesan

298
Garlic Parmesan Spaghetti Squash

300
Creamy Spinach and Mushroom Gratin

302
Sesame Ginger Bok Choy

304
Cauliflower Spinach Curry

DESSERTS & SWEET TREATS

308
Raspberry Lemonade Gummies

310
Easy Peanut Butter Cups

312
White Chocolate Raspberry Cups

314
Salted Chocolate Macadamia Nut Fat Bombs

316
Chocolate Ganache

318
Chocolate Truffles

320
Chocolate Sauce

322
Homemade Sugar-Free Dark Chocolate Chunks and Chips

324
Duck Fat Chocolate Chip Cookies

326
No-Bake Haystack Cookies

328
Butter Pecan Cookies

330
Coconut Oil Brownies

332
No-Bake Brownie Cheesecake Bars

334
New York–Style Cheesecake

336
Super Simple Vanilla Ice Cream

338
No-Churn Strawberry Sour Cream Ice Cream

340
Browned Butter Ice Cream

342
Banana Pudding Pops

344
Almost-Instant Blender Chocolate Mousse

346
Easy Raspberry Mousse

348
Tiramisu Mousse Cups

350
Crustless Lemon Meringue Pies

352
Cannoli Tart

354
Chocolate Crepe Cake

356
Gingerbread Cake Roll

358
Molten Chocolate Cakes for Two

360
Zucchini Spice Sheet Cake

GENERAL INDEX